HOME-LAND

Romanian Roma, domestic spaces and the state

Rachel Humphris

BRISTOL
UNIVERSITY
PRESS

First published in Great Britain in 2019 by

Bristol University Press
University of Bristol
1-9 Old Park Hill
Bristol
BS2 8BB
UK
t: +44 (0)117 954 5940
www.bristoluniversitypress.co.uk

North America office:
Policy Press
c/o The University of Chicago Press
1427 East 60th Street
Chicago, IL 60637, USA
t: +1 773 702 7700
f: +1 773-702-9756
sales@press.uchicago.edu
www.press.uchicago.edu

British Library Cataloguing in Publication Data
A catalogue record for this book is available from the British Library

Library of Congress Cataloging-in-Publication Data
A catalog record for this book has been requested

ISBN 978-1-5292-0192-5 hardcover
ISBN 978-1-5292-0194-9 ePub
ISBN 978-1-5292-0195-6 Mobi
ISBN 978-1-5292-0193-2 ePdf

Cover design by Andrew Corbett
Front cover image: Gary Waters / Alamy Stock Photos

This book is dedicated to Rahela

(born August 2013)

GLOBAL MIGRATION AND SOCIAL CHANGE

This series showcases ground-breaking research that looks at the nexus between migration, citizenship and social change. It advances new scholarship in migration and refugee studies and fosters cross- and interdisciplinary dialogue in this field. The series includes research-based monographs and edited collections, informed by a range of qualitative and quantitative research methods.

Series Editors:

Nando Sigona, Institute of Research into Superdiversity, University of Birmingham, UK: n.sigona@bham.ac.uk
Alan Gamlen, School of Social Sciences, Monash University, Australia: alan.gamlen@monash.edu

Forthcoming titles:

Time, migration and forced immobility: Sub-Saharan African migrants in Morocco by Inka Stock (2019)

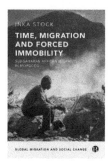

Contents

Who's who

This list includes frontline workers and the Romanian Roma families. It is not an exhaustive list; rather it lists the relevant information of those who recur frequently throughout the book.

Frontline workers

Emma, early years health visitor for 'hard to reach' groups (a category solely for Gypsy, Roma and Traveller mothers). British, married with children. Worked in Luton since 2008; lived near Milton Keynes.

Christian, volunteer for the Roma church. British, divorced with two grown-up children. Lived in Luton for two years.

Clare, head of a children's centre in central Luton. Took up the role in 2009; lived outside Luton. British, married with children.

Kassia, support worker for children's centre in central Luton. Arrived from Poland two years previously. Single with no children. Lived in Luton.

Lisa, NGO support worker. Single with one son. British, born and grown up in Luton.

Louise, head of a children's centre based in a church outside central Luton. British, married with one child. Lived outside Luton.

Paula, equality and diversity officer for the children's services department. British, married to a German national, two grown-up children. Lived in Luton and worked in children's services department for decades.

Rosemary, volunteer for the Roma church. British, single, no children. Previously a missionary in Bangladesh. Lived in Luton for decades.

Samantha, deputy head of a children's centre in central Luton. Took up role in 2012 and lived outside Luton. British, married with children.

Simon, pastor of Luton Roma Church and an 'English church'. British, married to a Swiss national, three grown-up children. Lived in Luton for four years.

Romanian Roma families

Catalina and her husband Radu arrived in the UK in 2013 with the four youngest of their eight children (aged 14, 12, 10 and 7 years old) to join their son, Andrei, who was living in London. He had married a Romanian woman, Sophia, who had gained refugee status through her Roma identity and they had one son called Armando, born in 2012. Catalina and Radu had been born in Romania in 1969 and 1968 respectively, but their eight children had been born in Germany, Belgium, Spain and Argentina. No one had a national insurance number.

Cristina arrived from Moldavia in 2012 to join her husband, Dan, who had already been working in the UK for six months. She was later joined by her two children (aged 4 and 2 years old) who had been staying with Grigore (Dan's brother) and his family in their Moldavian village. She subsequently had three more children who were born in Luton. She strongly identified as Pentecostal. Cristina had a national insurance number but Dan had been refused four times.

Ecaterina, her husband, Cezar, and their three children (aged 5, 4 and 2 years old) arrived in Luton in 2013 having previously lived in Blackburn and Tottenham since 2007. Cezar gained a national insurance number because of his scrap metal business. They had moved to a small terraced house with Nicolai, Dinka and their three children (aged 3 years, 2 years, and 4 months).

Florina, Sebastian and four children (aged 11, 10, 9 and 4 years old) arrived in the UK in 2011. Florina and Sebastian had been born and grew up in Romania but their three eldest children were born in São Paulo and their youngest had been born in Rio de Janeiro. They lived with Sebastian's mother and father, Sebastian's brother and his wife (Mirela) and their three children (aged 13, 11 and 7 years old). No one in this family had a national insurance number.

Georgeta, her husband, Rosvan, and their youngest son (aged 7) arrived in the UK in 2012 to join their eldest son, Emil (aged 21) in Luton. He had married Denisa, his *vera nepotes* (first cousin) and they had one daughter, Sarah, born in 2013. Georgeta was born in 1978 in Romania and had grown up in a *gazhe* (non-Roma) family. When she married Rosvan they lived together in Belgium, Finland, Germany, Spain and Italy. No one in this family had a national insurance number.

Margereta arrived in the UK in 2006 as an asylum seeker with her husband and four children. They were all granted indefinite leave to remain in 2007 when Romania acceded to the EU.

Maria arrived in the UK in 2007. She was born in 1982 and grew up in Romania. She had previously lived in Spain, Belgium and Italy. She was estranged from her husband. She had one daughter who lived with her estranged husband, his new partner and their two sons in Spain. She had gained a national insurance number through selling *The Big Issue* magazine.

Mariela and her husband arrived in the UK in 2012 with their seven children (aged 13, 11, 8, 6, 4 and 2 years old, and 7 weeks old). Mariela's husband gained a national insurance number.

Sanda and her husband Miron arrived from Romania in 2011 with their four children (aged 11, 10, 9 and 4 years old). Sanda gained a national insurance number through self-employed domestic cleaning.

Violeta arrived in the UK in 2011 with five of her six children (aged 16, 14, 12, 9 and 5 years old). Her eldest daughter had already married. Violeta was born and grew up in Romania. She had previously lived in Germany and Italy. She was widowed in 2009 while she was living in Rome. She strongly identified as Pentecostal. She gained a national insurance number through self-employed domestic cleaning.

Acknowledgements

Ethnography takes a long time and over the course of researching and writing this book I have been inspired and learned from so many people.

My greatest gratitude is to those who shared their everyday lives with me in Luton and beyond. I don't know how to thank the frontline workers and families at the heart of this book who allowed me to live in their homes and share their daily lives. When I left Violeta's house in March 2014 at the end of my formal fieldwork she said to me *"Dem murre shib palpalle!"* *(Give me back my language!)*. Language learning is perhaps the easiest to identify but only one of innumerable gifts that I cannot repay, give back or unlearn. This book represents a strange and uneasy kind of reciprocity, but one that I hope honours the extraordinary generosity, patience and kindness of those families which continues to shape me every day.

Academically, there are so many people who have shared their insights, experiences and knowledge with me. My two DPhil supervisors at Oxford, Ben Gidley and Marcus Banks, accompanied me through the challenges of fieldwork and writing. I feel very lucky to have had such understanding, encouraging and wise voices to guide me through that process.

I am also extremely lucky to have been involved in many lively academic communities which supported and challenged me. I am hugely grateful for the inspiring conversations with all those in ISCA, COMPAS, IRiS, and Max Planck Institute for the Study of Religious and Ethnic Diversity. Particularly, I want to thank Mette Berg, Nando Sigona, Jenny Phillimore, Stephen Vertovec, Bridget Andersen, Sarah Spencer, Caroline Oliver, Michael Keith, Hiranthi Jayaweera, Simon Pemberton, Lisa Goodson, Laurence Lessard-Phillips and Ceren Ozgen.

A number of institutions and organisations have provided support to make this book possible. I am grateful to the Sociological Review Early Career Writing Retreat where I wrote the conclusion to this book; the Covlet Fellowship; the European Academic Network on Romani Studies Early Career Research Fund; the Philip Bagby Travel Fund; the Peter Lienhardt Memorial Fund; the Gypsy Lore Society and the Fritz Thyssen Foundation. Thank you to Catherine Needham for the idea to hold a manuscript workshop and the College of Social Science, University of

Birmingham, for the funds to make it happen in the closing stages of the book. I also want to thank Umut Erel, Jon Fox, Ryan Powell, Madeleine Reeves, Deborah James, Stef Jansen and Sarah Turnbull (and Ben Gidley, Mette Berg and Nando Sigona again) for their generosity, attentiveness and care in engaging with my work and their intellectual vivacity.

The Roma Discussion Group has been a kind of academic home and unending source of encouragement, inspiration and friendship. I am truly indebted to Can Yildiz, Nicholas de Genova, Huub van Baar, Giovanni Picker, Juliya Sardelic, Jan Grill, Judit Durst, Violeta Vajda, Katya Ivanova, Colin Clark, Margaret Greenfields, Didier Fassin and Peter Vermeersch. There are so many people who have raised my spirits throughout this process. Soledad Alvarez Velasco, Paz Irarrazabal, Francesca Meloni, Sarah Walker, Vanessa Hughes, Jenni Berlin, Adele Galipo, Chiara Manzoni, Tess Altman, Marthe Achtnich, Amber Stechman and Irmelin Joelson, who are not only colleagues but all dear, dear friends.

I am profoundly grateful to my family who have all learned far more about Luton and migration than I'm sure they ever imagined or could have possibly wished for. Dad and Ruth, Veronica and Matt, Jake, my Janet and Bill, Ken and Angela, Gran, Granddad, Derek and Pat, this project certainly wouldn't have come together without them. And to my mum, whom I miss more than words can describe. Finally Will, whom I owe the greatest debt. In a literal and metaphorical sense, this book would not have been possible without him. Over the years he has always ensured I had a warm home I couldn't wait to return to, and has read this entire book at least twice. His editing, comments, suggestions and insightful questions have all been invaluable. Were it not for him, this book never would have been written.

Foreword

Baroness Ruth Lister,
Emeritus Professor of Social Policy,
Loughborough University, and
member of the House of Lords

As Rachel Humphris states, 'this book opens up new questions for academic and political debates about citizenship, migration and belonging' (p 16). These are all debates which are highly topical in the UK as it contemplates the realities of, and reasons for, Brexit. And it is as both an academic and politician that I read the work and found in particular her notion of 'intimate state encounters', which frames the study, highly illuminating.

One of feminism's contributions to citizenship theory has been to interrogate the public-private divide, which previously confined questions of citizenship to the public sphere and ignored the relevance of the private, domestic sphere and the care work undertaken within it. The opening up of the domestic sphere as a site of citizenship has been an important element in the multi-scalar conceptualisation of citizenship, as stretching from the intimate and domestic through to the global rather than simply being linked to the nation-state.

Rachel's analysis of intimate state encounters throws new light on what everyday citizenship can mean through a study of a highly marginalised, racialised group – Romanian Roma – when the domestic and the nation-state meet in their homes. It explores the gendered complexities of these encounters, which to a large extent involves mothers having to meet frontline (typically female) workers' expectations of 'good motherhood'.

While in some cases intimate state encounters could play a positive role in the women's lives this very much depended on judgements of deservingness and appropriate signs of gratitude, and on sentiment rather than on the exercise of rights. This will be of interest to students of street-level bureacracy. Here, though, we see the representatives of the state (and also volunteers) operating behind the domestic front door. It brings home how the state is not some faceless monolith but, 'digital by default' notwithstanding, in some domains encounters with the state are highly personalised, and this is especially true of those such as Romania Roma women and members of marginalised groups more generally. These are just some aspects of the study which will provide rich pickings for students of citizenship and the operation of the welfare state.

Read as a politician, the book helps us understand the realities of the government's 'hostile environment' policy, now rebranded a 'compliant environment', even though it was still in its infancy when the study was conducted. Whether 'hostile' or 'compliant', the policy outsources border controls to domestic arms of the state as well as to private citizens (notably landlords and employers). In the intimate state encounters described here immigration policies are closely bound up with various aspects of welfare policies. And 'compliance' is exactly what is expected of the mothers, if they are to prove their deservingness. In May 2018, the UN Rapporteur on Contemporary Forms of Racism dismissed as cosmetic the rhetorical shift from 'hostile' to 'compliant'.[1] This research illuminates how a 'compliant' environment can itself serve to undermine citizenship rights. Here the nation-state's borders are devolved right into the domestic sphere of the home for a particularly marginalised group of migrants – again linking the different spatial scales of citizenship.

Whether reading through an academic or a political lens, the study's rich ethnographic detail throws a spotlight on the daily struggles and precarious lives of a largely invisible racialised group of mothers who seek to belong.

---

[1] Office of the United Nations High Commissioner for Human Rights (2018) 'End of mission statement of the Special Rapporteur on Contemporary Forms of Racism, Racial Discrimination, Xenophobia and Related Intolerance at the conclusion of her mission to the United Kingdom of Great Britain and Northern Ireland' (www.ohchr.org/EN/NewsEvents/Pages/DisplayNews. aspx?NewsID=23073&LangID=E)

Series Preface

Home-Land is the second book in a new series with Bristol University Press, titled Global Migration and Social Change. The series aims to offer a platform for new scholarship in migration and refugee studies that explores under-researched topics and/or looks at old ones through novel perspectives and methods.

The idea for this new book series took shape in 2016, as Europe was coming to terms with a peak in unauthorised sea crossings at its southern borders. Meanwhile, US president Donald Trump was pledging the construction of an 'impenetrable, physical, tall, powerful, beautiful wall'[1] along the US-Mexico border, the UK was voting to leave the European Union in a referendum in which anti-immigration sentiments played a major role, and hundreds of people were displaced across the world as a result of new and old conflicts.

Against that background, we envisaged a series of broad questions and perspectives for the series which, among the others, would cast light on the politics and geopolitics of migration; examine the drivers and dynamics of human mobility in an interconnected world; explore migration-driven sociodemographic changes from intersectional and interdisciplinary perspectives; engage with anti-immigration and racist politics; analyse the accommodation of, and resistance to, diversity in rapidly changing societies; and investigate the relationship between immigration enforcement and citizenship.

We set out to showcase research that looks at the UK, Europe and beyond to understand the broader dynamics of global migration, exile and social change. We want to publish research monographs and edited collections informed by a range of qualitative and quantitative research methods that challenge disciplinary boundaries and established knowledge on human mobility and raise novel questions and connections on the relationship between mobility and social change.

---

[1] *Washington Post* (2016) 'Trump says he will build "impenetrable, physical, tall, powerful, beautiful" border'. Immigration policy speech, 31 August. [video] https://tinyurl.com/ycbrf99e

We are open to in-depth ethnographic and qualitative case studies, international comparative analyses, and everything between. We also welcome contributions that address the dynamics of migration, exile and social change at different scales (municipal, national, regional, global and so on), and which pay attention to different intersections of race, ethnicity, class, gender and age.

Rachel Humphris' ethnography of domestic spaces and everyday bordering is an excellent fit for the series. The book builds an intimate and fine-grained portrait of the encounters between citizens and the British state. Through 14 months of intensive ethnographic fieldwork sharing the everyday lives of 20 extended families, Humphris provides unique insights into contemporary processes of marginalisation. She focuses in particular on the myriad of contacts that happen in the domestic space and how the space itself is performed in, and transformed by, these interactions, including how the appropriate arrangement of toys in living rooms can become a form of bordering.

Migration scholarship has engaged with immigration enforcement and migrants' homes: for example, by examining the impact of early morning immigration raids and recounting the fear of migrant families with precarious legal status suddenly woken up by agents banging on their doors; by casting light on how the 'right to rent' immigration checks carried out by landlords can lead to exploitation; and the consequences of urban segregation in asylum dispersal areas. Humphris' ethnography instead gives us a fascinating and detailed account of what, at least on paper, should be more benign encounters. *Home-Land* gives us a portrait of Roma domestic spaces as border zones, capturing the everyday practices of adaptation and adjustment that Roma families have developed in their interactions with social services and support workers who are increasingly demanded to act as border guards for the Home Office.

Control and surveillance of poor people has long (perhaps from inception) been one of the functions of welfare regimes. This book goes a step further. It shows how Roma homes become a site of bordering and how social workers' home visits become closely intertwined not just with access or limited welfare resources, but also as a way of assessing the right of Roma families to live in the UK.

Nando Sigona
Birmingham, December 2018

INTRODUCTION

Romanian Roma, motherhood and the home

It is after six o'clock on a sunny June evening in Luton, a town 30 miles north of London, UK, in 2013. I am in a downstairs room of a small dilapidated Victorian terraced house on a street where many houses have boarded-up windows. Two social workers, Sarah and Rodney, are sitting on chairs near the doorway that separates this small room from the other downstairs room, which is being used a bedroom. Catalina, a migrant mother from Romania who arrived four months earlier with her family to find work, sits on her low stool next to the kitchen. Her long skirt flows onto the floor. She has seven children who were born in Stuttgart, Brussels and Buenos Aires. Radu, her husband, sits opposite her with the best view of the kitchen, the back door, and of the large TV, precariously placed on a window sill, that is playing Nicolae Guță, a popular Manele[1] Romanian singer. Radu is smoking a cigarette and has half a bottle of white wine next to him. They all have Argentinean identity (ID) cards. I am perched on the leather couch close to Radu, joined by two of their five sons. Catalina and Radu's two daughters intermittently shuffle past the feet and bags that are blocking their path to the kitchen. Paula, an equality and diversity officer for the children's services department, sits on a hard wooden chair close to Catalina. Catalina's grandson, who was born in London, can be heard crying upstairs from one of the two bedrooms where her daughter-in-law, Sophia, a refugee from Romania, is nursing him. She is the only one in the family who has this status and she does not have an Argentinean ID card. The family does not speak English.

1

We have all been sitting in this room for what seems like 20 minutes but it could have been longer. It is cramped and there are long silences between people talking, creating a tense atmosphere. I purposively stay silent unless asked a direct question from someone. Sarah – the social worker – breaks one of the silences. "How can they be here? How can they live here without access to anything?" She doesn't seem to be directly addressing any of the eight of us sitting in the small room. She looks dismayed at the Argentinean ID cards in front of her. The question hangs in the cigarette smoke for a moment. Paula responds, "You know, they are legally here due to their Romanian nationality." When Radu hears Paula say 'Romanian' he vigorously points to his Argentinean ID card. "No Romania," he insists. Sarah is silent for a moment, looking down at all the paperwork as if trying to make sense of it. Turning to Paula, she says that she can write a referral for a food parcel and then she turns to leave, followed by Rodney. Paula remains to fill in the school registration forms.

We will return to the story of Catalina and Radu later on and in Chapter Three, but for now this brief scene introduces many key themes of this book. The book explores how these new migrant families became known as 'Romanian Roma' and how they made a home in the UK 'without access to anything'. Paying attention to the details of encounters in homes like Catalina's, and what might seem to be mundane interactions, we can see they are not isolated events but address profound questions which affect us all: what are the terms on which we are able to make and feel at home? How does our everyday mundane domestic life affect our relation to the national home-land?

I did not set out to research encounters in the home. I wanted to understand how new migrants were settling down in urban areas that were undergoing rapid demographic, governmental and structural changes. I chose Luton, a large town 30 miles north of London, because it exhibited these dynamics (see Chapter One). However, through living with Romanian Roma for 14 months I was pulled towards examining home visits by frontline workers because they fundamentally shaped the life chances of families.

Romanian Roma families were very specifically racialised according to myths, legends and social representations that could be strongly linked to historical British stereotypes about Gypsies and Travellers and also a pervasive discourse of 'bogus asylum seekers' and 'welfare tourism' that more recently emerged in the post-Cold War period (see Chapter Three). This lens framed frontline workers' interpretations of mothers' behaviour, such as being both 'vulnerable' and 'undeserving', which also closed down other ways of understanding these families.

Most importantly for this book, this lens had implications for the *space* where interactions with local state actors took place. Local state actors undertook home visits because these had become the established response to engage with families identified as 'Roma'. In particular, this book focuses on how migrants' life chances rested on frontline workers' judgements of 'good motherhood' from within migrants' own homes. Home visits were crucial because they were often the only site where families could negotiate their legal statuses. They may have had interactions in a hospital, job centre or police station but these sites did not hold opportunities to build relationships with those who could offer the intense support they needed to gain a secure legal status.

The stakes in these encounters between Romanian Roma mothers and frontline service providers have gained life-changing significance because of the way welfare requirements and immigration controls have become entwined in the UK. Migrants now face 'internal borders' (see Chapter Six).[2] These internal borders emerged through the duties placed on private landlords, health professionals, banks, further and higher education, through driving licence applications and a host of state and non-state services. In the case of Romanian Roma, these internal borders emerged through encounters with frontline workers in their own homes. Although this book is concerned with Romanian Roma at a particular historical moment (January 2013–March 2014 during European Union [EU] transitional controls), the processes that led to intimate state encounters are relevant to the UK and many other Western liberal democracies implementing restrictive and hostile immigration controls.

This book draws from and builds on gender and queer scholars who have long pointed out that the distinction between 'us' and 'them' is most fundamentally drawn in the intimate sphere. From colonial times until the present day, ethnic and racial relations have been governed through intimacy (McClintock 1995; Stoler 2002). This book draws a line from these debates to the role of the family and the domestic in conceptions of nationhood, identity and belonging.

This book also has salience in the context of Brexit. The previous period of enlargement of the EU was a time of uncertainty for local state actors and migrants. Legal rules were often unclear and could become open to interpretation by those on the ground. As demonstrated by the tense silences in Catalina's encounter, the uncertainty evoked by impending legal changes widened the already unclear discretionary duties of local state actors towards migrants, with deep implications. The book tells the story of what happens when increasing responsibility is delegated to local government with decreasing resources. The space of the home exacerbates these confusions and contradictions, leading to what I have termed 'governance through uncertainty'. The related notion of the 'intimate state encounter' is used, introduced and developed throughout the book to elaborate these processes and their implications.

Grounded empirical research on these topics is crucial. It has been acknowledged that we do not have enough knowledge about the daily lives of precarious populations 'caught in the cracks and ditches of the new economic landscape' (Wacquant 2009: xiv). This limited knowledge has resulted in these populations often being presented 'as one undifferentiated mass, their individual characteristics and differences ironed flat' (Measor 2013: 133–5). As Flint (2012) has pointed out there is a growing literature on contemporary marginal working class lives. However, the specific mechanisms of statecraft are less well documented at the intersection between urban marginality, race and migration. This book fills this gap by providing in-depth ethnographic knowledge of the mechanisms and effects of the welfare-immigration nexus for those situated at the margins of the state.

Who are Romanian Roma?

The families in this book were identified as Romanian Roma by local state actors. The term 'Romanian Roma' developed through the narratives and discourse of frontline workers over the course of my fieldwork (see Chapter Three).[3] The identification of Romanian Roma does not exist in Romania; rather, it emerged and gained meaning through migration. Families used many different terms to describe themselves including Romanian, Roma, Gypsy, *Tsigane*, European, Canadian, Brazilian or Argentinean among others. However, a defining feature was the distinctions they made between themselves and their co-nationals. For example, Claudia drew on her language and the way she dressed to explain her identity to me. She wanted to ensure I was aware of the different language I was learning, that is, *Romanës*, an oral language spoken by those identified as Roma, and told me explicitly that I would not be able to speak this language in shops in Romania. She explained her family speaks *Romanës* not *Gazhikanes* (like a non-Roma). She also pointed out that a *romni* (a married woman) wears a long skirt (*fuwsta*) and headscarf (*diklo*). I also heard families using the words, or variants of the words, Gypsy or *Tsigane* when referring to others' perceptions of them, such as "that church not like Gyps" [sic] or "we are Gypsy".

Race operates as an organising social force and the term Romanian Roma can be seen as an artefact of racialisation that is co-constituted with class but is always contextual. For example, in the encounter between Catalina and her family at the beginning of this Introduction, Paula was present at the house because she had been referred by the local pastor who had identified the family as Romanian Roma through their appearance and recognising that they spoke *Romanës*. As Romanian Roma they were thought to require home visits because, in Paula's experience, Romanian Roma families did not attend appointments in bureaucratic offices because they led chaotic lives (Chapter Three). This home visit, which coincided with the visit by Sarah and Rodney, the social workers, had fundamental consequences for how Catalina and her family could negotiate their relationship to the state. In particular, this label revealed the family's intimate life to state scrutiny and hyper-surveillance.

All those who fall into the UK bureaucratic category of 'target groups' (Ofsted 2014) are subject to home visits and therefore such intimate state encounters[4] have a much wider resonance than Romanian Roma families. However, there are particular dynamics at play for the families that reproduce and exacerbate their marginalised status. Intimate state encounters function either to secure fragile political membership or instigate state abduction of children and forced movement (see Chapter Six). I will now briefly review the intertwining factors that make Romanian Roma families an extreme case.

Romanian Roma did not have a community organisation where they could receive advice and support unlike many other 'minority' groups in Luton. Throughout my fieldwork, it became evident that family members (particularly men) avoided each other to prevent conflict. This was clear in streets, shops, events organised for children and between men in the *khangheri* (church). If two people from different families passed each other in the street they did not acknowledge each other. They may not have known that they both spoke *Romanës* in their home. However, frontline workers put them together into the same group as 'Romanian Roma'. This avoidance of others, limited communication between different families, and their awareness of historical devaluings of the imposed identification of Gypsy or Roma (such as being seen as liars, cheaters and criminals) impeded families' ability to organise and work together as an identifiable 'community group' (Chapter Three). Moreover, many Romanian Roma had not attended school, often because of historical processes of racism and prejudice (Clark 2014). Many adults could not read letters and relied on spoken words to understand the bureaucratic channels that might be open to them (see Chapter Three). Their legal statuses were also extremely complicated due to their A2 migration status, under which they were allowed to reside in the UK for three months but had no access to the UK's social protection or benefit system. In order to gain a secure status they needed to keep meticulous records of their migration and work history, which was impossible for most because of their illiteracy and the precarious nature of their work (again, traceable to a prior history of racism or lack of formal qualifications). They understood this complicated bureaucratic identity through limited circles of friends and family and the non-translated words of bureaucrats (Chapter Three).

Lack of schooling within families and lack of support meant that there were no Romanian Roma candidates to be community workers, teaching assistants or translators. While there are also issues with drawing on those who are deemed to be 'culturally proximate' to provide support (see Chapter Two), the lack of Romanian Roma in these roles allowed the propagation of stereotypes within support organisations. Moreover, translators may have had negative perceptions of Roma. The situation Jan Grill (2018) describes as 'migrating racialisations' strongly resonates with my observations, whereby Roma were subject to new forms of racism in their migratory context because of the racist 'expertise' provided by their migrating co-nationals.

This phenomenon alludes to a further particularity of Roma migrants: they are positioned as not having a national home-land in Europe or elsewhere. Roma have been categorised as a 'nation without a state', leading to highly contested arguments that they are 'true' Europeans or paradigmatic 'transnationals' (McGarry 2017). The history and wide-ranging debate regarding 'Roma' identity, and the national building and bordering of pan-European Romani identity, is addressed in Chapter Three. Suffice to say the families at the heart of this book did not know the Roma national flag, the Roma national anthem, nor (as far as I knew) had ever met a Roma rights activist or been engaged in formal politics (or what might be recognised as political claims-making of any kind). Their understanding of migration, home and belonging was undoubtedly affected by this.

Or, perhaps more saliently, *our* understanding of migration, home and belonging is challenged by the categorisation of Roma. The nation-state is often taken as the analytical and methodological category to define 'Others'.[5] Historically, Roma have not been able to rely on a nation-state to protect their interests. The home-land has been the site of historical slavery, forced sterilisation, eviction and persecution (see Chapter Three). Roma parents across Europe at different historical time periods have been

– and are currently portrayed as – 'despicable' and incapable of reproducing European subjects (Vincze 2014; Wasileski and Miller 2014; Vrăbiescu and Kalir 2018).[6] On the national scale, Roma experience discrimination and hostility because of their position of extreme 'Otherness'. In these contexts the focus on the domestic home and family takes on increased salience. This book charts how new forms of statecraft are making incursions into this space, perhaps one of the few remaining potential sites of safety. The question then becomes, how can these so-called 'despicable mothers' gain citizenship through practices of motherhood within these spaces, while those same spaces are rendered unsafe?

Good mothers and bad migrants

When I first began living with Romanian Roma in Luton in January 2013, I had no idea that mothers were visited at home, or of the stakes that were involved in these visits. Nor did the significance of these home visits become immediately clear to me. As my language skills improved I began to become more aware of variants of the phrase: 'I don't want ladies coming to look at my kids' (*chi kamav avelas te dikas murre shave*). As I began to know families better I became increasingly aware of the rumours that spread about children who had been taken away from their families and put into state care. One particularly potent rumour circulated that if children did not have their own bedrooms with their own beds, state actors could take them away from the family. If the child was under 2 years old, mothers heard that they would lose their babies forever. These rumours fuelled fears about home visits and their potential repercussions. As I spent more and more time in Romanian Roma homes I was aware that some mothers were visited many times by different kinds of state actors and volunteers, while some migrants (particularly those without children) never experienced home visits.

The presence of children was the most significant aspect of these migrants' state interactions. Children were influential because they were subject to particular legal and policy conditions, which meant that they could not be ignored, regardless of who their parents were. The UK has legal rules governing the safety of children that do not rely on legal residency status. All parents in the UK have to bring up children to a standard that ensures the child's 'safety'. It is the state (through social workers) that decides what 'safety' means. The right of the state in these matters is greater than the right of the primary carer of a child.[7] The situation becomes complicated for EU national parents, particularly if they are poor. In cases where a migrant with children is at risk of destitution, they should qualify for support from the local government under the Children Act 1989 (including those who have legally been deemed 'No Recourse to Public Funds'). However, nationals from an EU member state are excluded. Local governments who judge an EU child 'at risk of destitution' cannot provide parents with support.[8] The only legal avenue to secure the 'safety' of the child is to take them into state care.

Home visits could be dangerous for mothers because they opened the possibility that their child could be assessed as 'unsafe'. However, home visits also provided mothers with the opportunity to gain information about their legal statuses and the regulations that governed their residency in the UK. Mothers could engage in relational labour through hosting to make interventions into the racialised stereotypes of Romanian Roma to gain a fragile form of political belonging. Home visits could have hugely different outcomes depending on how state actors judged mothers. While some home encounters led to hyper-surveillance of mothers' domestic space, others led to a refusal to care and families slipped into invisibility, becoming irregular migrants with no legal residency or recourse.

A further important dimension of home visits was that they were the primary and often only contact Romanian Roma made with state actors. As mentioned above, home visits did not happen to all migrants; they seemed to be a special practice reserved for those whose lives were identified as chaotic. Being identified as Romanian Roma immediately placed a mother within this category because of perceived cultural practices. Being identified as Romanian Roma acted to increase the focus on the home and stopped other practices (in other spaces) developing, such as having meetings in children's centres, health centres or non-government organisation (NGO) offices. Therefore home encounters describe interactions primarily between women (both mothers and state actors) as they engage in potentially life-changing meetings about legal status within homes. One of the main concerns of this book is to pay close attention to everyday experiences to reveal how assumptions based on race and gender differences led to, and played out in, home encounters, what this meant for migrants' everyday lives, and how Romanian Roma were able to make a home, and feel at home, under these conditions.

Feeling at home?

Research on the meaning and experience of 'home' has proliferated over the past two decades, particularly within the disciplines of sociology, anthropology, psychology, human geography, history, architecture and philosophy (see Mallett 2004 for overview). In migration studies, the idea of diaspora unsettled the fixed notion of home (Hannerz 1996; Blunt 2005; Nowicka 2007). Easthope (2004: 136) similarly promotes a de-territorialised, relational explanation of home, noting that 'while homes may be located it is not the location that is "home"'. Previous research has provided insights into the home as a multi-dimensional concept or a multi-layered phenomenon (Somerville 1992; Bowlby et al. 1997; Rapport and Dawson 1998; Wardhaugh 1999; Duyvendak 2011), identifying home as a conceptual and discursive space of identification, and as a nodal point in social relations (Olwig 2011). The diversity of different conceptions of home, dwelling, and belonging point to the, 'rearrangement through the production, relocation and re-experiencing of physical, social and emotional landscapes' (Ramírez 2014: 670).

The concept of home is unquestionably linked to identity, memory, structures of feeling, space, scales and intensities of affiliation, and material objects. However, the emphasis on the way that people make their homes can overshadow the ways that places also shape people, particularly in situations of unequal power. Feelings of home are mediated by feelings of control over physical space and this is structured beyond immediate social relationships.

The issue of being in control is central to feeling at home. One way to get close to the importance of these feelings, particularly in cases where migrants are concerned, is through the etymological similarity between host and hostage. As Jacques Derrida (2000: 53-4) states:

> I want to be master at home, to be able to receive whomever
> I like there. Anyone who encroaches on my 'at home', on my
> power of hospitality, on my sovereign as host, I start to regard as
> an undesirable foreigner, and virtually as an enemy. This other
> becomes a hostile subject, and I risk becoming his hostage.

The 'undesirable foreigner' is always at risk of overstaying their welcome and therefore hospitality cannot be thought about without the corresponding risk of hostility. These feelings equally relate to the home-space and the home-land. Through the lens of the home encounter, we can see how, the 'undesirable foreigner' within the home shifts when we move through different scales of home as nation and home as domestic. The 'undesirable foreigner' is also placed within a different set of meanings when viewed through different historical lenses such as colonial relations. Crucially, there is not a simple dichotomy between hospitality and hostility but both are always in tension and negotiation.

This is a crucial point and a key contribution of this book to debates on migration, belonging and citizenship. Citizenship has been variously defined throughout social science literature as a major form of political belonging that emphasises the equality of all members of the political community (McClintock, 1995), while in practice citizenship is characterised by a differentiated flow of resources to persons and social groups (Turner, 1993: 2).[9] Definitions of citizenship include legally defined rights and duties and a structure of feeling that entails the certainty of belonging (Muehlebach 2012: 158).[10] Citizenship is always contextually situated (Clarke et al. 2014). Through the notion of home I trace the interplay between notions of who belongs to the nation and the everyday negotiations of belonging in its messy and mundane sense. This book demonstrates how everyday practices of belonging are directly linked to the politics of belonging in and through the home. These negotiations and contestations not only take place in the public sphere, or within the scale of home-land as a metaphorical or ideological construct; but also in the embodied, material and everyday space of the domestic home. My focus and aim in this book is to explore how the nation-state is reproduced *within* the geographical home space, and the consequences this has for state theory.

A critical starting point for thinking about how the state is reproduced within the home-space is to follow an anthropological approach that does not see the state as a homogeneous entity that sits above society; rather, it emerges through everyday processes and is embedded in everyday lives (Sharma and Gupta 2006). This draws on a long tradition of examining the way bureaucracies function.[11] First argued by Mitchell (1991) and developed by Mountz (2003) and Heyman (2004), this perspective argues that the state is not just constituted of, but is constituted by, everyday social processes of reproduction (Marston 2004; Coleman 2012). Mitchell argues that the mundane and decentred practices of state officials and ordinary citizens give meaning to state projects and practices (1999) and that states are constituted from the product of these practices (Painter 1995). The state is not a unified object but made up of many different individuals and institutions. Anthropological perspectives see the state as a discursive construction – it does not exist but is continually 'made' and legitimised by the actions of those who in some way represent state power, and a society that discursively reproduces the notion that the state sits 'above' the everyday.

Scholarly attention has turned to examine how the state is 'spatialised'; how and where it emerges, for whom, and in what form (Ferguson and Gupta 2002; Navaro-Yashin 2002; Das and Poole 2004; Reeves 2014). This relational perspective on the state has examined how state representations are tied to state practices (Thelen et al. 2014): through infrastructure (Pinker and Harvey 2015), affect (Laszczkowski and Reeves 2015), structures of feeling (Obeid 2010), and desire for the state (Jansen 2014). This book draws on and builds on this scholarly work by emphasising the focus on the ambiguous caring and governing 'faces of the state' in the figure of the (precarious) welfare officer. The book also foregrounds the importance of integrating the intimate space of the home into these discussions of relational encounters.

Focusing on the home space also opens up a new area of analysis for social scientists who explore encounters across 'difference'. The book is concerned with encounters in the home between migrants and various others who in some way or another gatekeep migrants' citizenship and legal statuses. Elsewhere, everyday or mundane encounters have been studied in parochial and public urban spaces and 'micro-publics' (Berg and Sigona 2013; Hall 2013; Neal et al. 2013; Valentine 2013). Studies of encounters in urban space have generally focused on serendipity and 'neighbourly' relations across difference (Wessendorf 2013). However, encounters within the home take on a different character marked by their intimacy and the relations of power and hierarchy that are implied through notions of kinship and the ethics of care.

The intimate state encounter also has implications for the study of intercultural encounters and 'conviviality' more generally, which has typically focused on public or parochial spaces such as markets, and not paid enough attention to spaces of governance. These studies have tended to bracket out 'private' spaces, which are often understood in the conviviality literature as segregated or as revealing the limits of conviviality (Lofland 1998; Jensen 2013). This book demonstrates that the home is a place of (sometimes forced) lived diversities. It advances the literature on conviviality by opening up the home as a new site of lived diversity and also by foregrounding the importance of context to our understandings of conviviality.

This book also brings together a wide range of literature across disciplinary boundaries to understand the significance of the home encounter. Social policy researchers have previously examined home interventions through council housing management (Damer 2000; Ravetz 2003) and programmes such as 'troubled families' (Hayden and Jenkins 2014; Crossley 2016), 'problem families' (Garrett 2007), 'family-nurse partnerships' (Barnes 2008; Zadorozhnyi 2009), 'family intervention projects' (Parr and Nixon 2009; Morgan 2010; Batty and Flint 2012) and 'parent-focused programmes' aimed at gangs, drugs misuse, anti-social behaviour or youth violence (Holt 2008; Carr 2010; Aldridge et al. 2011). However, there has yet to be sustained analysis of encounters across many different social policy programmes in these domestic contexts, which is crucial to understanding the position of those marginalised. The intersection between the 'hostile environment' for migrants (Jones et al. 2017; Yuval Davis et al. 2018) and working-class marginality has also not been fully explored ethnographically. Moreover, none of this research has paid sufficient attention to materiality and the specific context of the spatial effects of these encounters.[12]

Such accounts have typically assumed the roles of client and service provider, rather than taking a processual approach and conceptualising how boundaries emerge and are negotiated. There has also been no sustained gendered analysis that brings the socially situated positions of all actors into analysis and examines the how intimate relationships shape citizenship and belonging. This book brings together the literature on street-level bureaucracy, relational encounters and racialised motherhood through the notion of the intimate state encounter to fill these gaps.

Social workers have also begun to think about the home visit as a distinct sphere of practice and experience in its own right, involving senses and emotions, and how movement through the home space is central (Ferguson 2018). This literature draws on anthropological understandings of 'liminality', an 'in-between' state, a sense of normlessness that arises from moving from one state to another (Turner, 1969). I argue that the home is not a 'normless' space situated in the movement between 'public' and 'private' spaces. Rather, home encounters do more than confuse the public and private; they actively depend on and reproduce that confused space. When frontline workers enter this space they do not enter a state of liminality that will eventually subside or come to a satisfying ritualised conclusion. The power of this public/private uncertainty is that mothers and frontline workers are always in a state of fragile negotiation that can never be fully reconciled.

The governance of intimacy through uncertainty runs throughout the book. The main argument is that the governance of marginality takes place through intimate state encounters creating spaces of indeterminacy, uncertainty and confusion. Such confusion allows frontline workers to maintain a coherent moral standpoint while enacting painful acts of exclusion, and thus also maintain their belief in the liberal promise of the state that provides protection to those who need it. Crucially, governance through uncertainty allows sentiment to overtake rights, depoliticising and pacifying those on the edges.

Politics of care and belonging through home space

To make this argument, two concepts are employed in this book – belonging and care – both of which have become increasingly significant in social sciences. Recent anthropological studies have used 'belonging' as a synonym for kinship (Edwards and Strathern 2000) while in the social sciences 'belonging' has been widely used to replace the concepts of identity, citizenship and integration (Geddes and Favell 1999; Pfaff-Czarnecka 2011; Yuval Davis 2013). This semantic shift has been justified by trying to move away from essentialising notions towards a more processual view of social relations.

Thelen and Coe (2017) argue that 'belonging' opens up the productive and multifaceted aspects of political identification and incorporation. For example, through his work on farms in Zimbabwe, Rutherford (2008: 73) underlines the significance of 'routinized discourses, social practices and institutional arrangements through which people make claims for resources and rights, the ways through which they become incorporated in particular places'. Similarly Krause and Schramm (2011: 119) argue 'other forms of incorporation may coexist with (and be in conflict with) citizenship regimes'. It has long been argued that formal citizenship is complicated by other belongings through which rights and access to resources are claimed. The aim in this book is to show how the politics of belonging and legal rights are made up in relation to other forms of social membership and practices of belonging within homes. These multiple forms of relations often evoke and draw on notions of care and mutuality but are also marked by distinguishing insiders and outsiders. The ones who do not receive care have to be constructed as undeserving of membership.

Invoking critical notions of care has a long history in feminist scholarship to connect the interpersonal to the structural, the public and the private.[13] More recently a body of scholarly work has looked at care through the lens of neoliberal policies, which are remaking the responsibilities and obligations of citizens (Ticktin 2011; Muehlebach 2012; Stevenson 2014). These literatures analyse the complexities of care, including its negative effects, which often entail power asymmetries. Care mobilises (and requires) social, material and economic resources and is significant in generating belonging (Tronto 2013). As Thelen and Coe (2017: 6) argue, 'the concept of care helps us to understand how political belonging is understood through representations of reciprocity and mutuality'. This book explores how care, and the refusal to care, plays out through intimate state encounters with repercussions for political belonging.

Outline of the book

The first three chapters outline the situated positions of different actors in the encounter, our different understandings and perspectives and how we are seen by others. Chapter One presents the research methodology including theoretical discussions of 'anthropological truth', and my own shifting situated positions throughout the fieldwork and writing process. My methodology conceptualised the social actor as a mobile spatial field. I did not choose the space of the home as my 'field site' – the home emerged as the most salient site of interaction through this methodology. This has two implications. First, following the social actor through different spaces provides a different entry point to social worlds (resonating with feminist analytics), rather than choosing a space and exploring the social actors that create it. Second, this approach revealed the home as the site where 'culture' was located and contested. This approach opens the home space to studies on diversity and conviviality. It also demonstrates the different terms that encounters in the home took on through the social roles of host and hosting, the materiality of the space, and gendered dynamics.

Chapter Two presents the position of frontline workers. The chapter is underpinned by a theoretical discussion of the 'relational state' and conceptualisation of 'the frontline'. It emphasises the importance of integrating the intimate space of the home into debate on relational encounters. I present the notion of 'everyday discretion' to describe the situated decisions that frontline workers had to make in the face of ethical dilemmas. These areas of discretion and uncertainty allowed sentiment to overtake rights and created individualised and fragile relationships of care. These decisions drew on and were justified through frontline workers' own life histories, cultural discourses and their own understanding of performing the 'good citizen' within a post-welfare state. This chapter acknowledges that frontline workers themselves have multiple 'roles', including being mothers, and may also have experiences of migration or marginalisation that shaped how they 'make up' the state for Romanian Roma mothers. This chapter identifies the unexplored issues of race, migration background and citizenship status in discussions of class in relation to home inspectors,[14] and examines institutional factors in the power dynamics of the domestic visit.

Chapter Three moves to examine migrant families and how they come to be perceived as Romanian Roma, the generative and co-produced nature of labelling, the symbolic violence that is accomplished through this label, and how it comes to hold currency in the UK state apparatus. The first section focuses on how the label developed; the second charts how being categorised in this way led to home encounters through the particular lens on child safeguarding; and the third considers how mothers' understanding of their position and room for manoeuvre were shaped by their backgrounds, such as illiteracy and previous experience of state violence. The chapter examines how encounters came to contribute to the mutual constitution of respective identities and how this shaped understandings of, and fears and desires for, the state.

Chapters Four, Five and Six analyse how intimate state encounters became the key mechanism of negotiation with the state, how these interactions played out and with what consequences for the actors involved, and how the state is reproduced along gendered and racialised hierarchies. Chapter Four looks specifically at home encounters and how they became the dominant mode of interaction with the state for mothers identified as Romanian Roma. Encounters between subjects and objects of state care have been explored through many different literatures, including social work, geography, anthropology, social policy and urban studies. In particular the emotional framing of encounters has been most recently explored through two sets of literature that have developed separately, namely the anthropology of the state (Reeves 2014) and social policy (Stenson 2013; Lawson and Elwood 2014; Crawford and Flint 2015). This chapter (and the book more broadly) brings the space of the home into anthropological debates on the state and incorporates the notion of relational encounters into social policy literature on street-level bureaucracy. Making links between these two bodies of literature allows us to think beyond strict dichotomies of the 'state' and 'community' to how boundaries emerge and are made significant. It also allows us question the costs and injuries of these new forms of governance. This chapter shows not only that processes such as bordering and gatekeeping services take place within the home, but that the nature of these processes – and therefore the reproduction of the state – take on different forms and complexities *because* they take place within the home, informing who is deemed morally legitimate to receive care.

Chapter Five builds on the previous chapter and explores the gendered complexities of the intimate state encounter in more detail, including how particular meanings that are imbued in the 'private' and domestic space heighten the gendered nature of governing relationships, placing more work on women and simultaneously excluding men. It explores how family organisation and inscribed gender roles therein can exacerbate or ease the uncertainty and confusion within home encounters. The means by which home encounters shape relationships among Romanian Roma women and men are also examined, as are the relationships between Romanian Roma women and, typically, female support workers and male church volunteers. The chapter argues that those who perform 'appropriate' subjects of care (as mothers) can be positioned as objects of care (of the state) and consequently that men are excluded from these processes.

Finally, Chapter Six details how re-bordering has occurred in the UK through welfare regulations that emerge in the home space. The chapter is underpinned by elaborating on 'bordering' as a theoretical perspective, and how the borders of Europe have become de-territorialised. It reveals how inclusion operates through exclusion, as those who formally gain legal residency are called on to consistently perform deservingness and gratitude through long-standing, individualised and fragile caring relationships with frontline actors. The chapter details the costs and injuries of these practices and how they contain both the promise of safety and also the fear of losing children to state care. These encounters demonstrate how care shifts the 'location' of the state and creates different forms of belonging.

The Conclusion reviews how intimate state encounters have affected the everyday lives of those engaged in them. In particular I foreground several key ways the analytical framework of the encounter develops understandings of citizenship and conceptions of care and belonging.

The chapters are punctuated by interludes that provide a brief story of an encounter or a series of encounters between a family and me. These interludes are an effort to recount the intricacies of relationships that I developed through the fieldwork and to make clearer how I worked. Each is loosely linked to the theme of the subsequent chapter and all address the notion of home.

Final remarks

This book opens up new questions for academic and political debates about citizenship, migration and belonging. It demonstrates how the right to belong has come to rest on the judgements of everyday routines in domestic space. It links everyday practices of belonging with the politics of belonging – or, in other words, it shows how everyday actions in the home affect the ethical and political value systems with which migrants are judged to 'belong'. Such home surveillance is far from a liberal democratic discourse where membership rests on rights and entitlements and putatively protects the privacy of domestic and familial space. This book clearly shows the conceit of privacy: it simply does not exist for those who do not have the material and symbolic resources to carve it out.

The uncertainty generated by governing in these spaces raises questions about the wider theoretical and substantive significance of living in a world in which the home visit is becoming an increasingly important element of how many people will live everyday life in their homes and work in the homes of others (Pink et al. 2015). Frontline workers have shifted from Lipsky's (2010) 'street-level bureaucrats' to roles that combine state, non-government and voluntary services in myriad combinations, exacerbating this uncertainty. Moreover, it is increasingly difficult to distinguish between these categories due to complex funding streams, governance arrangements and local political economies (Humphris 2018a). Life-changing decisions are diffused to frontline workers, who are often themselves in precarious citizenship or employment positions. More ethnographic research on governance is needed, particularly on the moral and ethical economies that play out and the impacts of these processes on everyday lives.

This book also provokes reflection on the governance of intimacy through elaborating on the term 'intimate state encounters'. A long line of inspirational scholarship has shown how mothering has always been political (Crenshaw 1989; Collins 1997; Stoler 2002; Reynolds 2005; Erel 2011b). How mothers care for their children, and their values of social reproduction, are directly linked to state reproduction. These processes do not just affect those who do not have a secure legal status. Racialised 'Others' are consistently called on to reproduce and perform their adherence to conflicting and contradictory sets of intimate behaviours and values even when they gain legal status. Those who make incursions into their homes can be similarly conceptualised as holding a marginalised status (typically comprising women from migration and minority backgrounds) indicating a shift in the governance of marginalisation. This book explores how governance through intimacy exacerbates marginalisation but further research is needed to trace its manifold consequences.

Finally, this book invites us to consider meanings of home, how we are able to make a home and feel at home and how marginalisation operates to constrict the spaces of home. This book looks specifically at those identified as Romanian Roma, but these questions are widely relevant where the injuries of these processes may not be as visible because marginalisation is not as stigmatised or extreme. This book really asks, what does home mean in a hostile home-land? What kinds of homes are achieved in these conditions? And how can we understand the actions of a state which surveys, filters and sorts families within their own homes?

1

Home truths: fieldwork, writing and anthropology's 'home encounter'

This book is based on the 14 months between January 2013 and March 2014 I spent conducting fieldwork, living with three families who were identified by the local state as Romanian Roma or Gypsies. Anthropologists have been thinking about issues surrounding ethnographic fieldwork, writing and knowledge production for a long time. Knowledge 'creates' the world by giving it shape and so discourse and symbolic constructs configure the way we make sense of our lives. Anthropologists tend to repeat representations when talking about these constructs (such as ethnic groups, cultural meanings or values), presenting these concepts as if they actually existed (Brubaker 2002). However, these representations might best be seen as schemes which function as methods that produce expectations (D'Andrade 1995: 79). Crucially, schemes are structured around paradigms. Therefore, within this framework, perceiving the world means putting it in relation to these schemes that give reality form and meaning (with the acknowledgement that the schemes themselves are reshaped and reorganised in the light of every new experience of interpretation). This book can be seen as a narrative which gives reality a possible shape.

The chapters that follow can therefore be seen to represent my understanding of the world produced by those I spent time with, which has been given shape by using the language provided from my background and education, making these experiences interact and blend with my fieldwork. These experiences were not solely mine, but made in relation to all those who I spent time with. However, I did not just participate and 'observe' others. I was also being observed, talked about and reacted to in various different ways. Ethnographers and 'the observed' manipulate each other, negotiate and adjust their categories of thought, and eventually produce a fusion that results in new meanings (Rabinow 2007: 6).

Most importantly, the ethnographic text must be seen as only one perspective, a reflection on the events that were experienced. In the words of Appadurai (1988: 16), 'the ethnographic text is the more or less creative imposition of order on the many conversations that lie at the heart of fieldwork'. With this in mind, I detail how I went about living with Romanian Roma families and the frontline workers (social workers, teachers, doctors, children's centre workers) and volunteers they encountered in Luton.

My data consists of field notes, life histories, detailed descriptions of specific encounters, and formal and informal interviews and conversations that took place most intensively between January 2013 and March 2014 but still continue as I am writing this. Formal interviews consisted of 52 local government employees, 13 third-sector workers and eight volunteers who all had responsibilities or duties that involved newcomers to the local area or those who had direct contact with them. I also conducted participant observation with these actors including accompanying them on more than 10 home visits and attending more than five 'multi-agency meetings' about migrants in the local area. I used a patchwork of different methods shaped by the participation of different actors. My position as a researcher with both migrants and their connections with state authorities required constant mediations and adjustments as relationships developed and I became more entwined in everyday life. I was also asked direct questions about a particular family by frontline workers and other families, such as how many children they had, their economic activities, if they had a national insurance number or if they received any state benefits. If I knew the information I openly said to family members that knew but would not tell them. To frontline workers I said that I did not know (even if I did).

Given the variety of subjects, it was necessary to adopt different techniques to suit different schedules but also to ensure that I was performing the role of researcher and my ethical duty to the research participants. However, I also needed to be flexible and open to engaging with subjects on the meanings and understandings of their roles and behaviours.

In addition, my treatment of different types of 'data' or materials gained from particular research instruments deserves a note of clarification. I was attentive to the inherently performative aspect in all interactions, particularly in narrations of events or when different actors related segments of their life histories. When writing field notes I made detailed descriptions of the time, place and context and my relationship and thoughts and feelings regarding the interaction. This practice was particularly useful when analysing interviews with frontline workers. Frontline workers' reflections invoke the politics surrounding what we remember, forget and construct, which is shaped by our situated experiences. I take a similar perspective to Radstone and Schwarz (2010: 3) who argue that 'memory is active, forging its pasts to serve present interests'. I do not, therefore, consider these descriptions to be any less illuminating. All narratives are a 'redescribing' of the world, where something new is brought into the world by the means of language. As Carr (1986: 120) identified, temporal distance does not lead to distortion or falsification but carries the 'positive and productive possibility of understanding'. This resonates with the notion of 'productive nostalgia' where memories acquire a tangible form and become 'embodied and enacted in practice rather than solely in narrative or imagination' (Blunt 2005: 208). Thus the advantage of hindsight, the opportunity to make sense of things anew, is crucial to the understanding of narratives. I have tried as much as possible to place narratives within their spoken context.

I also use the experiences of living within the homes of three families and spending my everyday life with them and their networks. We shared experiences from the intensely boring to the highly emotional, such as the beginnings and endings of human life, evictions, incarcerations, racial violence, redundancies, the joy of stopping a deportation order, birthday parties and religious celebrations. I learned to speak the dialect of *Romanës* that was spoken by families in their homes. In addition, various friends or family members often came to stay in the houses I lived in and therefore I often shared the room where I slept, and sometimes my bed, with mothers. All these experiences provided a richness and nuance that could not be captured in field notes or interviews.

Methodology of the encounter and the encounter as methodology

I have carefully chosen the word 'encounter' in this book because it evokes different senses of meaning and does much more 'work' (theoretically) in comparison with other words that might describe the meeting of people, such as 'contact' or 'interaction'. It not only describes what happened in the homes of migrants, but also an approach and entry point to the social worlds of others. The encounter is a common anthropological device to explain social phenomena. In contrast I am using 'encounter' not as a reflection on a wider social process but as the methodological and analytical framework. I use encounters in and of themselves, not as an example or a representation of social meaning or organisation but where meanings are being negotiated and formed.

While it has received scant theoretical attention the ubiquitous use of 'encounter' to describe contact does considerable work. Encounters have been approached as a site of disturbances (Stewart 2007): about 'rupture', 'surprise' and 'shock' (Ahmed 2000; Lapworth 2015). The implicit understanding that encounters are experienced as relational events that disturb us is central to their framing as sites of transformation, evoking instances in which something is 'unexpectedly broken open' or destabilised (Wilson 2017). This literature sees the encounter as a singular isolated event where we face the unexpected. In the ethnographic context, encounters do have these dimensions but they are also deeply reproductive. They are repetitive but they also involve a doubling of experience. They happen in sequence and in history. For example, the migrant mothers at the heart of this article have heard stories about the UK before they arrived and rumours about encounters. Frontline workers and families gain reputations. On both sides expectations are shared about these encounters. Rumours include both the stories of those who have gained legal residency and those who have had their children taken into care (Chapter Three).

Home encounters are not new, singular events that come out of nowhere. Frontline workers are also migrants and mothers themselves and remember what it was like growing up and encountering racism (Humphris 2018b). Or as more recent migrants they have their own stories of navigating the UK migration bureaucracy. Frontline workers reflected on behaviours of the mothers, comparing them with their own experiences of appealing to, or resisting, the state when they were in similar positions.

Encounters are therefore not only about rupture but also about repetition. Context, history and the expected are crucial. The iterative nature of these encounters draws attention, and brings us closer, to the experience of state bureaucracy in everyday life. Small interventions that aim at, and are guided by, larger projects are the way that bureaucracy works. Frontline workers are always involved in piecemeal actions that coagulate into larger wholes. How this iteration and merging of various interactions and meetings crystallise into an understanding of 'the state' in everyday life is perhaps what bureaucracy really is and the way that bureaucracy is lived on both sides of the encounter.[15]

The notion of encounter is also helpful here to document my participation and my positionality. I held many different and contradictory positions some of which I chose, and others I was manoeuvred into. My position shifted within and between encounters and was one of being a sister, daughter, friend, or I was seen as an outsider, for example Georgeta told her son when he refused to go to school that I could report him to the police. I was also, in some ways, acculturated into families in the same way as a child. Towards the end of my fieldwork Dan often told me and his brother's family (often in a humorous tone) that he had six children (not five) and that I was his biggest daughter. I was taught appropriate skills such as the language, how to get babies to sleep, how to wash clothes by hand and how to butcher chickens. I was also guided in behaviours and performances of emotions. I was told how to politely interact with others such as wishing men in the house 'good morning' (*drobiu tu*) or if someone wished me a good morning how to appropriately respond (*ter treise*). I was told to make sure that I didn't hold new babies when I was menstruating without pinching their noses, and many other practices that were considered '*lazhav*' (shameful) or '*marime*' (polluting – as opposed to *melalo* which meant dirty). I was taught what was funny and deserved laughter, how to celebrate a birth or birthday, how to mourn and show grief, what situations provoked worry, fear and anger, and what situations should be given over to luck (*baxt*) or to God (*o del*).

I was asked to call frontline workers and speak to them on behalf of mothers; at other times I was expressly forbidden not to speak. I created tactics such as only calling a frontline worker if I had been expressly asked to do so. I was always aware of how imperfect these tactics could be and was always torn by the allure of wanting to observe while being unsure of what the exact repercussions might be or how I might be asked to participate. I purposely excluded myself from some conversations with frontline workers because I thought it would compromise my position with migrant families, but sometimes it was very difficult to know when this might happen or it emerged later that it was significant. Mothers would also ask me about the legal and residency status of other mothers. I learnt that rumours spread quickly and I also never told anyone about the legal status or personal details of others. Through these experiences and being asked to be a link to the state (much like the frontline workers) I gained a deeper knowledge of frontline workers' ethical dilemmas, ambivalence and the way they might manoeuvre themselves within encounters.

Throughout the 14 months I lived with families I observed a large variety of encounters with a number of frontline workers. These encounters took place most frequently between new migrant mothers and female service providers within mothers' domestic spaces. I therefore started from the practices of migrants themselves. As mentioned previously, I did not set out to specifically research mothering practices. Mothering emerged as the most important site through which new migrants could negotiate their legal rights in the UK.

Encounters also allow analysis to start from the mothers themselves. I follow feminist critical analysis, which argues that investigations should begin from the lives of marginal groups and their histories (Haraway 1988) and that there is a 'need for a different entry point for analysis that approaches the individual in their role as citizen starting from marginal groups rather than an institutional or representational angle' (Andrijasevic 2013: 49). Drawing from this, the encounter as a methodology can be seen as a way to start from the negotiations and actions between migrants and others, rather than from an institutional perspective and an endeavour to undertake an intersectional perspective.

What has come to be termed 'gendered intersectional analysis' is confronted with a set of challenges due to the inherent complexity of the concept. This is echoed by Leslie McCall (2005: 1771) who states 'despite the emergence of intersectionality as a major paradigm of research in women's studies and elsewhere, there has been little discussion of how to study intersectionality; that is, of its methodology'. My approach is to use the encounter as a methodology that allows interactions to be analysed as a relational process where different characteristics become salient at different moments as actors move through vectors of time and space.

This heeds Massey's (1994: 2) call that 'space must always be conceptualised integrally with time; indeed the aim should be to think always in terms of space-time'. I use this approach to trace how migrants and others experience place and how embodied movement embedded in social relationships creates place. Space is conceptualised not as a container but as movement (Pandya 1990). This applies in terms of meanings attached to the material and physical as well as in bodily practices, routines or thoughts and feelings performed or verbally expressed. These meanings were inscribed differently by the individuals moving through different spaces.

Using the movement of people through spaces and moving with them helped me to understand the way migrants make place, what motivates them to go to certain places, how this is shaped by different embedded relationships and how their performances change in different spaces. I followed migrants' movements around Luton and also to Romania, undertaking three trips to villages in Moldavia, Oradea and Bucharest with different families. I also followed migrants to different areas of the UK, including Manchester and Croydon. These experiences have shaped the analysis and I draw on them when making sense of the social and material processes by which actors (re)create the experienced spaces in which they lived. I also became aware of the routes and paths that migrants came to know, how that affected the meanings they made from different spaces, and how that shaped the opportunities that could be open to them (such as knowing where the job centre was located). I gained knowledge of the town from the perspective of different individuals and mapped the areas and routes that particular families or individuals took and knew about. Being attentive to these practices also illuminated the way those who are illiterate navigate space without being able to read. For example, I did not observe anyone looking at maps or searching for locations on the internet. I was aware that people used particular markers to find their way to other people's homes, rather than looking at street signs. In addition, none of the women drove a car. Therefore their movement through the town was always on foot (some in high heeled shoes and long skirts), usually pushing a buggy or accompanied by children. This affected routes, duration, motivations for moving and understanding the town.

I was also aware of my own movement and how it created a particular understanding of the town. Families often asked me why I didn't buy a car (also many men were eager to sell me a car). This was very tempting, particularly in the winter months when walking the streets in the snow or rain became intensely tiring and cold. I also thought that a car might be a place where I could write notes quickly and have some time away from the hustle of family life. However, I decided against this due to the methodological standpoint described above. I was keen to experience walking through the town with mothers, driving in cars with frontline workers and driving in vans with men. This also heightened my awareness of the range of choices that were open due to the availability of different forms of transport, the requirements of different forms of company in different situations, the role of dress, and the rhythm of the day.

My involvement in home encounters also raise questions that resonate with colonial encounter and who is in a position to make knowledge about others. The resonances between the colonial state and the early welfare state in which 'visiting' was a key modality of governance, with women from dominant class locations entering the homes of women from subaltern locations to assess and meet their needs is explored in Chapter Three. The classed, racialised and gendered regime of knowledge and power, specifically of visibility, whereby some bodies have the right to enter the homes of others in order to produce knowledges about them, is a regime that is in some senses mirrored by the practices of anthropology and 'fieldwork'. As Asad warns (1973: 17), 'anthropologists have contributed, sometimes indirectly, towards maintaining the structure of power represented by the colonial system'.

I also made incursions into Roma homes and this book produces knowledge about marginalised and racialised people who were not involved in the writing process. Abu-Lughod expresses how anthropologists have become highly conscious of, and troubled by, our role in shaping the words of people we live with, particularly in conditions of large power asymmetries. She proposes that 'one way to alleviate some of the difficulties of this process of constructing a narrative is by making explicit how one has worked' (Abu-Lughod 1993: 18). Therefore, I have not removed myself entirely from the text or pretended that certain discussions were not directed specifically by or at me. I have tried to make my complicity in policing the borders of Roma identity explicit through being attentive to how Roma are positioned in the EU and the UK (Chapter Two) and how the label Romanian Roma was (re)produced in the particular situated contexts I observed and participated in (Chapter Three).

There is a key methodological issue regarding my position and presence in the space of interactions and how that has affected what I observed between migrants and frontline workers. Some of the tactics I developed included the length of time I spent with both migrants and frontline workers, including moments of shared positive moments and also heightened tensions. I oscillated between observing and being drawn into interactions by migrants or frontline workers or both. At some points this was to act as an authoritative voice or to corroborate a narrative. For some I held a privileged position because I was seen as 'British' and therefore I was expected to know the intricacies of the migration and welfare system. I was constantly called on to explain regulations or decisions. As my language skills increased some frontline workers and migrants asked me to interpret words or phrases, which was a source of tension for me. However, as funding for interpretation was being cut, I became intimately entwined through this involvement.

All interactions were shaped by individual context and therefore I did not use one particular methodology but responded to the action as it unfolded, using my previous knowledge, experience and relationships. Over the course of the fieldwork my relationships developed and changed, and reflecting on these changes was a source of further data. I visited migrants' houses many times, and was therefore aware of how I was treated when frontline workers were and were not present, any changes being recorded in my field notes. Alongside formal interviews I attended frontline workers' meetings, often talking to frontline workers before or after an interaction, and conducting informal conversations in cars during home visits or when we met on the street or in a café. I used all of this information to reflect on my role in encounters and the knowledge that was being relationally produced. I noted whether or how frontline workers involved me in the encounter, what questions they asked about the research and how they introduced me to their colleagues and clients.

I also tried to be as explicit as possible when explaining what I could not share with different actors, and was aware that there were issues and circumstances that they would not share with me, particularly regarding child protection. However, occasionally sharing was unavoidable due to the emotional intensity of the encounter or the need to make sense of situations together. In these instances I have not included what I considered to be confidential conversations in this book. I have also not included events or stories about families that might further stigmatise or marginalise them (in this way I am complicit in policing the boundaries of those identified as 'Roma'). In particular , where I feel as though I do not have the space to fully contextualise and address the complexity of an event or narrative or where it does not demonstrate anything new that has not been addressed elsewhere in the book I have not included them. Although I have not included some events or narratives, they have unavoidably influenced the way I have written about different people's motivations and understandings. I believe this is a great strength of anthropological research and should not be masked. On the contrary I believe it is this element, of the events and stories that are not shared on these pages, that provide analytical nuance and a greater understanding of the complexities and contradictions that emerge as social life unfolds. Therefore, although there are some details that have been omitted from the narratives, these understandings have been re-formed in the analysis and in choosing what to include. To reiterate, without doubt my presence affected the way people behaved and the way that they presented themselves. This may be one of the deepest challenges and yet the source of the most insightful power of ethnographic research.

Luton

Before explaining the fieldwork in more depth, it is important to describe why I chose Luton as the place to conduct this research.

Previous research has mainly privileged metropolitan and large urban centres to analyse intensified globalisation, shifting patterns of migration and mobility, and growing global inequality. Luton can be defined as a downscaled urban area (Humphris 2018a). It is a peripheral urban context but is similarly grappling with the acute need to prioritise and cut services and issue of shifting patterns of mobility that have been attributed to global metropolises. The town is an illuminating case because widespread restructuring and budget cuts in local government has had a greater impact on poorer urban areas (Hastings et al. 2013), leading to a more acute need to prioritise certain services over others. Luton is not a city but its demographics are exemplary of new, dynamic patterns of urban diversity (Hall 1993; Kofman 1998; Touraine 2000; Schierup et al. 2006; Castles and Miller 2009). For example, Luton has a younger population than the UK average, with 22% under 15 years of age compared with 19% nationally (Luton Borough Council 2013). In 2011 the pupil-level school census showed that 51% of children are identified as 'Black, Minority, Ethnic'. The director of children's services commented "We have 62 schools in Luton with more than 120 languages spoken" (interview, November 2013). Furthermore, since May 2004 there had been more than 10,000 new national insurance registrations by people from new EU member states, with more than 80% from Polish nationals (Mayhew and Waples 2011). 'New migrants' became a term that was discussed at all levels of local government and was also included in bureaucratic roles such as an education officer for those who were 'new to the UK' (interview with the co-ordinator for refugees, asylum seekers and all others new to the UK (aged up to 19 years), Luton Borough Council).

Luton has been termed an 'escalator' area, referring to the notion that as soon as residents have sufficient resources they move away (Robson et al. 2008). The town has a permanently new population. This sentiment was evident in interviews:

> 'Your service has to be flexible enough to cater for your client base. Luton is a very transient community. What you do find is that once people reach a certain economic status, they leave Luton… [this] creates a very unique challenge to those who work in the statutory sectors because we have got to be flexible enough to meet the needs of a very changing population.'
> (Home improvement officer, Luton Borough Council)

Migrants' settlement in an area can also be seen as an assessment of its desirability as a place to live. This assessment influences the narrative of an area that contributes to, and reflects, its trajectory of disempowerment or redevelopment (Lee and Yeoh 2006). Luton has a long-standing negative image connected to its 'working class marginality' and has been previously represented as a manifestation of the failure of multiculturalism (Rootham et al. 2015). Luton suffered in the economic recessions of the 1970s and 1980s in which the car industry declined, affecting Luton's Vauxhall car plant which employed the majority of the largely male workforce. The most recent economic downturn saw Luton's unemployment rise in line with national trends (Luton Borough Council 2013). The area is also associated with extremism and racist violence (Francis 2012). The English Defence League (EDL) emerged in Luton, a far-right movement whose stated aim is to oppose the spread of Islam in the UK (Allen 2010; Copsey 2010). Moreover, there had been intensive media coverage of a small number of Islamist militants and four arrests of suspected terrorists that took place in Luton. Due to the history of far-right activities in the town, the implementation of policies that affected migrants and 'minorities' had taken on increased salience within local government.

'Cutting the field': a chronology of fieldwork

A key consideration for all ethnographers is how to 'create' or 'cut' the field site, particularly in urban ethnography. To address this issue I was inspired by Nancy Munn (1996: 450) who draws on Lefebvre's duality of social space as a 'field of action' and a 'basis of action'. She constructs the notion of a 'mobile spatial field' (1996: 451), which can be understood as a culturally defined, corporeal-sensual field stretching out from the body at a given locale or moving through locales. In other words, 'it is a space defined by an actor' (1996: 451). She argues that space cannot be seen simply as referring to culturally meaningful terrestrial places as this 'disarticulates the dynamic relations between spatial regions and moving spatial fields' (1996: 465). Munn uses spatiotemporal analytics (of location, distancing, movement, relative duration and boundaries) and considers space–time as a symbolic nexus of relations produced out of interactions between 'bodily actors and terrestrial spaces'; this allows her to question the locus of powers of exclusion and how boundaries emerge and are signified in cultural practices in the same paradigm (1996: 449). Although Munn is discussing exclusion in terms of sacred spaces, I utilise her concept to delineate intimate state encounters and also reveal the way excluded spaces were created within homes. The following chapters trace the way that spatial exclusion manifests at different times and becomes pivotal in the articulation of boundaries of access, blurring boundaries between public and private space.

Lefebvre (1991: 191) describes the 'basis of action' as 'places whence energies derive and whither energies are directed'. This provides a useful frame through which to view the mothers (and others who entered their domestic space) as simultaneously deriving different energies from the home space and directing different energies towards the space, each motivated by different logics and aiming for different consequences. Using this frame brings to the fore the different values, perceptions and expectations entwined in the home space. It also allows an intersectional analysis of the salience of different characteristics as they unfold within the interaction.

During the study I (as well as all the people I spent time with) moved constantly between different subject positions. This movement is important, between 'cutting' the figure of an objective researcher one moment and 'going native' the next. The usual injunction of 'going native', in terms of participant observation, implies that one can experience being moved about as a member only if one is 'there' in the first place as a member. 'Participating' means being around long enough to observe what is happening to others. It also means being involved so that things happen to the researcher as a member. As I became 'visible' and 'available' others used me for their own ends, or felt that I was in their way.

The way in which I was perceived was premised on the way in which I gained access to different people in 'the field'. I first visited Luton in January 2010 when I was invited to talk to the British Red Cross about my experiences of working with Roma migrants in London. After that I became increasingly involved with different families through contact with the British Red Cross and Simon, the pastor of the 'English church' (*englezi khangheri*) and the Roma church (*khangheri*) who had taken it on himself as a personal mission to help those he identified as Roma in the area (see Chapter Four). The church was struggling to find volunteers to look after the children and I volunteered there over the course of a year. I also began learning the language spoken in the church with Maria, a Romanian Roma mother, who also spoke very good English.

I began fieldwork in January 2013 and moved into a house with Cristina, Dan and their five children in February 2013, by which time they had lived in Luton for 11 months. My aim was to live with different families, tracing the ways in which they made connections and following their networks. I had hoped that this would lead me to different families that were not identified as Roma; however, it emerged that the main network of contacts was with other family members. I was faced with a dilemma. I could choose to find another family, arbitrarily based on language, legal status, ethnicity, nationality or some other 'cleavage'. This, however, would negate my twin aims of letting social cleavages emerge from the data and my methodological approach of tracing the 'field' as connections that radiated from this first family. The second family I lived with, Georgeta, Rosvan and their two children, I met through Cristina at the Roma church. They had moved to Luton in March 2013 and had just moved from staying with a relative to a house of their own and had a spare room. They were from an urban centre in south Romania, rather than from rural Moldavia. I lived in this house between July 2013 and October 2013. I then moved to live with Violeta, a relative of this family, and her four children between November 2013 and February 2014.

Finding houses and switching roles

Simon, who referred to himself as the pastor of Roma church, knew I was trying to improve my language skills and suggested I move in with Cristina and Dan. They had five small children and I could live in their spare room and contribute two hundred pounds towards the rent of the house. He arranged a meeting where I visited them and explained my research. At this point Simon was translating for me and they seemed happy with the research. I justified my payment of rent because it would seem unethical to take a room from them that they might have been able to rent to others. Also, they insisted that I eat with them and this money also contributed to the food, water and electricity that I was consuming.

It was not unusual for Cristina and Dan to have others staying with them. When I moved in, Dan's brother, his wife and four children had just moved out. I stayed in the small bedroom where the whole family had previously slept. Over the course of my five-month stay many others also slept in the house for varying amounts of time. One family stayed for two months; Dan's second cousin and his family stayed for two weeks; Dan's half-sister also stayed for two months, as well as his nephew and a man he had met on the coach from Romania. Although I began fieldwork with high hopes that I was going to gain new insights into how this family was settling down and making relationships with others in Luton's public spaces, I soon found myself entwined and entangled in the household's routines and everyday life. As an unmarried woman it was much easier for me to spend time with the women and children who were often at home, rather than trying to accompany groups of men to internet cafes, parks, car boot sales, the buying and selling of merchandise or when they drove around to collect scrap metal.

I was usually referred to as a *rakli* (a young girl who was not part of the family). As I began to learn the language they spoke at home, Cristina made jokes that even though I was older than she was, she still had to teach me how to wash clothes by hand in cold water, butcher a chicken, make clear soup and get the babies to sleep quickly, among many other things. She said I was like her 'little sister'.

After living with Cristina and Dan I moved to live with Georgeta and Rosvan in June 2013 until October 2013. In contrast to Cristina and Dan who had moved directly from Moldavia, Georgeta and Rosvan had lived all over Europe and could speak many languages. Rosvan told me his family was from a town near Deva in Central Romania. As with Dan and Cristina, Georgeta and Rosvan had many other family members come to stay. Rosvan's nieces and nephews stayed when their parents went to Romania for two weeks. His brother and family also stayed in the house for a month. I usually had my own room in this house, but when others came to stay Georgeta and I shared a bed to make sure everyone was accommodated and that unmarried men and women were not sharing a room.

In November 2013 I moved in with Violeta and her children. Her husband had died in Rome six years previously but pictures of him hung in every room of the house. Violeta's husband and Rosvan were brothers. Similarly, in Violeta's house I had my own room apart from when family members came to stay. I spent my days mostly with the women in their houses and walking around Luton meeting others, or going on visits to local doctors or attending the church services that were organised for Roma in the area. I also met many frontline workers and volunteers and went on home visits with them, attended local meetings, met them for coffee and went to their houses for dinner and discussions.

My situation changed in each family. In the second house I paid the same rent but also was asked for contributions for many other aspects of daily life, such as being sent to the shop to buy coffee or being taken on a trip to the supermarket and then left to pay for the food. However, this altered after a period of time and particularly when I assisted in the birth of Georgeta's granddaughter, when requests shifted to my calling other people to ask them for help with the rent or for specific material items, particularly for the new baby. These requests made everyday life tiring. Despite the effect of time which acted to increase my feelings of being at ease, there were times when my outsider status suddenly emerged. For example, Georgeta once threatened her son who refused to go to school that the *rakli* would tell the police and he would be taken away. My personification as a terror to the children was a harsh reminder that I was sometimes seen as an outsider placed inside the house.

In the third house, Violeta refused to take any payment from me. She was in receipt of temporary accommodation from the local government (the only family I know who had gained such accommodation) and stated that God had given her the house and therefore it was a gift from God for me to stay. In return we went shopping together and I would buy her household items such a new toilet seat, paint, food, flowers; or I would take her for lunch after her cleaning job in the morning or provide childcare for her daughter or grandchildren.

I often asked people if it was okay to write it in my book and they always said yes when I asked them; however, I often wondered whether they knew what it meant. I told everyone I was a student but sometimes this was confused with social work students who also volunteered for the church. I then made it clear that I was writing a book about what was happening to them and their families in Luton. I was surprised when people started to tell me 'put this in your book' or 'you write this'. This happened more often than not when mothers felt as though someone was cheating them. Maria also joked with me 'I know you write me – you put me in the book'. However, when I was introduced to someone I had not previously met they were much more interested in my family and where I had come from, who I was staying with and for how long, rather than my 'work'. What I felt defined me, as a PhD student, I realised was not very interesting to them. They were far more interested in defining me against the social relationships that I upheld with my family and the other families that they knew in Luton and, in the short term, whether I could help them with a phone call or reading a letter. This became particularly apparent to me as a defining feature of my reputation. People did not know me by 'my book'. When I was introduced to people I was often described as 'not married', 'alone' or 'with a dead mother' (*chi maritime, korkorro, laki day si muli*), which arose feelings of pity, on occasion to my deep embarrassment.

Not only did my role change according to the perceptions of others, it also changed in context with the same person. On some occasions I would be given a lift by a group of men and sit in the front seat, being asked about my family and interactions with frontline workers. At other times, for example on the way back from church and when we were travelling as a family, I would sit at the back with the children and be treated very much like a child. Sometimes I was told that I could speak the best and that I was the only one who could help; at other times I was told in no uncertain terms to keep quiet. When in the house I was not included in group conversations with men, or when there was a prayer meeting and men and women were separated. I also became very frustrated when I was always left in the house when something exciting seemed to be happening and all the men would bundle into the car in the evening.

My relationships with families shifted and oscillated throughout the period of fieldwork. I noticed that women stopped asking me for money when I saw them begging on the street. This was forcefully made clear to me when I met three women in the street, one of whom I had not met before. This woman began to 'perform' in the way of engaging in a begging encounter and when she offered her hand to me it was slapped away by one of the other women. She then took her bag and hit the woman on the back and all of them proceeded to laugh. The two women I knew then proceeded to ask me where I was going and what I was doing and told me to come to see them when I was 'free'. During the latter part of my fieldwork it was unusual for me to walk anywhere around the 'Indian centre' (*indiano centro*) or the train station and not meet someone I knew either walking with children or sat at the side of the street. (The 'Indian centre' (*indiano centro*) was so called because the shops, cafes and restaurants seemed to be frequented predominantly by Bengali and Pakistani residents. According to the 2011 census, 53.8% of residents in this area identified as Asian or British Asian. Most Romanian Roma families lived there as well because the area had the cheapest private rented housing. The area was contrasted to the 'English centre' (*englezi centro*), which included the train station, town hall and large shopping centre.) These meetings would provoke a new round of conversations, meetings or going back to their houses for coffee.

Negotiations with frontline workers

From the outset of my fieldwork I wanted to explore how migrants made place including their interactions with frontline workers. In the first instance I wanted to research interactions in public spaces, particularly men negotiating with others. However, after I began living in the houses of Romanian Roma, I became entwined in female domestic routines. While this was initially a source of acute frustration, I began to notice, and was drawn to, the home encounters between Romanian Roma mothers and (mostly female) frontline workers. At first I found it very difficult to contact and engage with these frontline workers. A key turning point came when I began to know increasing numbers of families and they asked me to call particular frontline workers who they had heard were 'for the school' or had helped a relative gain child benefit. Initially, this was a point of anxiety for me as I thought that I was using my knowledge of families to further interactions with frontline workers. Eventually I became aware that families often found a way to call the frontline workers in any case.

As this started to happen, different frontline workers became more conducive to talking to me about my research, my aims and my own background and experiences. I also formally interviewed directors of services in the local government to make them aware of my research and the relationships I was developing with frontline workers. I had disclosed my information sheets and consent forms and discussed my ethical guidelines with the heads of departments for Housing and Community Living, Public Health, Social Justice, Community Development, and Children and Families. I also used this opportunity to ask them for further contacts and by the end of the fieldwork I was being consistently referred back to people whom I had already interviewed. I believe that the Oxford University label was pivotal to some of these meetings, although I often had the impression that my slightly dishevelled appearance was not what they expected.

My field of inquiry became a mixture of the policies and practices that were being enacted on, and through, frontline workers and migrants. In order to understand the range of frontline workers, volunteers and NGO workers that were being spun into the web of connections that unfolded I needed to make these spaces 'unfamiliar' with the aim of learning their 'bureaucratic language', or their ideas, values, everyday gestures and practices. With migrants, 'wasting' time was key to differentiate me from the frontline workers, but with frontline workers I had to be careful to be efficient and to conduct my research in a way that suited their everyday routines and practices. I had to fit my own research tools around their day. This included going on home visits and having conversations while driving in the car, e-mail conversations, arranging 'formal' interviews at times that were convenient to them, attending meetings and having quick 'catch-ups' before or after encounters.

The length of time I spent in Luton was also crucial to gaining access and building relationships with frontline workers. This became evident due to their similar reactions when I told them I was living in Luton (not London) and would be staying for at least 12 months. Often, stories would then be related of journalists or politicians who 'dropped in and dropped out' whenever they wanted a regional story or perspective that was only a 30-minute train ride from central London. This sentiment emerged from directors of services or those located in the strategy department, as their proximity to London meant that Luton was constantly being evaluated by national civil servants and the national media.

There was also a further element to these interactions. When I explained my research was with migrants, frontline workers often assumed that I had chosen Luton due to its connections with the English Defence League and the group then known as al-Muhajiroun (later Islam4UK). When I explained my research was not focused on this aspect of Luton and that I was living in the town, this helped to build relationships. At different times frontline workers also quizzed me in detail regarding my own background, family, education and the reasons behind this research and my PhD. These questions and how I answered them provided a useful insight into the process of being researched and the partial nature of interviewing. It also highlighted the role of the relational nature of knowledge production in ethnographic fieldwork.

I spent a lot of time with one educational support worker, Paula. Despite her willingness to understand ethnographic fieldwork, at times she also seemed frustrated that I did not have a clearer or more specific research question and that I could not describe exactly what my research was going to be about. I found it very helpful when she introduced me to those I had not met before by explicitly stating my position as a PhD researcher for migrants and Luton council. The way I was described when someone introduced me was a crucial moment to ensure that my role as a researcher was upheld.

Ethical entanglements

There were many ethical entanglements in the process of conducting this research and also in managing the material and deciding what could be written down and fixed in these pages. There is no easy solution but they warrant discussion and reflection. From the outset, the aim of the research, that of exploring how migrants negotiate to make place in a rapidly changing urban location, continuously generated novel situations that required me to reflect ethically on my role and research. I developed ways of thinking about situations and making decisions to ease these dilemmas. I decided that if someone asked me for help directly, for example about children's services or employment difficulties, then it would be unethical not to provide them with details of suitable frontline workers. This meant that, on occasion, I created the situations that were at the heart of my research. Eventually I realised that people were often already aware of these options, either through hearing about a particular person or office from a family member or, in some circumstances, by having already made contact. I therefore came to understand that migrants asked me questions as much to check what I knew as to gain new information. Many were as active in positioning me for their own ends as I might be seen to be positioning them, although with very different consequences due to highly uneven power relations.

I was cautious about my role and I explained what kinds of questions they would be required to answer when they went to different agencies. I was aware that parents in particular were overly cautious with regard to presenting their children at bureaucratic agencies. I was also worried that the more I became involved in 'helping' with bureaucratic processes the more I would be viewed as someone who was a frontline worker. Furthermore, I was attentive to try to manoeuvre against being placed by frontline workers or migrants in the role of a 'middleman'. A further cause for anxiety occurred when I was asked for my opinion and what I thought was the best course of action in terms of bureaucratic processes. I was often asked 'What will happen for Romanians? What does England want for us?' or 'What do you think is good?' These questions intensified as January 2014 approached, which signalled the lifting of the transitional controls. Rumours proliferated at this time regarding 'closing the door' (*pando o'wudar*) to Romanians and being evicted. The reasons for asking me were due to my English language ability (and knowledge of how to 'speak well' – *das duma mishto*). These comments were often used to try to secure my involvement in a bureaucratic process and I often had to negotiate my position to extricate myself from the situation or refrain from giving advice.

To what extent were all of the people I shared time with giving me their 'informed consent'? This question arose in many different situations throughout my fieldwork. As Barnes (1963: 133) discusses, the motives of social scientific research are never entirely clear to informants even in the contexts in which there are no linguistic or cultural barriers to separate the researcher from the researched. This is because informants generally lack familiarity with the intellectual and social contexts in which the research is embedded, such as how questions arise, how they are addressed, how results are disseminated and to what end. Anthropological enquiry is embedded in social relations, just like relations with anyone else, which in my experience are infused with bonds of friendship and good-will and also intense tensions and difficulties. As has been noted by Besnier (2009: 27), 'ethnographers are working with complex allegiances and obligations, and from complex identity formations'.

I employed various tactics in an attempt to make the research process clear to the participants. If there was a member of the family who could read in English I paid them to translate my information sheet and consent form. Any unfamiliar words would be explained by me and discussed. By asking a family member to translate, not only did I gain a way of explaining my research more clearly to other family members but I could have an open conversation with that person about the research without there being any obligation to participate. After we had discussed it, I then asked whether I could also write about their experiences. I found this to be an effective way to broach the topic of consent and to make sure that I could talk to people about the research without them feeling as though they had to be part of it.

For frontline workers, I found arranging interviews was the best way to explain the research as it seemed to be what they expected from my role as a PhD researcher. It therefore acted as a space where they could ask questions and give me their consent through signing my consent form and keeping the information sheet with my business card. Interviews took place according to individual circumstances and preferences, which gave me a glimpse into the patterns and rhythms of their working days. I conducted interviews in offices, in the local theatre café, in a café in the middle of the new shopping centre, in coffee shops and in pubs or community centres. Ultimately, ethical decisions had to be made when reflecting on exactly what to write (Okely 2013). This was a combination of using my memory in hindsight to evaluate how well I had explained my research alongside a judgement on what different people shared with me as a researcher.

Final remarks

This chapter has discussed the methodological aspects of my research. Reflecting on knowledge and fiction, I discussed how we perceive the world by placing it in relation to models that endow reality with form and meaning. Anthropological knowledge may be described as the attempt to present a possible world by making the metaphorical description of scientific discourse interact and blend with the models and schemes an ethnographer acquires in the field. Within this epistemological framework I detailed my experiences and fieldwork, including how I used encounters as a method to examine cleavages as they emerged from interactions in the home. I also elaborated my ethical standpoint and how this ultimately rests on what I have decided to fix in these pages and what remains in field notes and memories.

Interlude | Facebook with Cristina

It is 28 June 2013 and I'm sitting on the bed in my small room in Cristina's house. There is a chest of drawers in the room that Cristina found in the street, which she cleaned and squeezed into the room next to the bed. Cristina comes in and stands on the small part of the floor between the bed and the wall. She has received a letter from the telephone company and she wants to know whether this means she can use the internet. She wants to use Facebook to try to find her sister. Dan, her husband, had mentioned to me before that Cristina's sister moved to Italy when she was 15 (Cristina was 6 years old at the time) with an Italian man. Cristina thought that she would be able to find her sister through Facebook and often asked to use my phone, which could access the internet, to search for her sister's name.

We sit on the bed and after fruitlessly searching once again for her sister's name on Facebook she tells me that she wants to show me a place called Mănăstirea Petru Vodă on Google maps. We search for it on my phone and we locate it – a monastery in the middle of the forest in central Romania. She tells me there was a man who knew her maternal grandfather. He knew that her mother didn't have money for school so he took her to the monastery and she stayed there for a year. He came to visit her every month for the first three months and then stopped. She made a point of telling me that her brother wasn't at the monastery, just her. Then the money ran out so she returned to her grandmother's house and didn't receive any more schooling.

Until she was 15 years old she had lived with her brother and grandmother and went out to work in other people's houses and gardens. She told me that when she was 14 she asked God to help her because she didn't want a boyfriend of the same age. At this time she was going out to work in people's houses and gardens. It was also at this time that she asked God to help her because she didn't want a boyfriend of the same age. "This is no good going to the disco. Why would I want to do that?" She wanted a boyfriend who was older. She met Dan, who was 32 at the time, and they were married as soon as she was 15. This is what she wanted, "he had a house and everything".

Cristina often tells me the many ways God has helped her. For example when she was 2 years old she became very ill and she was sure that "God brought me back to life". God also helped her find Dan and gave her a house and a family. She also tells me about when Dan left to come to England and left her alone in their small rural village in Moldavia. She was pregnant, had no money and was looking after their two children, aged 4 years old and 12 months old. She became very ill; it was a very cold winter and there was no way of heating the house. Although there was an open wooden stove she found it difficult to carry the wood in order to light a fire. The children's dirty clothes were piling up because she didn't have the strength to go to the tap at the end of the street to collect water, bring it back and heat it to wash them. In any case, there was no detergent because she had no money. She tells me that the devil came to her at that time, in dreams and during the day when she felt dizzy and needed to sit down. She thought she was going to die but she told the devil that she had two kids and not to take her. God saved her at this time. Dan had called his brother (who was living next door), and she had spoken to him, telling him that she couldn't stay alone in the house. Dan sent money to bring her to England on the coach. She left her two children in the care of Dan's brother and his wife and within a week she was standing at Victoria coach station in London.

On a different day when we have had breakfast and washed and cleared away all the breakfast things Cristina and I begin to talk about families. She complains that she has told her mum that the kids were going to get taken away because she didn't have a house and that her mum had to come to England. Cristina is angry because her mother had just told her that she has got married again and isn't coming. She seems very angry with her mother but not surprised. The conversation turns quickly to stories of her grandmother's house in mountains. She says that the town was very small, maybe 20 houses, because Ceaușescu didn't "put" anyone there. She speaks quickly when she talks about the mountains in Romania, the plants and flowers that grew around her childhood home, and her grandmother. As we are talking the rain starts coming in through the roof in the kitchen again. Cristina put a bucket underneath and as the water is dripping she turns to me and says "*musika!*" (music). Lucia, her 3-year-old daughter, comes to see what we are doing. Cristina takes her by the hands and we dance around the bucket, using the sound of the drips like a drum. Lucia is dancing and laughing.

2

Shifting faces of the state: austerity, post-welfare and frontline work

I am sitting in a multi-agency meeting at one of Luton's children's centres. Paula, an equality and diversity officer for the children's services department, is explaining a recent experience of a family that has since 'disappeared'. Others at the meeting include Lisa, floating support worker for Pathways;[16] Clare, head of a children's centre; Samantha, deputy head of a children's centre; Kassia, a children's centre support worker; and Simon, pastor of the Roma church. She explains that Emma, a health visitor, went to a flat and found two parents and four children sleeping in one room in a one-person bedsit (one room in a shared house). The health visitor had identified this family as Romanian Roma through their surname and called Paula. Paula had called the landlord. "I really went to town on him, saying how could he let this many people sleep in one room, and the ceiling was falling in and this was no place for children and what was he doing?!" The landlord told her that he rented the house to just one man and that he didn't know that a family was living there.

The next day the mother of this family called Paula to tell her the landlord was going to evict them. Paula had called the children's school; she noted that they had no attendance issues and the teachers believed that they were apparently all sleeping very well. Paula described how the mother had showed Paula where the children were sleeping, and how she was pulling the sofa out and away from the place in the roof where the water was coming in. Paula told the multi-agency meeting that the mother had been upset and didn't know where the family were going to live. They were not eligible for any welfare support and therefore Paula could not refer them to emergency temporary accommodation. There were no charities or other organisations that could help to support them. Paula had then received a phone call from the school telling her that the children had been absent and when Paula went round to the house the family had disappeared.

Paula then noted "What is culturally acceptable? We have a homeless family now and they could be anywhere. The children can be taken into care. I am asking myself these questions every day." Paula goes on to explain how she has brought this up at the local safeguarding board in the local government but they "are not interested" and she is left to reconcile these issues alone.

During my fieldwork, I was often taken aback by how often frontline workers like Paula faced these kinds of dilemmas every day. I could see how they were spending a large amount of (unaccounted-for) time trying to decipher whether their clients' migration and legal statuses made them eligible to receive their services and to deal with the large emotional strain of trying to support mothers who may have needed help but were not entitled to social protection in the UK. They often mentioned their targets, strictly time-managed caseloads and funding cuts. In an environment that seemed entirely based on accountability, it was remarkable how little of the work they were doing was accounted for within the structures of their organisations. In addition, the large scope for discretionary decisions did not seem to be fully acknowledged within their work and they were largely left to face these conflicts alone.

This chapter focuses on such discretionary decisions and how they were created by a combination of the UK government's expressed policy aim of creating a 'hostile environment' for migrants (Kirkup and Winnett 2012), combined with a shift in the underpinning logic of the welfare state (which has been exacerbated by the financial crisis in 2008 and subsequent austerity[17]). The main aim of this chapter is to demonstrate how new forms of subcontracting and commissioning were not weakening state power, but rather signals a consistent mode of state governance that diffused power through targets and funding mechanisms leading to widening frontline workers' discretion based on behaviours and adherence to values that would deem a family to be 'morally legitimate' subjects of care (Ticktin 2011: 4). This discussion lays the ground for Chapters Four, Five and Six which explore how this provided opportunities and constraints for all those involved in home encounters.

Before reviewing how the hostile environment policy, austerity and local government restructuring shaped local practice towards Romanian Roma migrants, I explain why frontline workers came to believe that home visits were the best and only way to engage with Romanian Roma. As detailed in the Introduction, all state acts allow observation of the mechanisms of inclusion and identification, as claims and decisions are made about who belongs to a given community and who will have access to limited public resources. For Romanian Roma, these decisions took place within their domestic space, primarily through assessments of their relationships with their children. The implications of home encounters on the daily lives of Romanian Roma migrants will be explored in Chapters Four, Five and Six. In this chapter I detail why these encounters took place in their homes in the first instance and the licence through which frontline workers entered their homes.

Seeing like a state–actor: the safeguarding lens

One critical entry point for examining the mechanisms of statecraft has been to examine what James Scott (1998) famously introduced in his book *Seeing like a state* as 'state abstractions'. Building on Benedict Anderson's foundation text (Anderson, 1983), Scott argues that, in order to govern, states need to categorise, count and map their populations, attaching particular rights, duties, entitlements and resources accordingly. These abstractions in a sense are departures from reality but state agents come to apprehend and act on reality through these abstractions. The consolidation of their actions is what we term 'the state'. This process of governing populations plays an important role in the process of creating social structures because designating and quantifying populations does much more than reflect social reality; it plays a key role in the construction of that reality (Kertzer and Arel 2002; see also Chapter Three). Those on the frontline have to translate these categories of governance into practice within their everyday work. Their responses are formed through the ways categories and labels of people are created in the social world and how they are evoked, contested and negotiated (Hacking 2004; Sigona 2009).

The focus on state abstractions dovetails with the anthropology of policy. Policy is theorised by anthropology as explicit, proscribed, governing rules that produce new social and semantic spaces, sets of power relations, political subjects and webs of meaning (Shore and Wright 1997). Through policy formation and implementation, a variety of agents seek to classify and regulate certain spaces and subjects around certain organising principles, rationalities of rule and governmentalities within regimes of knowledge and power. In so doing, policies legitimate dominant governing projects as well as generate and modify them.

Policies, like other 'state abstractions,' reduce the heterogeneity of possible responses to possible future scenarios down to guiding, governing principles as well as strict protocols to be applied uniformly in real situations. They also produce practices as state agents try to translate these principles and protocols into everyday life. This is inherently a moral and ethical technology of governing that defines what 'should' be done.

The most crucial aspect of the delivery of public services in this formulation is the operation of discretion. Discretion refers to the negotiation that bureaucrats undertake when applying rigid policies to the unending variation of clients' individual circumstances. In his seminal book *Street-level bureaucracy* Lipsky (2010) argued that bureaucrats can never be neutral in these processes and are required by the structure of frontline bureaucratic work to interpret rules and programmes as guided by their own background and experience. Scholars building on Lipsky's paradigm have made attempts over time to test, develop and add nuance to this approach (see Gilson 2015).[18] Others, most notably Maynard-Moody and Musheno (2003, 2012) have sought to highlight the relationship between street-level bureaucrats and their clients. They find that when making decisions, street-level bureaucrats rely more on their personal moral judgements, based on their interactions with clients, than on the bureaucratic rules and regulations they are called on to implement (Mayard-Moody and Musheno 2012). It is important to note, however, that the term 'citizen-agent' fails to account for the non-citizen clients, such as migrants, which is something the authors have noted themselves (Mayard-Moody and Musheno 2012). It is this stream of street-level bureaucrat literature that this book builds on, by linking it with anthropological theories of the state and exploring how street-level bureaucrats and migrants relationally co-produce identities and actions at the frontline.

Anthropological research has examined how the everyday private lives of state officials affect the way in which states operate (Herzfeld 1992). More recently, scholarly attention has turned to the wide variety of actors who are imbued with the authority to identify 'good citizens' (Kahn 2000;

Ticktin 2011; Klotz 2013); however, this literature has not foregrounded the relational labour between frontline workers and migrants or fully explored all social actors' situated positions. I bring together literature on street-level bureaucrats and anthropological theories of state and policy to shed new light on the mechanisms of statecraft.

During my fieldwork, there were wide areas of discretionary decision making with regard to Romanians in the UK as legal regulations and requirements created ambiguity regarding their entitlement to social rights. Most Romanian Roma families became visible through their children (Chapter Three). All the frontline workers who made discretionary decisions to enter Romanian Roma homes had duties to ensure the safety of children. This duty was drawn from the notion of 'safeguarding' established by the Children Act 2004, which created a significant burden on frontline workers to identify potentially 'vulnerable' children and families, and gain information on their domestic and private lives to safeguard the children.[19] 'Early intervention' was a core rationale in the Children Act 2004, and involves collecting information on children before problems arise with the aim to intervene as quickly as possible to promote safeguarding (Gray 2014). The Act also requires organisations in the public, private, voluntary and community sectors to put in place shared governance arrangements, policy structures and practice arrangements and to create a local safeguarding children board.

'Early intervention' therefore widened the bureaucratic gaze to include the broader domestic and family context within which the child lived. One children's centre support worker, Samantha, explained to me that for any given family she needed to gain detailed information about everyone residing at the same address, including their financial details. In other words, "we need to know how they are putting food in their child's tummy". Similarly, Clare, the head of a local children's centre, noted in a formal interview with me that "we will dig deep. We will want to know what the underlying problems are and we will want to know about finances. Our primary concern is the children and we will fulfil all of our safeguarding obligations."

The Children Act 2004 thereby provided frontline workers with the drive and the licence to enter homes. Alongside discretionary decisions about how and what support to offer which families, frontline workers' own perceptions and value judgements were frequently foregrounded in the designation of which families deserved discretionary support. This will be explored further in Chapter Three, when we turn to look at the racialised nature of the term 'Roma', which often places families in the category of 'undeserving' migrants, and how this overlaps with perceptions of children as 'vulnerable'.

Everyday discretion in a hostile, austere, post-welfare state

Three processes entwined to create the specific nature of home encounters between frontline workers and Romanian Roma: first, the hostile environment; second, the post-welfare state and the gendered, racialised and classed positions of frontline workers; and third, the implications of an 'audit culture' within the post-welfare state. How these processes came together shaped frontline workers' discretion, which effectively became a form of 'border work'[20] (Reeves 2014) but which was inextricably linked with notions of care within home encounters (see Chapter Six).

The hostile environment policy created complex bureaucratic categories for Romanian Roma alongside new duties for frontline workers that included forms of 'bordering' (Chapter Six). Historically, individuals migrating from Romania have been subject to many different migration regulations. Between 1970 and 1989 anyone crossing the border from Eastern Europe received residence permits as a 'single humanitarian action' (Matras 2000). The end of the Ceauşescu regime in Romania precipitated stricter interpretations of the law and gaining refugee status became more difficult throughout the 1990s, although it was possible to apply for asylum seeker status between 1990 and 2007 (Clark and Campbell 2000; Sigona and Trehan 2009; Humphris 2013). Concurrently, the end of the Cold War triggered a rapid deepening and widening of European integration and Romania acceded to the EU in May 2007.[21]

Romanian and Bulgarian nationals (A2 national) were subject to particular regulations between accession in 2007 and when these transitional controls expired on 1 January 2014. I conducted fieldwork between January 2013 and March 2014, during the time transitional controls were lifted. However, as the following chapters demonstrate, the regulations regarding A2 migrants were shifting throughout 2013. Moreover, the end of transitional controls were imagined and experienced in very different ways and set in motion a diverse range of actions. Unlike those who had come to the UK exercising treaty rights following the 2004 (A8) enlargement, A2 nationals were restricted from accessing both the labour market and state welfare benefits.

Transitional controls arose as an approach towards border securitisation, which had been increasing in the UK since the 1990s. A2 nationals had to gain worker authorisation for employment and after 12 months of paid employment were discharged from the scheme and gained the 'right to reside', which enabled them to claim state benefits. [22] Alternatively, A2 nationals could hold a qualifying status. These included being self-employed, which is the status many Romanian Roma claimed in order to reside legally in the UK for more than three months (see Chapter Three for discussion of the informal economy of knowledge about legal status).[23]

A2 nationals also had to pass the habitual residence test, which in addition to right to reside sought to establish intention to remain in the UK for the foreseeable future. Without the right to reside A2 and A8 nationals had no recourse to public funds.[24] As EU nationals are not subject to immigration controls these right to reside tests are implemented by social welfare actors when deciding whether to grant an individual social welfare benefits. If A2 nationals fail to find work in this period they do not gain the right to reside and are unable to access state support.[25]

The introduction of the right to reside test is crucial and marks a shift in the way the UK controls access to state resources. Critically, it was the foundation of using welfare exclusions as a means of migration control (Chapter Six). The significance of the right to reside test and the decision regarding whether an individual was 'habitually resident' emerged as pivotal to frontline workers as these shifting regulations were variously understood. Despite various regulations and court rulings,[26] large uncertainties remained in the application of the fundamental right to free movement and associated social rights, especially with regard to defining work and legal residence for Romanians and Bulgarians.[27]

In addition to the shifting definition of right to reside; the interpretation of a 'worker' also emerged as a site where boundaries around access to state resources could be drawn.[28] Due to these regulations the definition of 'genuine self-employed work' was crucial to deciding whether an individual was considered to be exercising Treaty rights or not. As illustrated by the following chapters, the definition of 'work' and 'genuine self-employed work' was constantly shifting and open to interpretation. Transitional controls acted to increase ambiguity in the regulations for EU nationals, placing further significance on the discretionary decisions that were made by service providers as gatekeepers in homes. A situation was created where, in the eyes of state bureaucracy, EU nationals were only able to reside within the UK national territory if they were 'self-sufficient' and did not constitute 'an unreasonable burden on the social assistance system' (ECJ Case C-333/13). Therefore, in addition to the differentiated categories of EU nationals created by transitional controls, the impact of these controls was also filtered through the situated gazes of those who administered the transitional controls which led to different assessments of what constituted a 'burden' in terms of earning capacity.

The increasing work that migration policies put on frontline workers was exacerbated by a shift in welfare policies beginning in the 1980s that represent a 'post-welfare' state (Wacquant 2009; Muehlebach 2012; Anderson 2013; Dubois 2014a). These policies are based increasingly on behavioural criteria, rather than addressing structural inequalities. In Dubois' words, 'bureaucratic practice has become a key instrument of contemporary social and employment policies that, in practice, increasingly reflects government over the poor that strives to remake dispositions and behaviours rather than socio-economic structures' (Dubois 2014b: 41). Broadly, the fragmentation of public services, the imposition of financial targets in welfare services, the rise of new public management, state-society arrangements increasingly guided by commissioning and subcontracting, and transformations within civil society have elevated the significance of this form of governance.

These developments can all be associated with neoliberal restructuring. Ong warns of approaching neoliberalism as an ensemble of fixed attributes that 'will everywhere produce the same political results and social transformations. She suggests adopting an approach based on the conceptualisation of neoliberalism as a logic of governing that migrates and is selectively taken up in diverse political contexts' (Ong 2006: 3). This is a crucial point; there is nothing linear in the way that neoliberalism works or how neoliberal logics play out in different contexts. However, hallmarks of a neoliberal logic of governing are, in Bauman's (2001: 9) words, 'competitiveness, cost-and-effect calculations, profitability, and other free-market commandments'. These trends can be identified in the organisational structures that frontline workers operated within and how notions of deservingness were mobilised when frontline workers tried to make decisions about Romanian Roma mothers when faced with wide areas of discretionary decision making. As will be explored in the following chapters distinct parameters based on values shaped which Romanian Roma were recognised as 'morally legitimate' to receive care and therefore subject to forms of hyper-surveillance of their domestic spaces, and which Romanian Roma slipped into invisibility or potential punishment, such as removing their children into state care.

Deservingness and the politics of care signals a shift from a discourse based on rights to moral categories.[29] In essence, post-welfare has replaced 'the sovereign state' with 'the caring acts of the sovereign individual' (Muehlebach 2012: 133). Displaying compassion or performing a desire to help has become part of the complexity of frontline work, which also requires particular emotional dispositions from those who are being helped. This particular ethics is difficult to challenge as it not only motivates frontline workers under the caring logic of the system of child protection but also reflects an internalised and active reception of this care on the part of Romanian Roma migrants (as will be shown in Chapter Three when mothers actively invoke frontline workers to become more involved in their intimate and daily lives).

Notions such as charity, empathy, compassion and benevolence actively construct the terminology of a new kind of politics. In response notions such as 'humanitarian reason', 'the politics of care', 'the politics of benevolence', 'the politics of compassion' or the 'governance of intimacy' have now come to dominate scholarly work based on international, national and local governance of Others. In the chapters that follow I examine how governance of marginality takes place through intimate state encounters and how this creates spaces of indeterminacy, confusions and contradictions, which allow frontline workers to maintain a coherent moral standpoint while also enacting painful acts of exclusion. In these indeterminate spaces marginalisation is reproduced or exacerbated through confusions of public and private, informal and formal, affective and juridical, kinship and state.

The shift from a rights-based approach to increasing emphasis placed on discretion based on deservingness and moral value had particular effects for how frontline workers carried out their roles. Frontline workers were faced with value decisions regarding whether an individual should be eligible for support (which was made more difficult by complex and shifting migration categories), rather than a role of supporting individuals to enjoy their entitlements.

Greater reliance on the market and voluntary sectors through outsourcing and subcontracting services meant that frontline workers increasingly relied on the voluntary sector to fill in the gaps in support that they could no longer provide due to decreasing resources. However, there were fewer voluntary organisations in Luton at this time due to austerity (and those that were still operating had limited and targeted funding). Thus at the time when voluntary support became more crucial because of privatisation, there were fewer organisations and resources that were able to do the work, leading to large gaps in service provision. Frontline workers had to deal with this absence of support and find ways to justify their non-action to Romanian Roma, and to themselves, thereby increasing the emotional burden in their daily routines.

Moreover, the co-option of volunteers as 'faces of the state' intensified the salience and circulation of moral values (see the following section in this chapter). What we think of as 'public' or 'civil society' that was built on an idea of social citizenship and bonds between equals was transformed to an ethical citizenship built out of a desire to relate, empathise and care for those considered legitimately needy.

These processes are also highly gendered. Women have historically been employed in human services, which are also among the lowest paid (Phillips and Taylor 1980; Connell 1990; Kofman 2000; Graham 2002; Lamphere 2005). Unpaid reproductive labour in the domestic space and the affective labour that takes place in the human services represent the gendered nature of work and signal similar processes that affect both mothers and frontline workers. With regard to frontline workers, not only has recent critique illustrated there is less recognition of the additional work needed in these roles, often referred to as 'emotional labour' (Hochschild 1979), but also the majority of workers are increasingly 'black, minority and ethnic' women (Kofman 2000). Moreover, in a post-welfare state, these roles are increasingly removed from direct local government control. Welfare provision has always involved a mixture of state, market and voluntary agencies often working in combination. However, the restructuring and constriction of welfare states with an increased emphasis on commissioning and outsourcing has intensified the reliance on non-governmental organisations. Low-paid, precarious or voluntary support workers bear the brunt of this additional emotion work alongside the new pressures of 'border work' (Reeves 2014) created by the hostile environment (see Chapter Six).

Frontline workers fill these gaps in service provision and take on additional emotional burdens through framing their work in terms of charity and compassion. One such frontline worker is Paula, an equality and diversity officer for the children's services department, who defines the boundaries of her role differently for different families. In the course of various conversations, Paula told me she often worked all night, for example by writing letters of support for unaccompanied asylum seekers or filling in forms and paperwork because she did not have the time to fulfil all her work during the day.

Throughout my fieldwork I often received text messages and emails from Paula in the early hours of the morning. She and her husband also drove families to London to visit embassies or attend immigration court hearings. Throughout our conversations she oscillated between the actions she undertook through her waged employment, and actions that she considered to be informal or voluntary. As will be explored in Chapter Four, these actions were inextricably woven into her identity as a citizen and in her bureaucratic and paid role as an equality and diversity officer. For Paula, this involved a complex set of blurred roles and identities where she met families and established relationships in her paid role, the realm of market exchange, but in certain circumstances offered discretionary support to some families in the form of gifts marked by compassion for those who were especially needy. While many of Paula's clients were deemed to be 'vulnerable' she only provided those who represented particular forms of deservingness with discretionary support. Paula can be seen as representative a new kind of governance that has resonances with pre-welfare moral categories and is enacted through a form of governance through philanthropy. Although society is still a site for rational and technocratic state intervention, this type of intervention is geared mainly towards its production as a site of affective practice. Paula enacted a different kind of work outside her daily routines that was based on her desire to empathise and care. The work that takes place at the frontline is bound up with intense moralisation and therefore may be deeply desired by frontline workers, volunteers and Romanian Roma in differing ways.

The complexities of undertaking frontline work are also represented by the active targeting of frontline workers to certain roles because they are perceived to be 'culturally proximate' to clients. For example, Kassia was chosen to be the family liaison worker for Romanian Roma. Kassia was young, Polish and had been living in the UK for two years when I met her in June 2013. She was assigned by Clare, head of a local children's centre, to work with those identified as Roma families because of her own experience as a recent European accession migrant (despite the widely differing regulations for Polish and Romanian nationals). This phenomenon brings Cohen's (1999: 26-7) framework of marginalisation to the fore. She uses the term 'advanced marginalisation' to describe how members of a marginalised group are called on to serve and discipline the most unincorporated group members (1999: 63-9). In so doing they are required to 'demonstrate their normativity and legitimacy through the class privilege they acquire, through the attitudes and behaviour they exhibit, and through the dominant institutions in which they operate' (1999: 64).

It is important to reiterate at this juncture that the practice of frontline workers entering poor and racialised mothers' homes is not new (Flint 2012). In the UK, women have long been tasked to morally discipline other women from the development of the Poor Law, medical hygienism and the emergence of the Charitable Organisation Society (Gidley 2000). Domestic inspections to examine and classify behaviour and standards were also prevalent in the history of housing management in Britain through the late 19th and 20th centuries (see Damer 2000; Ravetz 2003). There continue to be resonances between this history and the way some families' private spaces are singled out for state surveillance (see Introduction for overview). Previous scholarship has acknowledged that iterations of home surveillance are not only performed by middle-class women who govern the poor but that social workers often share dimensions of social class, geography and speech with families and power dynamics in the co-production of the domestic visit are uncertain (Keane 2003; McNay 2009). However, these studies have not acknowledged the importance of the migration backgrounds, precarious employment and uncertain citizenship positions of frontline workers.

Previous scholarly work has acknowledged the dilemmas of frontline workers within 'authoritarian therapeutism' (Wacquant 2013) and how they justified their practice on different grounds such as social justice, the transformative potential of paternalistic interventions or communitarian principles (Flint 2018). However, this literature does not unpack why different practices are undertaken for some families and not others. There has not been in-depth analysis of why some families become 'seen' or identified as worthy for care while others do not. This analysis requires long-term ethnographic work with both frontline workers and families. It is through these methods that the situated positions of frontline workers and how their own previous experiences of the state shape who they see as morally legitimate subjects of care. They can decide whether to enact discretion to provide informal support to families to help them achieve a formal legal status, or they can decide to restrict their role and leave families to negotiate their own legal status and bureaucratic identity (which could lead to children being taken into state care in the longer term).

Kassia, as mentioned earlier, had been assigned to work with those identified as Roma families because of her own experience as a recent European accession migrant. However, she did not share a common language with mothers, and although she understood the legal regulations for Poland, the combination of different accession regulations for Romania and the diverse migration trajectories of Roma families created uncertainty, generating a wide area of seemingly unwanted discretion. In order to accurately evaluate whether mothers were eligible for social assistance Kassia needed detailed information regarding their migration trajectories, financial circumstances, income and legal status (fathers were formally absent from these considerations; see Chapter Five). She also required knowledge of rapidly shifting UK immigration, welfare and case law, and had to make discretionary decisions regarding her own legal duty to both children and families. For example, she could choose to provide large amounts of informal support but had to balance this in light of increasing demand for services set against reduced personnel, time and funding.

In one relationship that Kassia forged between herself and a Romanian Roma migrant mother we can see how histories of encounters with the state and their affective resonances are carried through mothers. However, this was only possible on constrained terms and through a particular imaginary that Kassia upheld about herself and Mariela. Mariela had eight children ranging from 15 years old to 4 months. They had moved to the UK four months before Kassia met them. Kassia began to assist this family because she had been introduced to them through the local church (Humphris 2018a). She supported them formally through her role as a children's centre family liaison worker but was unable to account for her time through any of the projects that were funding her role. Mariela's husband had a job in a nearby fruit stall. Kassia mentioned to me that he was working hard and trying to provide for his family but she was worried that the owner of the fruit stall was not paying the minimum wage. She therefore expressed an idea that the family were 'deserving' because the husband was engaged in work that she could corroborate because she had seen him working in the fruit shop (this was not possible for other men who bought and sold second-hand cars or if frontline workers saw them sitting at home where they believed they were not 'working'). This family were therefore conforming to particular kinds of kinship relations that Kassia recognised and valued and particular models of what constitutes legitimate work.

Kassia was able to visit Mariela very quickly because the children's centre was a five-minute walk from Mariela's house. This was crucial because she had a strictly managed case load and therefore could only make short visits. In addition, she was on a part-time, short-term contract which was regulated by target-driven funds and she therefore had to justify all of her work within predefined categories. Despite these constraints Kassia, drawing on her relationship with Mariela and resonances between their family situations, made the discretionary decision to provide free Stay and Play[30] vouchers to the family (which Mariela was not eligible for because she did not receive child benefit) and invited her to events (such as a Christmas party) that she organised specifically for Polish mothers.

Kassia explained to me that she was providing 'emergency support'. It seemed that she knew she was pushing the boundaries of her role (and Mariela's legal entitlements) and therefore justified this within the terms of short-term 'emergency' help and therefore she did not have to confront (to herself or to her managers) why she was doing this for Mariela and not for other mothers who were in a similar position. It seemed that Kassia directly related to Mariela's individual situation.

Mariela had applied for child benefit before enrolling her children in school and was caught in a bureaucratic loop. Her child benefit application would not be accepted before she sent a letter from a school confirming attendance. However, the school could not register the children without their identity documents, which were being held by the HM Revenue and Customs (HMRC) until they received a letter from a school. Kassia had supported many Polish mothers who had been caught in similar bureaucratic loops with HMRC and had previously had her own difficulties with UK welfare and migration bureaucracy. She therefore related to Mariela's situation through feelings of 'unfairness' and her desire to disavow a harsh migration governance system that she had very recently been subjected to, yet was now in the position of enacting (for example, by excluding those without legal residency from free support). As Kassia and Mariela entered into a new relationship, Kassia drew and reflected on her own previous encounters with migration bureaucracy. Her personal frustration and distress caused her to perceive Mariela's situation as 'unfair' and this opened a space for Mariela to become a legitimate recipient of discretionary support.[31] Experiences of the state are shaped by how mothers draw on the affective registers they invoked within their own biography of state encounters.

The post-welfare state and audit culture

The context in which frontline workers were operating is crucial. Soss et al. (2011) argue that at each step of the policy process actors 'below' control information needed by actors 'above' and hold discretion over how to pursue pre-set goals. Actors above seek to discipline this discretion by setting benchmarks, controlling resources, monitoring performance and promoting particular discourses and frames. The contemporary system is thus guided by a coherent governing logic that applies as much to those on the frontline of service provision as to their clients. I mentioned earlier that throughout my fieldwork frontline workers often described how they had to audit their time because of monitoring and evaluation procedures resulting from tighter funding regimes and the increasingly formalised and 'professionalised' policies that governed practices relating to children.

There was an ongoing tension between less routine work in order to cope with the increased demand but fewer resources and an increased pressure on targets, results, monitoring and evaluation of short-term project funding. Administrative and legal categories proliferated; clients were perceived to be complicated and not easily slotted into bureaucratic categories and resources were stretched, leading to frontline workers having to make decisions more quickly. These processes (complicated categories, little time and diminishing resources) also led frontline workers to put in increasing amounts of work even though they were less able to justify such work within their organisations' auditing structures. This work became discretionary, outside their formal roles, and was therefore available only to certain kinds of deserving subjects. For example, Lisa worked for Pathways (an NGO subcontracted by the local government), which operated a strict time-managed case load because of funding targets, underpinned by their contract. Lisa explained, "If I haven't had contact with a client for two weeks then my manager wants to know why." The service was designed for intensive support for short periods of time to help people to become 'self-supporting', rather than as a long-term service.

Many of Lisa's clients could not read and therefore relied on Lisa to pay bills and respond to schools, health appointments or any other form of written communication. In addition, administrative structures delayed support. The increased waiting times for national insurance number interviews or applications for social assistance meant that she often had no contact with a client for months until the decision was received. She also explained there was no time to open a new file every time she made a phone call or read a letter, which meant she often did not account for a large majority of the work that she undertook for families. She explained that it was 'easier' to do things this way; however it also meant that this work was not recorded or acknowledged. Lisa's role was not structured for those who were illiterate and required long-term (but not intensive) support. This kind of support did not exist within the organisation or anywhere in Luton.

As we will see in the chapters that follow only certain Romanian Roma families gained Lisa's discretionary support and this relied on who she believed was the most deserving. Crucially these decisions were informed by her situated position as a single mum and through identifying as black. For example, Lisa developed a strong connection with Maria, a Romanian Roma mother, based in part on personal circumstances. Both Lisa and Maria had experienced relationship breakdowns and had a child. They laughed and joked together due to a sense of shared experience as the following extract from my field notes exemplifies:

Maria:	'You married, Lisa?'
Lisa:	'Not married.'
Maria:	'Divorced? ... No? ... Boyfriend?'
Lisa:	'Sort of. I like to party too much.'

Maria, pointing to the spot on her face: 'I need a man. I go out to party with you, Lisa.'

We all laugh as Maria dances in her chair by putting her arms up in the air and clicking her fingers.

Maria mentioned to me that she liked Lisa because they both had gold teeth, both had tattoos, were both 'big' (*bari*) and liked to dance. On one occasion Maria commented to me, while dancing with Lisa in her home, "She is big like me!" Their shared bond developed over several months of working together. Maria then encouraged Lisa to also support Ramona, who was married to Maria's brother. Lisa helped Ramona secure housing benefit for herself and her grown-up children. Maria explained to Lisa that Ramona was supporting her children while they were looking for jobs. Lisa supported both women informally over a long period.

In contrast, I witnessed another mother, Georgeta, experience a distressing meeting with Lisa. When Lisa arrived at Georgeta's house in September 2013, Lisa found Georgeta had no national insurance number and no other documents or receipts. Georgeta was working as a household cleaner but was often paid in furniture or food rather than money. She was not aware that she needed to keep receipts or have business liability insurance. Moreover, Lisa found that her housing contract was not 'valid' because she was renting from a private landlord who would not provide her with receipts or a legal rental agreement. Lisa sat on the couch in the front room and sifted through the documents, bills and other papers, including solicitor letters regarding a car accident that involved Georgeta's husband. There was no order to the papers. As I perceived the situation, Lisa was uncomfortable with the organisation of the home as several other relatives were staying with Georgeta at that time, and Lisa did not want to become entwined in a very complicated 'case'. Lisa decided not to offer any further support, and instead told Georgeta that she could not help her. Lisa explained to Georgeta that she should wait until January (three months) when transitional controls for Romanians would be lifted. Lisa believed that it would be easier to Georgeta to get a national insurance number because she would have access to the labour market.

Room for manoeuvre within frontline workers' understanding of EU migrants' entitlements and their discretionary decisions to provide informal support also intertwined with the UK's policy of austerity and funding cuts. Paula, an equality and diversity officer for the children's services department, held a budget to provide free school uniform vouchers to families unable to afford them. To begin with, these were offered to Romanian Roma families. Later, when her budget was reduced, this support was withdrawn from those families entirely, which Paula explained to me she could justify as they now had the legal right to work, even if in practice Paula recognised they were unable to because of their lack of formal education and stigmatised status. By exercising this discretion and justification, she was able to both operate within an interpretation of their legal entitlements, and manage the problems of reduced funding within her own ideas of acting morally towards different families who were categorised as 'vulnerable'.

Paula's practices were also situated through her own position as a white, middle-class woman who had strongly expressed beliefs in equality and diversity, particularly gender equality. Paula was married to a German migrant and had two grown-up children. During my fieldwork, she was working with Claudia, a Romanian Roma mother who had spent a short amount of time in prison, where she had given birth to a baby girl. Paula worked with Claudia on her release from prison. During a phone call, Paula related to me the details of one particular visit she made to Claudia's home.

Paula told me Claudia had taken her upstairs to the bedroom and showed her a baby book, which was not brought down to the communal space where others were having coffee and chatting. Paula told me that she considered this to be an indication of a bond between herself and Claudia because all her other encounters with Claudia had taken place in the front room of the house. Paula described how they both talked for a long time about the foot prints and hand prints in the book that Claudia had filled in with the help of prison officers. They also took photographs and stuck them into the pages of the book. At this point Claudia told Paula that she did not want to live with so many people in the house and that she wanted a place only for her and her family. Paula had known Claudia for two years and was convinced that she wanted to be a 'good mother' to her two boys and the new baby. Claudia's comments about wanting to live in a house just with her family were interpreted by Paula to mean that she wanted to live in a way that also resonated with Paula's own ideas regarding how she related to her own children, and with notions of 'good motherhood' that align with the safeguarding lens.

As Paula narrated this story she also made reference to the length of time she had known Claudia and noted how Claudia was very "different to other Roma mothers". One of the characteristics she mentioned was Claudia's recent planned pregnancy. Contraception was a marker for Paula, which made Claudia different from other Roma mothers and more in line with Paula's understanding of a good family life. Paula continued working with Claudia, supporting her informally as well as within the strict parameters of her role, and would offer to help out with things like filling in the baby book (though this could also be a source of tension, as Claudia on that occasion offended Paula by showing a lack of interest in the baby book).

This relationship demonstrates how a series of personal connections and an apparent convergence (as perceived by Paula) of the two women's values around the home and motherhood, became part Paula's approach and her willingness to offer Claudia additional support. In contrast, on another occasion I was with Paula when she visited a different household which seemed 'chaotic', and did not align so easily with her values. After one visit she noted "My children knew how to play with blocks when they were about 4 or 5 months old." Paula made this comment primarily to express the worry she felt for these children being left behind when they reached school. In her view, it may have already been too late for these children. Paula reproduces the idea of distinct phases of childhood that correspond to particular markers of development, drawing on her own memories of being a mother to make sense of the differences between her own family and values of parenting and the Romanian Roma family we were visiting. When the family asked Paula for help with their legal status, Paula was very clear in establishing the limits of her role, saying "I'm just here for the school."

Paula was nevertheless often conflicted about her role and the ethical dilemmas that were intricately entwined within it as shown by the vignette that opened this chapter. In another instance, she explained a case that she had found deeply troubling. A young boy was going to be taken into care because his mother had been given a prison sentence. The young boy's paternal grandparents wanted to look after the child. However, members of the local government safeguarding board did not think that the grandparents' home was good enough for the young boy. Crucially, an issue was that the boy would not have his own bedroom in the house. Paula explained that even if the boy had his own bedroom, he may not be used to sleeping on his own and that was not because he had been neglected but because this was how he has been brought up. She explained:

> 'Social services just don't understand some issues and the assessment they made of the boy staying with his grandparents – I could have said that would be the case in any Roma house, basically – any Roma house could be said to be neglecting the children – no stimulus, no toys for them, no boundaries in place in the home. They think that they have real emotional issues because they don't like being alone in a room – all Roma are like this – they hate being alone. I tried to explain but they said there is no negotiation. They think I am making excuses but I am just trying to understand where they are coming from. The cultural issues are very difficult – I try to translate cultures and try to understand.'

Here, the boy was threatened with going into care because the safeguarding board did not appreciate that the paternal grandmother had been looking after the child previously and was confused that someone else would look after the child while his mother could not. Paula's position as a 'smiling face of the state' created intractable issues for her as she tried to 'translate' different cultures for herself and for others. In another case, Paula was called to testify in court regarding one family whose five children had been taken into care. She explained to me one day in a café that she had been in court for three days and she did not know what to do. She had tears in her eyes as she described being quizzed by the judge while the family was looking at her. She told me that she had assured the family she would help them but now they were losing their children. At the end of the conversation she acknowledged the intensity of the emotional burden in her role but that she could 'only tell the truth'.

The structure of frontline workers' roles, an increasing drive to gain more knowledge about mothers through national safeguarding guidelines, organisational restructuring and their own moral beliefs about 'the right thing to do': all these factors shaped the encounters that unfolded between mothers and frontline workers. They were also aware that there were few other organisations to which mothers could be referred or avenues where they could receive support. As they became increasingly aware of the hardships faced by families and the cultural practices that sometimes challenged their notions of good mothering, at the same time they had decreasing and fragmented resources with which to offer formal support and less recognition within organisational structures to validate the work they undertook. Furthermore, they often conducted home visits unannounced and in their 'spare time' outside their formal working hours (Chapter Four).

The implications of unannounced visits is exemplified by Louise. Louise was a children's centre worker (for which she also had training under the safeguarding agenda), and a volunteer at a Baptist church. She began a relationship with Cristina, a young Romanian Roma mother who attended the Roma church every week and had a strong relationship with the pastor, Simon. Though Cristina technically lived outside Louise's jurisdiction they met when Cristina was brought to Louise's clinic by a local church volunteer.

Louise described Cristina to me as 'standing out' and began to make home visits not only because they shared a religious belief, but also she told me, because she had a specific target to 'safeguard vulnerable families'. Louise's decision to work with Cristina was discretionary: she explained to me that she would often 'pop in' unannounced at Cristina's home if she had time during her day, because her support of Cristina was outside her geographical remit. Louise's area was more affluent and other than her decision to support Cristina, she had no other Romanian Roma cases, and did not work with anyone else outside her area of remit.

In a recorded interview, Louise discussed her thoughts about Cristina and her husband, Dan:

> 'I feel really sorry for them. They have struggled so much – it seems so unfair. They deserve to be [pause] they really want to work. They would love to be self-sufficient … The house

is always spotless – I am, like, you should come to clean my house.'

Constellations of gendered deservingness are evident as Dan is characterised as a hard worker and Cristina the ideal housekeeper. Louise reproduces the notion of the 'hard-working family' identified by the New Labour government in 1990s as 'the corner stone of social order, responsibility and security' (Clarke and Fink 2008: 232). Despite their convergences, there were also tensions and contradictions in their relationship: Cristina knew from rumours between families that Louise had the capacity to refer her to social services and to remove her children. However, Cristina was also aware that her relationship with Louise – and a network of church volunteers – represented an opportunity to gain resources and informal support that would secure her family's position in the UK. In practice, Cristina accessed more support through these networks on account of her performances within the home encounter, drawing in particular on her Pentecostal faith.

Paula also went to people's houses unannounced, particularly in the early evening. As far as I could understand, this was because she was overworked with few resources and decreasing numbers of staff in her team. Her remit had expanded because of the early intervention agenda; she was now required to register all babies as soon as they were born, rather than when a child had reached school age. She left visiting Romanian Roma houses until the end of the day because, as she described to me, they often took longer than she scheduled and she found them 'unpredictable'. Also, she was often undertaking work that was outside her formal remit.

Visiting homes in the evening or unannounced had effects for how families were perceived. As we shall explore further in Chapter Four, when a mother was not at home at this time of day, certain assumptions were made regarding where she might be, which were drawn from notions of the way Romanian Roma mothers used public space. These assumptions were linked with seeing those identified as Roma women begging in the centre of town or walking around the streets looking for scrap metal or recycling to sell. In one instance where I was accompanying Paula on home visits, Paula asked another family about the whereabouts of one mother she hadn't seen for a long time. The answer was, "She is shopping." Later Paula told me that if this response was given a number of times she assumed the mother was in prison. This highlights a further implication of many of the frontline workers' roles and the idea that they enacted 'low-level' work. They were not social workers and therefore were not automatically provided with information that might be crucial for them to fulfil their roles effectively. If a mother was not present and there was no clear explanation, frontline workers felt as though they had wasted time and resources, which in turn added to the idea that they could not make sense of the activities and relationships within a household or they were being deceived.

This section has explored how the structure of frontline work was fundamentally shifting through outsourcing and target-driven funding, austerity and post-welfare ideologies of social protection. Frontline workers could decide to narrowly delimit their roles or could decide to provide informal discretionary support. Because such informal support was outside their formal roles it was justified through assessing mothers as morally legitimate receivers of care. This encompasses Romanian Roma in a relationship that is not based on universalistic rights mediated by the state, but on voluntarism and face-to-face action; not on a politics of equality, but on emotions and sometimes feelings of co-suffering. It has many resonances with the politics of humanitarianism, which is individualistic because it depends on the dispositions of individuals rather than on universal law, on visceral feelings rather than social citizenship. This move towards individual and moral decisions at the frontline (rather than decisions over rights and entitlements) was intensified through the practice of diffusing discretionary power to volunteers.

Shifting faces of the state

As frontline workers faced a high level of responsibility with limited time and resources, areas of discretionary and value-based decisions again came to the fore in two crucial ways: how information about the families was gathered and how support could be offered. With the increasing pressure on time and resources frontline workers knew they could not support all mothers and so they looked for help wherever they could, often turning to volunteers. Volunteers were very loosely related to formal service provision and were drawn into formal bureaucratic work through frontline workers' personal connections and relationships with them.

While it has been argued that volunteers fill the gaps left by the contraction of welfare support (Mayblin and James 2018), the implications of how volunteers come to undertake these roles, the discretionary power they assume and exercise, and the consequences for how we think about the state have not been fully explored. Throughout my fieldwork frontline workers used support from the local Roma church to achieve their targets (see Chapter Six for development of the Roma church).

For example, a key target for all children's centres was to register mothers in their catchment area who were considered 'vulnerable' by

Ofsted (Office for Standards in Education, Children's Services and Skills) categories. Children's centres' budgets relied on proving that they were engaging with vulnerable mothers.[32] Frontline workers were given targets to find and register such purportedly elusive people. "How do staff go about supporting mothers that you don't know are even out there?" asked Samantha, deputy head of a children's centre, in a formal interview. One frequent answer to this problem was to gain referrals from the Roma church.

During my fieldwork, Clare, head of the local children's centre, began an arrangement to have a formal monthly 'catch-up' meeting with Simon, the church pastor, to gain information on the 'Romanian Roma community'. Simon then worked with Kassia to arrange trips to register previously 'invisible' mothers at the children's centre. One day I accompanied Kassia and Simon on one of these trips. Kassia told me her line manager had said to "drop everything and go". They registered six families on this day, which Kassia noted was a "great achievement". On some occasions, Simon even knew about a family before they arrived in the UK. A case in point relates to two Romanian Roma men: Dan, who was already in the UK, and his nephew, Gigi. Dan told Simon that Gigi and his family were coming to the UK several weeks in advance. Simon picked them up from Luton Airport in his car. Gigi later tells me that he 'knew' (*genav*) Simon when he met him. This word in *Romanës* is different from 'recognise' (*prinjerav*), which is the usual way of describing someone that you have met before. When I ask Gigi to explain, he says that as soon as they arrived at Dan's house (where Gigi and his family were staying), Simon pulled out a small black notebook and wrote down the names and dates of birth of everyone in the family.

In this way, Simon sometimes began the process of both gathering information on migrants arriving in the area, and getting families registered with the local government. He came to be seen by several of the frontline workers as a vital asset in their work with Romanian Roma. However, the relationship with the church was also a source of tension, both for Simon and for those who worked with him, and demonstrates a complex interweaving of different actors' discretionary and normative approaches. Simon's involvement provided differential trajectories for families who did, or did not, belong to the church. One local support worker complained to me: "He can just choose who he works with because the only person he has to justify his decisions to is God." Additionally, on some occasions Simon would use his position to put pressure on frontline workers to provide more discretionary support to particular families.

The frontline workers' close association with the church initially served to support their work and extend their capacity, given the limited state resources. Along the way, it also created new layers of perceptions and values for Romanian Roma families to negotiate, based on the situated positions of the different actors. For example, several of the frontline workers recommended that the families work with Christian, a church volunteer who was known to be able to help people applying for national insurance numbers. Christian became a source of information and translation of state processes for both frontline workers and mothers. By the time of my fieldwork, he had detailed knowledge of bureaucratic processes and documents as he had been working with some Romanian Roma families for around 18 months. From support worker Lisa's perspective, whose previous experience was largely working with English Romany Gypsies and Irish Travellers, Christian had more relevant knowledge than she did, and because of his accounting background he also had vital skills and understanding regarding self-employed income and tax returns. This was because the legal status of Romanian Roma was complicated and needed specialist support, which was very different to the help that Lisa was experienced in providing for English Gypsies and Irish Travellers (who are UK citizens). In light of this, Lisa asked Christian for help advising her clients on the paths and courses of action they should take. However, Christian and Lisa had very different values regarding welfare entitlements. Christian employed a strong set of religious values in his understandings of 'deservingness'. Families referred to Christian often took on new challenges and performances to maintain this relationship.

For example, Maria wanted to help her mother apply for a national insurance number. Lisa was happy to help make the appointment but could not go with her to the job centre. She called Christian as he had spent time with Maria and filled in her tax return. Christian refused to take Maria's mother to the interview as he believed she was not a genuine applicant for a national insurance number because he thought she did not have the skills to gain or retain a job. Moreover, he did not have an existing relationship with Maria's mother, as she did not attend the church. Maria's mother did not have anyone else to support her because Lisa had bestowed this decision on Christian. In addition, as we shall see in Chapter Five, Christian was prepared to break any contact with a mother who was thinking about having an abortion because of his beliefs on the sanctity of unborn children. Thus state forms were reproduced through embedded relations among and between migrants and those who assume 'faces of the state', all with their own systems for assessing deservingness. When describing 'faces of the state' in his book on public life in Turkey, Navaro-Yashin (2002: 175) explained that the state 'appeared in many guises and faces … no sooner did the state appear in the garb of military officer than it disappeared and reappeared in the cloak of the mafia'. The difference between Navaro-Yashin's account and the volunteers described here is they were not seen by Romanian Roma as always inhabiting a 'face of the state'. They were considered to be a co-member of the church, a friend, or an intermediary who could help them gain access to state resources. Volunteers therefore had a highly ambiguous role that shifted (sometimes in an instant) between friend, church member, intermediary or face of the state, making relationships difficult and complex to negotiate.

The judgements that volunteers made when they assumed this role were based on relationships that had developed within domestic spaces as mothers tried to negotiate the performances of their own identities Christian made decisions based on understandings that were drawn from his relationships with families which had developed in their homes over many months, which then came to have implications for their formal political belonging and access to state resources. This further illustrates how the space of the home becomes an indeterminate and contested space where notions linked to public and private, formal and informal boundaries are reworked through these encounters, with meanings drawn from them and actions informed by them.

These complex relationships of informal support and contacts were activated because of discretionary judgements by individual frontline workers about who might be the most legitimate receivers of care. In turn, this created different experiences and trajectories for different families as they negotiated the specific individuals and networks that constituted their relationship with the state. As we shall see later in the book, these decisions about who 'deserved' additional support were often formed during home encounters, where performances and contestations of different values came most to the fore.

A further reason for turning to volunteers who had specific and in-depth practical experience with Romanian Roma was due to the large amount of confusion that stemmed from constantly shifting policy positions, expectations and entitlements that were conferred on A2 migrants. Confusion and errors were common. During this time, I saw one children's centre worker instruct a Romanian Roma mother to apply for Healthy Start vouchers,[33] which it turned out she was not eligible for; an educational support worker advise another mother to enrol in English Language classes that she was not eligible for; and a hospital ask another mother for payment after she gave birth, despite her status entitling her to free healthcare at that time.

A case in point that represents the changing interpretations of rules (and the uncertainty that surrounds them) was a shift to refusing *The Big Issue* sellers as 'genuinely self-employed'. This shift was experienced by mothers and was not a formal designation in 2013 (however, it was mentioned in political speeches in 2014 and became a legal ruling in April 2017[34]). *The Big Issue* is a weekly magazine sold by those who are considered to be legally homeless. Many of the women who had arrived in 2007 or 2008 had sold the magazine and used this work to secure their national insurance numbers; yet when newer arrivals attempted to follow this path they were refused, as women were increasingly told that selling *The Big Issue* did not fulfil the definition of 'genuine self-employed work'. Lisa, a support worker for Pathways (an NGO subcontracted by the local government), explained to a volunteer in my presence:

> 'The problem is that *The Big Issue* now is not seen as enough to make a living on. That is how they [job centre] are redefining it. You can't get benefits because you aren't making enough to live on through *The Big Issue*. This is the new way they are working it now, which means that all those ladies who are selling *The Big Issue* aren't going to get any help because you can only get a right to reside if you are working enough to live on and *The Big Issue* won't give you that.'

The ambiguous restrictions increased confusion for frontline workers and migrants alike. They also increased migrants' reliance on frontline workers to provide informal discretionary support. For example, Lisa had to make a discretionary decision about whether, and how, to help migrants informally, such as helping them to register a formal household cleaning business. As mentioned earlier, one of the ways that she would provide this support was through referring families to volunteers.

As regulations for A2 migrants became increasingly restrictive throughout 2013 the confusion regarding how different regulations were being implemented meant that volunteers who had the latest and most up-to-date experience were seen as the most reliable sources of information because they had the most knowledge of negotiating with individuals in different bureaucratic offices, including the job centre and local authority children's services and housing. In a conversation between Simon, the pastor of the Roma church, and Lisa, a support worker, Simon explained Violeta's experience with the local government housing department: "We had four meetings at the council and in the end a big guy came from the homeless team and gave her the keys to a house." Simon then told the story of Dana who tried the same path: "I went down to the council with the family and they gave her three options: go back to Romania, leave now, or we take the children into care. They explained that they had a duty to house the children but nothing for the parents." At this point Lisa said that Cristina would probably be given the same three options if she went to the council to complain about the rats in her house. Cristina therefore had to try to hide any trace of rats or living in bad conditions to frontline workers who entered her home space. She also became more dependent on the informal discretionary support provided by frontline workers, and particularly volunteers, to help her to create the 'appropriate' conditions in her dilapidated house.

In summary, the laws governing EU migration in general, and A2 migrants especially, were complicated at the best of times and frequently subject to changing interpretations, with the resulting confusion creating space for frontline workers' own interpretations of individual regulations and circumstances. The child safeguarding agenda created a specific lens through which families were viewed, foregrounding frontline workers' personal judgements about the potential vulnerability of children when deciding what support or interventions were appropriate. The pressures of cuts to services under the UK's austerity programme meant that the time spent making these decisions was limited, often relying on heuristics or support from volunteers; at the same time, frontline workers could often only offer support through informal means or the voluntary sector, again creating discretionary spaces whereby their own judgements of 'deservingness' could determine access to state resources. Such additional support was justified through notions of charity and compassion.

Alongside these areas of discretionary decision making, frontline workers were themselves subject to a variety of pressures that affected their approach. Advancing Lipsky's (2010) approach to understanding frontline workers' (or in his words, 'street-level bureaucrats') situated positions, I have taken account of how frontline workers were shaped by their own life histories and experiences, how they tended to be female, from 'minority' or migration backgrounds, from lower socioeconomic backgrounds, on temporary and insecure employment contracts, overstretched, and subject to intense pressures from an 'audit culture' to meet key targets with limited resources.

With little time, limited resources and high levels of responsibility for discretionary and value-based decisions, frontline workers often brought their own norms, values and personal histories in deciding how to allocate their time, where to offer support and which individuals to target. In addition, they had their own conceptions of themselves as providers of care (see Chapters Five and Six), which were shaped by their own understandings of being a 'good citizen' in a 'post-welfare' context.

Within these constrained conditions, frontline workers chose to make home visits. They considered it to be the best use of their time because Romanian Roma led 'chaotic' lives and did not keep appointments. Home visits also allowed frontline workers to learn more about Romanian Roma lives, in trying to more fully understand their array of legal statuses and concomitant entitlements.

Final remarks

This chapter has laid the ground for understanding encounters between frontline workers and Romanian Roma by exploring frontline workers' situated positions and their scope for discretionary and value-based decisions.

In the chapters that follow we shall see how seemingly small decisions made by a wide range of different frontline workers with their own organisational routines, personal histories and perspectives can have large consequences for the life chances of migrants. This chapter has shown how the decisions frontline workers make are guided by their own backgrounds and experiences and are 'relationally embedded' (Thelen et al. 2014: 7). In addition to their own situated experiences, frontline workers also have to reconcile the idealised versions of bureaucratic practice held in policy with the everyday and often incoherent enactment of those policies when faced with individuals (Mountz 2003: 627). Interactions become sites where different values emerge, are contested, and either re-inscribed or transformed. These interactions are not only 'state acts', that is, sites of delivery of public services, implementation of state policy and where decisions regarding access to state resources are made (Lipsky 2010). They are also 'state encounters', highlighting the processual and emerging nature of the state, which are not fixed entities to be reproduced or wholly embodied by frontline workers, but dynamic relational events that are negotiated, holding the possibility of production as well as reproduction.

They are also the sites where 'the state' itself can be understood. Following a Foucauldian reading of power 'the state' operates not as a locatable object but as a located series of networks through which governance takes place. Therefore, to trace these subtle workings of state power it is crucial to envisage the state as 'relational' and continually reproduced through embedded social relationships (Thelen et al. 2014; see also Introduction). The discretionary decisions of frontline workers are where state forms are quite literally reproduced and where 'the state' itself is constituted. These encounters are where people perceive and experience the agency of the state, where decisions around who belongs and who does not belong are made and represent the site where relational practices at the margins shape the state itself.

Crucially, these decisions are made by the lowest paid and least valued frontline workers who are women and often from a minority or migration backgrounds. Through examining frontline workers' everyday decisions this chapter has advanced Lipsky's (2010) theoretical framework of the 'street-level bureaucrat' by exploring how these actors are themselves classed, racialised and gendered. They also have multiple roles (or subject-positions), as they are not only frontline workers but also mothers, carers, wives or daughters and their backgrounds shape which behaviours they recognise as either deserving or not.

This chapter has shown how this theoretical approach can be understood in practice, looking at particular processes that create wide discretionary scope in the decisions of frontline workers and the ways in which their individual situations and relationships affect their encounters with Romanian Roma. The structure of frontline work opens spaces where care and compassion become the primary mechanisms for whether and how frontline workers establish relationships with Romanian Roma mothers. This again blurs the roles that frontline workers engage in and heightens dilemmas in their potentially 'bordering' roles. These encounters are not approached lightly or easily justified by frontline workers, who sometimes agonise over these experiences. The next chapter will look at the position of the Romanian Roma, before we see how both sets of actors then bring their own situated positions to bear on encounters within the home.

Interlude | Disappearing Dinni

It is a Friday morning in May 2013 and Dan has risen very early. I hear the front door slam at around 5:30. I gradually fall asleep, trying to ignore the rats running through the walls and in the bathroom next door. I know that Dan is on his way to London to pick up someone from Victoria coach station in London because, about two weeks ago, I went with Cristina to Western Union to transfer money to an address in Moldavia. She told me it was to pay the coach fare for a lady to come to the house. When I asked exactly who, she replied a lady who was Dan's sister but only 'half-half' (pash pash). At around 11 o'clock Dan returns accompanied by Dinni, a small lady who looks as though she could be around 50. Her face is tanned and rough as though she had been working outdoors for a long time and she is wearing a headscarf. She looks visibly tired and after being hugged by Cristina with "Peace, my sister" (pace, murri pey), a greeting I have heard used only between those who attend the Roma church, she flops down on the couch. Over the next few weeks, new patterns emerge in the house because of Dinni. The first noticeable difference is that any object is stored away and out of sight. Dinni seems to work tirelessly and always finds new things to clean or tidy away, such as cleaning out the freezer or pushing furniture around to sweep behind couches and tables. She sleeps downstairs on one of the couches but every morning there is no sign of her having slept there or where she stores her belongings. She is always the first person in the bathroom in the morning and seems to be washed and dressed before anyone else in the house. Cristina still looks after the babies during the night but Dinni takes over as soon as they are awake.

Dinni's relationship with Cristina seems strained. The only time they laugh together is when Dinni manages to kill a big rat with a broom in the kitchen. Cristina seems relieved and hugs Dinni while they joke about the rat. Dan calls it Mickey Mouse so that the children will also think it funny. Although I think Cristina seems harsh towards Dinni, she also buys her presents. One Sunday evening when we are going to church Dinni wears a new white headscarf, which she tells me Cristina has bought for her.

I once helped Dinni go to the doctor because she had pains in her stomach. On the walk back we discuss Luton and what brought her to the UK. She immediately says that she doesn't like the town because "it is not beautiful or old". She asks me whether I like it and I reply that my boyfriend is in London, so I like London better. She says that she is not staying for much longer. She seems out of breath from walking so we stop at a newsagent's and I buy us two cans of Coke. We drink them outside the shop in the sunshine. It is a very hot day. Dinni continues to tell me about her eight grandchildren. They are between 2 and 8 years old. However, her face falls when she moves on to her husband. "He drinks beer all the time. He is not a good man. I have had nothing for 10 years." She tells me that her grandchildren "have nothing" (*si les khanchi*) and she is worried about when the cold weather comes again because they don't really have a proper house. I tell her that I visited the village and saw the houses where Dan and Cristina used to live. They were simple concrete buildings with two rooms, one leading into the other. The buildings had doorways and holes for windows but very few had doors or glass in the windows. The floor was earth and rooms were heated with open wood burning stoves. I ask her if her house is like Cristina and Dan's house and she tells me it is not far from there. She is worried because she has no money to send back to them. She wants to be with them and is finding England "very difficult" (*foarte pares*). In particular, she mentions that she feels lonely because Simon the pastor and Grigore have both "gone". There is no church at this time because it is the middle of summer and too many people are away. We talk about the church and she tells me how Dan used to visit her when they both lived close to each other in Romania and he talked to her about God. He described how God had changed his heart and invited her to come to the church near to where they were living. She explains how Dan's brother, Grigore, talked to her and she decided that she wanted to "go into the water" and was baptised.

Dinni seems to be increasingly on the phone over the next few weeks. Cristina tells me one of her granddaughters is very ill. In the evenings she sits in the corner of the room and Cristina's children run around her as she talks to her family on the phone. The situation comes to a head when we are sitting at the table eating. Dinni, as usual, takes a plate of bread and baked beans and sits on the couch to eat. Cristina, Dan, the children and I all sit at the table. The phone rings and Dan answers. It is Dinni's son. Dan gets very angry and shouts at him. Dinni gets up and goes into the garden as everyone else continues to eat baked beans.

Dan comes back to the table and explains that Dinni's son wants her back because he has "big problems". He continues

> 'I am not keeping her here but I pay her £100 a month to look after the kids. I paid £150 for the ticket and now they want her to go back. I don't have the money. If she wants to go back, there is no problem. But I can't pay for her to go for one week holiday. I pay for her to stay with the kids. Cristina needs to work. This is a big problem.'

Cristina joins in: "We need the same person to stay. This is not my mum. If it is my mum then maybe she would help me for free, but not this lady." Dan continued,

> 'I will get another lady. I have a big, big family. One man says, "Here take my daughter to look the kids," and I say, "No, I pay." This is important. I pay for someone. I am not going to just take one lady. Dinni has big problem. Her husband is drinking and smoking. Her house is broken. It is really falling down. I told her "You work here, you keep your money separate and then you go back and you keep your kids and your kids' kids. You have a big family! You stay here and work and then you can go back. But not go, come back, go, come back. I don't have the money for the ticket." Why didn't she tell me to my face? Why did she get her son to call me and get very angry with me on the phone? This is not good.'

Cristina goes outside to talk to Dinni who then called her son to tell him that she is coming home. At the weekend Dan took her to the coach and I didn't hear anything about Dinni again.

3

Romanian Roma mothers: labelling and negotiating stigma

> 'See, other people dress like this – Spanish, Indian, Muslim and me. What can I do! I can't change my religion. It is not my problem. I can't dress like you, in jeans. How can I do that? I am not changing my religion, so it is his problem.'

Maria said these words in an exasperated voice as we were walking down the street after she had been accused of stealing and told to leave a shop in the 'Indian centre' (*indiano centro*). She believed she had been accused of stealing because of her long skirt, headscarf and jewellery, which meant that the shop owner had identified her as Roma. Maria made sense of these experiences in different ways at different times. In this case, she was resigned and decided that the views of the shop keeper were 'his problem' and had not tried to argue with him. All Romanian Roma families I accompanied around Luton contended with these experiences every day. Interactions with frontline workers were no different.

At this juncture, it is important to reiterate that I am aware that by using the term Romanian Roma throughout this book I am also complicit in policing the boundaries of Roma ethnicity.[35] The term Roma has a specific history, particularly within EU and national public policies.[36] The origin of the term is widely argued to come from the word 'rom' which means married man for which the plural is 'roma' in the language spoken by those who are identified as Roma. The diverse histories and trajectories of those who are called Roma have led some to question its use as an ethnic identifier because of the potential for essentialisation and homogenisation of the term (Tremlett et al. 2014). However, such critiques could be levelled at using any ethnic definition, many of which are contested and have emerged through asymmetries of power relations (Banks 1996). Alternative labels such as 'new migrants' may also be homogenising and depoliticising, indicating the inherent problematic with any categorisation.[37] Throughout the book I also use the term 'families' or 'mothers' as well as Romanian Roma to foreground the contextual variety of their identifications (just as I also at different times call frontline workers 'mothers'). However, for the most part I have settled, somewhat uneasily, on using the term Romanian Roma. This chapter details how I use this term and explores its many different meanings and their implications, including how 'Romanian Roma' is a bureaucratic label and how it came to be invoked and reproduced through state encounters.

State labels and everyday racism

I am not interested in trying to describe an essential Roma identity or ethnicity.[38] Rather, I am interested in unpacking the process by which the label 'Romanian Roma' became a legitimate category of social division for frontline workers and families, and how it was relationally produced and filled with meaning. As explained in Chapter Two, I draw on Anderson and Scott to conceptualise labelling. The very boundedness of the state meant that its component objects were countable, and hence able to be incorporated into state organisation (Anderson 1983: 184). James Scott built on this idea to argue that 'state simplifications' such as naming populations and then counting them 'are like maps that are not intended to successfully represent the actual activity of the society they depict but to represent only that slice of it that is of interest for the official observer' (Scott 1998: 3). It is important to understand how labels operate because they have a determinative effect on the life chances and material circumstances of the people being labelled. This is because labels do not describe reality but are *generative*. They do not simply put a name on a group of people that already 'existed' but play a crucial role in creating that group and therefore a way of thinking about reality.[39]

The different meanings and uses of the label Romanian Roma throughout my fieldwork draw attention to another characteristic of labelling. Categories are not applied to people, families or groups in a void. They draw on histories and assumptions that are constantly being renegotiated. The history of those identified as Roma has long been associated with the representation of Roma as collectively inferior and as Europe's perennial 'inside-outsiders' (Guy 2003; Balibar 2009; van Baar 2011; Vermeersch 2012). These histories are important as they shape the underlying logics, policy programmes and actions that play out in current debates (Powell and Lever 2017). The violent histories of racist discrimination, including enslavement (Beck 1989; Achim 2004) and the

Holocaust (Friling et al. 2005), have been interwoven with various and widely varying formations of differential inclusion throughout history and across nations.

A pervasive commonality is that all countries in Europe, in varying degrees and historical time periods, discriminated against and persecuted those they identify as Gypsies or Roma (variously defined and named). More recently, there has been building and bordering of a pan-European Romani identity, which has emerged under particular political and socioeconomic conditions. Since the end of the Cold War and the eastern enlargement of the EU, Roma have been the target of the largest number of EU social inclusion programmes, while at the same time accompanied by calls to control Roma migration, particularly to Western Europe (van Baar 2017). Despite the EU's attempts at social inclusion 'many Roma still belong to the poorest, most segregated, most discriminated against and least "integrated" populations in Europe, and their chances for socio-economic mobility continue to be extremely low' (Sigona and Vermeersch 2012: 1189). Roma are not only a problem but have come to represent *the* problem of the EU (Yildiz and de Genova 2017).

There are also distinct gendered dimensions to stereotypes about Roma. In literature, cultural representations and public discourse Roma women are portrayed as stealing babies and acting as 'despicable' mothers (Perkins 2004; Martínez Guillem 2011; Okely 2014). Roma are accused of abducting children (Picker 2017) and selling their own children (Richardson 2014). These historical tropes and public discourses play out in media representations and infuse frontline workers' perceptions of those they label 'Romanian Roma'.

A further characteristic of labelling is that those who are labelled form their own understandings of the label. This is an important point because it raises the question of the latitude migrants have to identify themselves. In Romania, the term 'Romanian Roma' does not exist and would make no sense. Migration has therefore created this category and through processes of continuing encounters the label gains meanings. As we shall see, the way this category operates has consequences. Migrants internalise the category and in so doing it takes on importance (Brubaker et al. 2004) and becomes meaningful.

There is also a 'splitting' in the operation of the label, as those who are labelled both internalise the label and challenge it. But this is not a challenge that unsettles the logic of labelling or the hegemonic structure that produced it. The stories that follow unpack how migrants become complicit in the label's reproduction through their challenges of it. This process can be conceptualised as the symbolic violence of labelling (Bourdieu 1991). The category of 'Romanian Roma' is created and takes on pejorative meanings that hold currency in a British context. These meanings are co-produced in and through encounters with frontline workers.[40]

The label Romanian Roma can be seen as an artefact of racialisation that was continually being shaped relationally during my fieldwork, as the precise groups it referred to and meanings attached to them developed and created a possible reality through which they were thought about and responded to.[41] This chapter is dedicated to tracing how the term emerged, was solidified and normalised within bureaucratic discourse and how it came to be understood, invoked, negotiated, reproduced and contested by those labelled as Romanian Roma.

The aim in this chapter is to acknowledge the complex and contextual features of labelling while unearthing the underlying logics and symbolic violence that can be detected across these various instances and contexts. It traces the historical precedents of racialisation that shape current relations between frontline workers and Romanian Roma. The label Romanian Roma is shaped by representations and the power asymmetry between the state (where some of those representations are incorporated) and those being labelled. The tension between representations and positions plays out throughout the chapter.

While this group of migrants were termed Romanian Roma by frontline workers, the migrants in fact had widely varying legal statuses, migration trajectories, nationalities, languages, religions, family structures, educational backgrounds, as well as aspirations, expectations and perceptions of the UK state, thoughts about what constituted a meaningful life and were engaged in a range of economic activities. The importance of the label Romanian Roma is brought into stark relief when the wide array of social differences among and between individuals is acknowledged. I review these not to fetishise difference, but rather to point to the power of categorisations to privilege a particular subjectivity (namely 'race') above other characteristics.

It is also important to be aware of the complexity of different individuals' lives because this had an impact on how, and whether, frontline workers were able to provide them with support to access a legal status in the UK. Their legal statuses (often many different legal statuses within one family and across generations) included UK citizens, refugee status (UK, Belgium, Canada), A2 migrants, irregular migrants, failed asylum seekers, deportees who had returned to the UK, and those who might be considered 'over-stayers' from Brazil and Argentina. (In addition, as noted previously, many of these legal statuses changed during my time there, as transitional controls on EU A2 migrants were lifted.) Migration trajectories included families and individuals who had arrived in the UK from Romania, Hungary, Italy, Austria, Moldova, Belgium, Canada, Brazil, Ireland. One family, for example, had arrived in the UK after stays in Romania, Germany, Belgium, Spain and Argentina, and their seven children variously had identification documents from all of those countries.

Nationalities included Romanian, Canadian, Spanish, Argentine, Brazilian, Italian, Spanish, Irish, British and Canadian. Languages spoken included most of the above, as well as Hindi (which was learned from TV programmes and by interacting in the local area, particularly at market stalls or material shops where the common understandable language between most people was Hindi). Religions included Jehovah's Witnesses, Pentecostalism and Romanian Orthodox, as well as many who did not understand the notion of religion as presented to them. (One family only understood the difference between religions as a distinction between 'Rashai' or Romanian Orthodox Priest and 'Pastaro' meaning Pentecostal Vicar). Similarly, religion was used to describe a sense of identity, as when Maria used it in her description of being identified as Roma. When asked to fill in their religion on a form, one family were confused and offered 'Romanian' before one of the children shouted "Tsigane", meaning 'Gypsy' in Romanian. Nonetheless, all of these individuals and families were called Romanian Roma.

The most prevalent common characteristic I found was speaking the Romanës language in the home. It was through this language that I came to know the families at the heart of this book. However, even then, some migrants I encountered did not speak Romanës, though were able to understand it; and others had only learned Romanës as a second language when marrying partners who did.

The implications of the homogenising nature of the term and the direct harm that was caused to families can be demonstrated by recalling the encounter that opened this book, with Catalina, Radu and their four youngest children. I will detail the specifics of the encounter between this family and social services in Chapter Four. However, the salient details here are that they had an extremely complicated mix of legal statuses that social services were not equipped to manage. Catalina and Radu had been born in Romania, but their eight children had been born in Germany, Belgium, Spain and Argentina. They insisted that they were Argentinian – and referred to their Argentine ID cards and the children's birth certificates. To complicate matters further, the eldest son, Andrei, who had been born in Brussels, had married a Romanian national, Sophia, who had migrated to the UK in 2004 and gained indefinite leave to remain. They had a son called Armando (Catalina and Radu's grandson) who had been born in London. Not only were the legal statuses complicated by the different nationalities, but each person in the house spoke a different combination of languages, and the only common language was their oral dialect of *Romanës*. Social services hired a Romanian translator for their visit because Paula, an equality and diversity officer for the children's services department, had noted that they were not 'illegally' residing in the country because of their Romanian nationality. However, the four youngest children could not speak Romanian, and had learnt to speak Spanish. No one in this family could read or write.

Paula, who was also present at this home encounter, suggested using a telephone interpreting service that was provided by the children's services department. The resulting 'assessment' of the children's safety was disjointed and distressing for everyone involved, particularly the family. While having four unknown people in the house asking intimate questions would be distressing for any family, the lack of recognition of the family's complex migration trajectory made this encounter particularly troubling. The social workers had assumed that because the family had been called Romanian Roma they would all speak Romanian. This was not the case. First, the two social workers asked the parents questions through the Romanian interpreter. The children were present but could not understand what was being asked. The parents were then asked to leave, but the house was so small they both stood in the garden looking through the window to try to check on what was happening to their children. The Romanian interpreter then left and Paula phoned the Spanish interpreter, put her phone on loudspeaker mode and placed it in the middle of the table in between the chairs and couches.

The children were visibly confused and quite upset at being asked questions about their parents by a disembodied Spanish voice. The youngest children, two boys who were 6 and 9 years old, were calling their parents to come back inside and did not seem to understand who the social workers were or why they were asking them questions about their parents. The oldest daughter who was 14 answered questions cautiously. The social workers asked whether she thought her parents were happy and if she was happy living with them. She stated in a quiet voice that her mum and dad couldn't live without each other.

Paula was also not happy and commented to me afterwards that she had felt "awful" throughout the assessment and had stayed afterwards to try to make jokes with the children. She also tried to be friendly towards Catalina and Radu, asking them many questions about the previous places they had lived. Catalina could remember the address of the flat where they had lived for a short time in Stuttgart more than 15 years previously. Paula's husband was German and they exchanged words in German, with Paula trying hard to make conversation and encourage Catalina. Catalina cooperated with Paula and then continued to ask her questions about 'social' for the children. Paula answered that the children needed to go to school. I stayed in the house after this encounter because I did not want to leave with Paula, in case Catalina thought we were talking about her and her family. After the encounter Catalina hurriedly rushed to get food ready for the family as they were hungry, further indicating the disrupting nature of this encounter to their daily routine. This example goes some way to demonstrating the complexity of statuses and languages, and how it creates deep uncertainty and distress for migrants and, to some extent, the frontline workers.

While bearing in mind that racism is always contextual and changes in time and space, the label Romanian Roma actively shaped how encounters played out because of the pejorative meanings that were generated when the term was used. These meanings were negotiated and contested during encounters and discourses, and it is therefore vital to understand how the label Romanian Roma was invoked and reproduced, and how it situated migrants in their relation to frontline workers and the terms on which they were able to negotiate their legal status.

Everyday labelling: connections and disconnections

The main mechanism in creating the label Romanian Roma was the separation of these families from their Romanian co-nationals and linking them to a pan-Romani identity. Frontline workers distinguished Roma from their Romanian co-nationals in subtle but significant ways, drawing on tropes linked to Gypsies and political and media representations of Roma migrants. For example Kassia, a Polish children's centre family support worker, compared Romanian Roma families in Luton with Polish Roma in Poland. Her expectations were drawn from her understanding of Polish Roma rather than her other clients who are Romanian mothers, demonstrating the power of the Roma label to supersede national identifications. Roma women were primarily identified by their appearance (including the way they dressed), their economic activity (such as selling *The Big Issue* magazine or begging) or a surname that they associated with Roma. However, this also led to confusion when families who did not dress in this way were also identified as Roma, either through speaking *Romanës* or through association with the Roma Pentecostal church (*khangheri*). This confusion provides further indication of the ways Roma were treated as a generic group who were expected to behave in particular ways, despite wide variations across all axes of differentiation (see earlier). Frontline workers recognised this diversity but nonetheless endeavoured to retain an idea of distinct 'Romanian Roma' and 'Romanian-not-Roma' groups regardless of the many instances where this division was challenged.

There was also a distinct gendered dimension to this racialisation. For example, I was told by other mothers that Cristina was *gazhi* (non-Roma) and that her children were *pash pash* (half-half). However, frontline workers never thought to question whether Cristina was Roma or what that might mean for their understanding of 'Roma-ness'. Cristina became subsumed by her husband's identity and racialised through her marriage to Dan. Male identity is assumed to encapsulate the woman's identity (see Chapter Five for further gendered implications).

The distinction between Romanian-Roma and Romanian-not-Roma was introduced and repeated between frontline workers when they met at bimonthly multi-agency meetings. The aim of the meetings was to bring together those who provided education, health and welfare support to migrants for information sharing and to ensure that frontline workers were not duplicating work. The migrants' ambiguous legal situation, that of citizens of an EU member state but not able to access state resources, was a new phenomenon for many frontline workers and their organisations. For example, some had a background in working with refugees and asylum seekers; others supported previous European migrants who were subject to different legal regulations. While legal information was available, it did not reflect the rapidly shifting interpretations of the transition restrictions. Rather than receiving guidance from team leaders, frontline workers were considered to be the experts on the different regulations and legal statuses that affected their clients. Many of those who were considered experts had previously worked with Irish Travellers and English Romany Gypsies who had full recourse to public funds (a similar situation is noted by Picker, 2017).

Frontline workers' discussions at these meetings revealed their understanding of the changing legal framework in January 2014 and how this bled into their daily activities, infusing their subjective expectations and perceptions of those identified as Roma. Paula, an education and diversity officer, was considered to have the best grasp of the population and others relied on her to identify and define the meanings attached to this label. For example, in a formal interview Lisa, a Pathways support worker, expressed confusion regarding the definition of different groups and believed that Paula had a more authoritative grasp of the distinction because she had been working with some families that she identified as Roma for a longer amount of time:

'Paula speaks about the Traveller Romanis or Romanis. I haven't grasped who is Traveller and who isn't. I just think they are all Travellers, there are just different classes. It is the same as the Travellers, you get all the different surnames, don't you? They have told me that those families are like this, those are like that.'

In the wake of uncertainty regarding these migrant families, Lisa drew on local understandings informed by her own previous experiences with other 'groups' of migrants, her own experience as a visible minority in Luton and media representations and political discourses:

'It is the same as when black people came – we weren't allowed in the same pubs as the white. They [Romanian Roma] have got bad stigma for themselves. All communities have got stigma but they are new to the UK. I only saw in the paper the other day, a Romanian selling his daughter as a slave – as a working girl for him. Then you are seeing them in the streets begging … They are up against a brick wall. As long as people have these views about Roma people they are going to find it really difficult …'

While Lisa uses the term Romanian and Roma interchangeably, she is drawing on her experiences of Travellers and making links that contribute to the idea that Romanian Roma are a distinct, separate group from their co-nationals.

Paula also relied on the distinction between Romanian Roma and Romanian-not-Roma. In one multi-agency meeting in November 2013, Paula expressed the view that those who were working long hours in low-wage jobs and not applying for a national insurance number were 'doing the right thing' by waiting until transitional restrictions were lifted. She provided the example of a 'Romanian-not-Roma' married couple who were working 'all the time and not going for national insurance numbers'. It was agreed that Romanian Roma should also wait until January 2014 when transitional restrictions would be lifted. It was alluded to during these meetings that Romanian Roma had been misusing frontline workers' time and resources by trying to obtain national insurance numbers in 2013, particularly when they were unlikely to be granted due to increasingly strict interpretations of the transitional restrictions.

Romanian Roma families were also distinguished from their national counterparts through the use of old tropes of nomadism and a desire for living in caravans rather than houses. Rosemary, a family liaison volunteer for a primary school, was working with a family that she identified as Romanian Roma because she had received their referral from the pastor of the Roma church. She presumed the family was nomadic and therefore would not stay in the local area. "I wouldn't be surprised if they suddenly disappear."

The link to a pan-Romani identity shaped the support that was offered to this family (see 'Rosemary and Ecaterina', Chapter Six). Rosemary's practices therefore had racist implications and reinforced underlying racial relations, a phenomenon Philomena Essed (1991) termed 'everyday racism'. Attention to these small mundane practices identifies how different socio-political and legal statuses are reproduced. Different practices for 'Romanian Roma families' developed and became routine as experiences were shared among frontline workers. For example, frontline workers would often visit Romanian Roma family homes unannounced because it was believed that Roma did not keep appointments (Humphris 2017; see also Chapter Four).

Beyond depicting the development of different subjective attitudes and behaviours among frontline workers, understanding the label Romanian Roma is vital to the assumptions and value judgements that were made about these families' intimate lives and approach to motherhood as they interacted with formal legislation. We can also see how this label was invoked and reproduced to make families visible to frontline workers through the goal of child safeguarding, and how this came to position Romanian Roma families, shaping their encounters with frontline workers.

Mothers under the Romanian Roma label

The perceptions and expectations that were linked to being Romanian Roma shifted and were constantly being invoked and (re)produced through encounters. As highlighted by Fox and colleagues (2015: 733), it has proven difficult to observe and measure the different combinations of 'biological and cultural indicia' that reproduce systems of racial domination. These subtle processes can be grasped through specific instances where frontline workers expressed surprise, or were unprepared for the behaviour of specific families and individuals in encounters.

The examples reveal how Romanian Roma were thought about in particular (and pejorative) ways. Frontline workers, from their position in the state apparatus, are entrusted with categorising mothers as 'safe' or 'unsafe'. Fathers were seemingly absent from this context (see Chapter Five). As reviewed in Chapter Two, frontline workers are gatekeepers and their decisions encourage 'good' citizens to reproduce children while disavowing undesirable parents and parenting. Roma, Gypsy and Traveller mothers are identified in Ofsted guidelines as being the focus for targeted interventions. Being identified as Roma therefore automatically places a mother in a category as vulnerable. Media representations and public discourse that regard Roma as dangerous and unsafe mothers also bleed into frontline workers' expectations. Being identified as a Roma mother is accompanied with labelling as a vulnerable but also undeserving mother.

Frontline workers' perceptions of Romanian Roma were often most visible when they had experiences that unsettled their expectations. For example, the assumption that Romanian Roma women shared a set of traditional religious values meant they were not offered contraception by frontline workers, unlike many other families. The reliance on the Pentecostal church for its networks of voluntary support further reinforced this effect. In my position as being outside these structures, several women mentioned to me that they were concerned about family planning. When I suggested this to Samantha, deputy head of a children's centre, she reacted with surprise and confusion. She thought that all Romanian Roma women wanted big families and therefore had not entertained the idea that they might want family planning advice. That some Romanian Roma women might want contraception conflicted with perceptions that had become integral to her understanding of people who had been labelled Romanian Roma. This is an example of where the ideological dimensions of racism are linked to daily attitudes. The structural forces of racism can then be identified within everyday 'routine' and sometimes 'mundane' situations.

On another occasion I witnessed, Paula (an equality and diversity officer for the children's services department) planned to help one family with forms to register their children in schools. When Gigi, the father, took the paperwork from her to complete it himself, she reacted with shock. The assumption was that Romanian Roma had limited education and were typically illiterate, or at least unable to write in English. She explained to me, "Those brothers are very different – it is like they are used to being around other people who aren't Gypsies." She continued,

'It is in the way they are dressing, the way they talk to you, their whole behaviour. Gigi went to go and get a copy of Traian's [oldest son's] birth certificate straight away – he actually went to the shop to get it. I have never come across a family like this before.'

Paula was similarly shocked when a Romanian Roma mother moved house to be nearer to her children's school. Again, the perception was that these mothers did not value education and would not actively reorganise their lives for the education and welfare of their children. In that example, the mother in question had refugee status and had already had a different set of experiences in another city in the UK. In contrast, many other mothers had children at multiple schools and would not have had the resources to move house, even if they thought it would be beneficial.

While the meanings attached to the label Romanian Roma were constantly being co-produced through encounters, frontline workers had more power to determine what challenged their fundamental conceptions of families. Crucially the instances described above remained as surprising exceptions to a distinct form of 'Roma-ness'. Encounters with families where parents were illiterate, had been in prison, were begging or were involved in early marriages were seen as 'real' Roma behaviour and to be expected.

Crucially, most of these assumptions relate fundamentally to value judgements that assumed Romanian Roma were poor or risky mothers, unlikely to properly plan a family, unable or unwilling to support their children's education, thereby potentially exposing 'vulnerable' children to inadequate and chaotic domestic environments. These perceptions were layered with other value judgements about 'good families' as the frontline workers continually reformed and shaped the categorisations of 'Roma mothers' through their interactions. One distinction emerged in frontline workers' narratives between those who migrated as a family and those who migrated alone, with the latter being seen as more 'appropriate'. For example, one education support worker described a Romanian Roma man staying with his sister, who had gained refugee status in 2001, as 'doing things properly' because he was sending money back to his family rather than bringing them with him. However, in another conversation she expressed a contradictory assessment when discussing non-Roma families, saying it was important for children to be brought up in strong families with two present parents.

In this way, value judgements about good parenting interweave with specific perceptions of Romanian Roma to reinforce negative perspectives about 'appropriate' behaviour. It is in these contradictory assessments, where families identified as Roma are seen as bad parents regardless of their actions or intentions, that pinpoint the implications of racialisation.

The idea that parents and children should live together was also reflected in ideas of 'good motherhood' for the mothers I stayed with, but other negative perceptions of Romanian Roma prevented these values from emerging in frontline workers' understanding. For example, one evening I was watching a Romanian TV show with Georgeta and her daughter-in-law Denisa who was seven months pregnant. The programme depicted a mother who left her two young children with her sister and her sister's boyfriend to work in Italy. The sister mistreated the children and at the end of the programme I noticed Denisa crying. Georgeta commented "We (*ame*) don't leave the babies. It is best to stay with mum (*day*) or grandmother (*bába*)." She made a value distinction between those who leave children and, in her view, the better practice of raising children with their parents.

Thus, although frontline workers and mothers held some converging views, those identified as Romanian Roma families were categorised as moving with their children in order to claim benefits, invoking a different, and stigmatised, set of values. Hierarchies developed to place different work and migration strategies on levels of appropriateness that related to assessments of deservingness. Those identified as Romanian Roma who migrated with their children were not seen as privileging their children or family life but categorised as taking advantage of benefits. Thus the position from which mothers could negotiate performances of 'appropriate mothering' was shaped by a set of racialised expectations and perceptions, by which they were quickly designated both as 'vulnerable' and 'undeserving'.

These general perceptions of Romanian Roma as being poor mothers were vital to how families became visible to frontline workers. Referrals or reports that related to Roma families were more likely to result in 'early intervention' strategies. From birth, Romanian Roma children were identified as potentially 'vulnerable', providing the drive and licence for home visitations by frontline workers. The next section further explores how these processes, through which negative perceptions of Romanian Roma interwove with the child safeguarding lens in UK policy, led to these families becoming visible to frontline workers.

State visibility and the bureaucratic magic of children

Children open up a realm whereby families have an opportunity to gain a more secure legal status but there is also the danger of being subject to processes of surveillance (see Chapter Six). First, this section demonstrates how children make a Romanian Roma family 'visible'[42] and, crucially, that frontline workers with duties over children are the primary, and often only, professionals with whom these families interact (see Chapter Two). These interactions are the only place where mothers can learn the complex rules and regulations they are subject to and the performances required to negotiate these relationships. Second, this section explores how migrants who do not have children are not captured by bureaucratic lenses and have no position through which to negotiate a firmer residency status with formal frontline workers, and are therefore cut off from most informal support as well.

A Romanian Roma family could become visible to frontline workers in a number of ways. First, when a Romanian Roma woman gave birth in the local hospital she would automatically be referred to Emma, early years health visitor for 'hard to reach' groups (a category solely for Gypsy, Roma and Traveller mothers), to begin the Healthy Start programme. Hospital staff often identified women as Romanian Roma because of specific surnames or mode of dress. Thus, by virtue of being identified as Roma, these women were singled out for special treatment.

Second, families with school-age children become visible to frontline workers. One social worker told me she had been made aware of a household identified as Roma whose children did not have shoes and were dressed in inappropriate clothes. Neighbours had called social services. Similarly, one volunteer was fostering a Roma child because her mother had been looking in nearby bins for food as they did not have enough to eat (although I often saw women looking in bins, not for food but for scrap metal to sell).

Third, children made families visible through alleged instances of domestic violence. Neighbours had contacted social services about one family because they had reportedly seen a man hitting a woman and both were shouting very loudly. As it was also reported there were many young children in the house a social worker had attended out of concern for their safety.

The trajectories of how children made a family visible to frontline workers were crucially important to the subsequent relationships that were established. As an early years health visitor Emma's remit was to operate under the safeguarding agenda. In addition to checking whether she believed children were safe within their homes, she had the capacity through multi-agency meetings to refer mothers to other agencies for formal support. Simon, the pastor, also made families with school-age children visible through referring to Paula. The church also made mothers visible through linking them to children's centres. These differences had effects for how encounters played out. As we see in the next chapter, there were differences between mothers who were visited with no warning and mothers who met frontline workers in the church or the children's centre *first* before they were visited at home.

It is important to note that some mothers did want to actively engage with frontline workers under certain circumstances. For example, Petti had moved to the UK before 2007 and had gained indefinite leave to remain due to her Roma status. The mother of two children, she had moved from Croydon to Luton two years before I met her. I visited Petti at home, and she told me that she used to get child benefit for her children but this had stopped. She was also concerned that her 5-year-old son should be attending school. As Petti had indefinite leave to remain and believed that she was entitled to support, she was keen to engage with state services and was not concerned about opening her home to surveillance. However, she had not been aware of how or whom to approach until my visit. I told her about Paula at the children's services department and how she could help Petti if she wanted to register her children in school. A clear pathway was thus established for Petti to gain the support she needed. Paula visited her at home and registered her children at the nearest school. She also helped to get child benefit reinstated and to receive backdated payments. While this scenario saw a mother actively seeking encounters with frontline workers, this was only possible because of her children.

There is a clear difference in how Romanian Roma who did not have children experienced their everyday interactions, in particular because they were not 'bureaucratically captured' by frontline workers. This can be seen from Gigi's description of working in the UK alone, and when he later moved with his wife and three sons. He told me "[B]efore there was no problem, but now with the kids I am being cut ...". 'Before' refers to when he first came to the UK after Romania acceded to the EU and was working in the construction industry in the temporary labour market in 2008. He had not encountered any frontline workers and had worked and lived freely in the UK, earning a living and sending this money home to his family. However, when he returned to the UK from Romania four years later with his wife and three young sons he had a very different experience. His statement about being 'cut' refers to how he felt his efforts to establish himself and his family were being thwarted. First, because of the various regulations and visits that his family were now subject to because of the presence of children, and second, the seeming devaluation of his work as he was considered not to be 'genuinely self-employed' because he did not earn enough money. He compared this experience with when he worked in construction in London and Glasgow in 2008, where he told me he easily gained a CIS (construction industry card) and his colleagues were able to gain national insurance numbers (he did not apply for one at the time). Gigi's experiences demonstrate how restricted access to social rights is not equally significant in the lived experiences of migrants and highlights the significance of children, where particular tensions can emerge for parents. Gigi previously assumed the role of a tolerated precarious worker without being affected by incursions into his daily life by frontline workers. But with children and plans to establish himself and his family in the UK, rather than work in temporary and precarious jobs, he was cast into a different relationship with the state.

Many migrants experienced exclusion and invisibility despite wanting to engage with frontline workers. For example, Mihai and Ilinca, a couple whose children were adults and living elsewhere, could not register with a doctor. In order to register with a GP (general practitioner) a number of forms had to be filled in. An interpreter could not be booked to help to translate and fill in the forms until the patient was registered, thereby creating a catch-22 situation where migrants who could not read or write English were restricted from accessing healthcare unless they gained informal assistance. Many gained this assistance through frontline workers who believed it was important to register children, and therefore the mother, with a GP. Mihai and Ilinca, and many others who did not have children, were unable to access this support and therefore were not registered and could not access healthcare.

The importance of children can also be seen through two contrasting experiences of Victor and Costel, two members of the same family. Victor stayed with Dan and his family for two weeks. When Dan got a construction job, Victor moved to Grigore's house as Dan told me that it was 'not good' (*nai mishto*) for Victor to be in the house all day with Cristina and the babies. Victor had no means of supporting himself, never interacted with frontline workers and eventually returned to his wife and children in Romania. In contrast, when Costel arrived in the area with his wife and three children support was provided by the church. Simon told Paula about the family and she registered the children in the nearest school. Through interacting with the school and frontline workers, Costel and his wife tried to learn English. His wife also helped Grigore's wife with looking after the children and making food for the family. Eventually, with help from Simon, Costel managed to get a scrap metal licence and thus support his family. Through these relationships Costel was able to gradually establish himself, his wife was able to learn the performances required of her to interact with the school and children's centre, and in the following year they were able to gain secure residency in the UK. As two members of the same family with similar personal networks and resources, the contrasting trajectories of Victor and Costel place the significance of children in stark relief.

The presence of children is fundamental to the processes that allow migrants access to state resources and forms of belonging. The lens through which this focus on children has developed creates both opportunities and dangers, particularly because interactions take place in the home. The trajectories through which families become visible and encounter frontline workers are fundamental to understanding how they negotiate their legal statuses, and why the frame of the intimate state encounter becomes so salient.

Engaging, resisting and reproducing 'Romanian Roma'

Before moving to analyse home encounters themselves in the next three chapters, there are some further processes that help to situate the actors and reveal the complex and contradictory dynamics at play. First, as explained in the Introduction, historically Roma are a marginalised group who often experience discrimination and prejudice throughout Europe. Focusing on the complexity of lived experiences is vital for understanding the shifting nature of racialisation and is pivotal to avoid reductionist accounts of social relations (Hall and Du Gay 1996; Balibar 1998).

I describe some specific instances where Romanian Roma women experienced discrimination and how they made sense of this everyday racism. Second, I describe how the category took on social meaning through being internalised and then challenged from within the terms of the category. Third, I explore how experiences of racism and state violence have consequences for how Romanian Roma substantiated information and formed relationships with frontline workers. These processes intertwined with their complicated migration trajectories and legal statuses, which can be seen as part of the hostile environment in the UK to create confusion and uncertainty. Each family had a different status, not only because of the rapidly changing UK residency rules but also the discretionary decisions of frontline workers and volunteers. In consequence, Romanian Roma often had wide-ranging and misguided understandings of their rights and entitlements, and experienced the 'system' as 'crazy' (*systemos si dillo*) and ultimately untrustworthy, which affected how they engaged with frontline workers.

Romanian Roma constantly experienced forms of racism in their daily lives and they engaged, resisted and reproduced the bureaucratic label depending on their varied backgrounds and their symbolic and material resources. Women were more easily identified because of the way that they dressed. For example, I visited a material shop with Iolanda, a 17-year old Romanian Roma *shey bari* (young unmarried woman), after taking her to the dentist. She did not often come into town without a member of her family. Her mother had given her around four pounds in coins to buy a drink for us both on the way back from the dentist. She wanted to visit the material shop to see if there was anything she could buy to decorate her clothes. As soon as we entered the owner of the shop told us we had to leave. Iolanda immediately turned around to leave without comment; however, I pressed the owner of the shop for further explanation. He said his sunglasses had been stolen on the previous day and now he was not allowing anyone with a 'big skirt' into his shop. He then shouted at Iolanda that she could remain in his shop if she removed her long flowing skirt.

Expectations of stealing linked to the long skirts was a recurrent theme (it was thought that Roma women hid stolen items in their skirts). Maria was very aware that she could be identified by her clothes and she tried to change her appearance in different situations. When we visited the job centre together, she stopped outside and took off her headscarf, re-tied her hair and put on a grey hooded sweatshirt. She also crossed herself, kissed her hand and threw it up in a gesture towards the sky. When we walked into the job centre the receptionist said to the G4S security guard who was standing ominously close by, "It's the Romanians again." She told us there was nothing she could do for Maria and handed us a leaflet that listed the phone numbers of HMRC and the Department for Work and Pensions. Maria left, stating "I have no luck today," and continued with her day, resolute that she would try again another day when she might gain different information or advice.

Another common reaction to racism and discrimination was blaming others who were giving Roma a bad name. Tactics for resisting discrimination also differed, depending on migrants' different backgrounds, resources and experiences, but often rested on spatial or social distancing. For example, one day, Mihai and I were sitting in the front room of the house where he was staying with Ilinca, his wife. He had returned from working at the hand car-wash and was relaxing while Ilinca was boiling a large pot of chickens in the kitchen. Mihai began to tell me about his family. He had two sons and three daughters and had lived in many different countries. He explained that he had four years of school in Hungary and four years of school in Romania. He had lived in Denmark, Austria, Germany, the Netherlands, Spain and France. I asked him why he travelled to so many countries and he replied, "In Romania, we can't get job because of racist, because of being *black*." He said the word 'black' quietly and moved towards to me to say it, although there was no one else in the room at the time. He also explained specifically that he didn't speak French and had not stayed there very long because there were "too many Romanian people there. It was no good." He had moved because he believed Romanians had a bad reputation, which would make it difficult to live there.

This theme of avoiding others who were also identified as Roma (and therefore might tarnish relationships with others) was common throughout the families I spent my everyday life with, regardless of where they were from or their migration trajectories. For example, I told Maria that I wanted to write something about how Romanians are finding living in the UK. She told me,

'It is like this. Say someone asks you "Where are you from?" and you say "England", then everything is good for you. Say there is one person who is stealing who is from Romania and they say "Where are you from?" and you say "Romania", then they think everyone from Romania is stealing. Not everyone is the same.'

While Mihai noted that in some circumstances he avoided places with "too many Romanians", Dan's tactic was to try to place himself and his family outside stereotypes of stealing through invoking his religiosity. One afternoon on our way to buy food from the supermarket we walked past Lenuţa who was begging in a passageway that led from the supermarket to the road. He knew her from the Roma church and said,

'I don't mind Lenuţa, but she is stealing and for this I have a big problem. It makes it bad for Romanians here – people see them stealing and then say "Everyone go back home."'

He continued,

'People, they don't like Romanians. Because some Romanians are stealing everyone goes down, down, down and then no one likes them. Across Europe it is like this. This is normal. It is the way. For me, I love God. I love everybody. No stealing. Nothing.'

Dan put a boundary between himself and others through identification with God and religion. He told me to be careful around other families because they 'xoxavel' (lie) and 'choralian' (cheat). He also taught his children to make this distinction. One night we were watching a police programme. Two men who lived in Luton featured on the programme because they were involved in a car accident. Dan was laughing and said that the accident was a fake to make a car insurance claim. At around the same time his youngest son, who was 13 months old, had found my rucksack that I placed near to the front door and was exploring what was inside. Dan jumped off the couch when he noticed his son doing this and went to pick him up, saying "You are not Hunedoara – you are not stealing," making his other children laugh. Hunedoara was a town in Romania where some migrant families in Luton were from, including the two men who had caused the car accident. Dan's joke drew on a deep awareness that the term Roma carried a stigma that was difficult for him and his children to disrupt. The social category had a deep meaning for him and he endeavoured to teach his children how to respond to it. Dan expressed to his children how they could move outside this stigmatising label through drawing a boundary between their family and 'others' from a different area in Romania.

These everyday experiences of racism linked to the stigma of being labelled as Romanian Roma cannot be underestimated in how they shaped perceptions and expectations in interactions with frontline workers. Migrants did not make sense of these experiences in isolation, but they were folded into their general understanding of life in the UK and were the basis on which relationships with frontline workers were formed (over time these relationships could change and individual frontline workers gained different reputations as different meanings were made relationally). In addition, these subjective perceptions entwined with migrants' objective positions because their access to information was severely restricted, due both to their illiteracy (caused by segregated education that is often inferior to the mainstream) and the small number of opportunities they had to acquire information about their legal statuses in the UK. As Essed (1991: 8) elaborates, 'the experience of everyday racism is a cumulative process. New experiences are interpreted and evaluated against the background of earlier personal experiences, vicarious experiences and general knowledge of racism in society.'

Previous experiences of being labelled as Roma, the racism and state violence that followed, and the limited access to information about legal status in the UK, meant that rumours about UK policy and practice towards Romanians were rife during the course of my fieldwork. For these migrants, rumours could not be verified through researching information on the internet or paying a lawyer to provide legal advice that would be trusted and valued.

The understanding of legal restrictions and residency rights circulated in a social field that had an excess of stories and rumours about how to make a life in the UK. Stories of interactions with frontline workers, such as children being taken into state care or deportations and removals, acted as ersatz news in the absence or rejection of more formal and verifiable news. The stories therefore offered an interpretative frame for those participating in their circulation. This resonates with what Harney (2006: 276) has called 'rumour publics', where people make use of the knowledge they possess to solve problems, make sense of changing or uncertain conditions and construct explanatory narratives in the face of fluid and ambiguous situations (Shibutani 1966; Stewart and Strathern 2004).

For migrants, rumours about changing regulations in January 2014 were the source of many stories and conversations about possible outcomes. Previous encounters in different migration contexts were drawn on and folded into understandings of the potential scenarios in January 2014 (Humphris 2018b). When attending a church service at the end of October 2013, Margereta, a migrant mother, immediately asked me whether I thought she would be "put out" of her house when England "closes the door". I asked whether she was paying rent and she confirmed that she was staying with a family who were paying rent to a private landlord. I asked why she thought she would be moved from her house. She answered that she had heard it on the Romanian televised news and from other mothers who didn't have a national insurance number. Margereta moved to England in June 2013. She proudly showed me a photograph of herself with her son when they lived in Montpellier in France, but she told me she had been sent back to her village in Romania the previous year. She had left her son with her parents while she tried to gain work in England. She was extremely anxious because she had already been deported from France; the rumours that she might be deported from the UK therefore seemed very plausible to her. Margereta increasingly believed she would not be able to get 'good work' (such as cleaning in contrast to begging, which was considered 'hard' (*zurelli*) work), would not be able to bring her son to join her in England, but, conversely, would be sent back to Romania.

The information that Margereta had heard on the news was 'substantiated' to the extent that it was received by word of mouth from interpersonal relationships; that is, from the other mothers whom she trusted. The information was then subjectively evaluated against standards of experience and knowledge from her previous experience in Montpellier where she had been deported back to her village in Romania. As explained earlier, many Romanian Roma adult migrants were illiterate and therefore had severely curtailed access to sources of information. Information was exchanged almost entirely through oral transmission and memory. The credibility of the speaker and the plausibility of their speech were assessed on particular forms and norms of performance linked to social position. Further, migrants' previous and current situations and their own understanding of the palpability of racism inflected their evaluation of interactions and accounts of encounters. Almost all of the migrants addressed in this book had previously, directly or indirectly, experienced eviction, deportation, imprisonment or had a child taken into the care of social services. These experiences changed the contours of plausibility when assessing narratives about the future and had particular consequences for interactions with frontline workers and how rapidly changing residency rights were interpreted and understood. These events become folded into their everyday understanding of experiences in manifold ways.

Attention to these stories, such as Margereta's, bearing in mind that she could not read and write, reveals migrants' subjective understandings of the legal systems in which they were subject and how previous experiences were mobilised to make sense of current situations. Margereta's anxieties provide a glimpse of how she understood her position within situated migrant hierarchies. It specifically locates her desires within a work trajectory and imagined future for her and her son. However, her previous experience of deportation formed part of her assessment of possible futures in the UK, shaping her understanding of regulations and she eventually returned to Romania.

Rumours, substantiated by previous experiences, also had a direct effect on the relationships between migrants and frontline workers. For example, one day Cristina asked me "Who is Lisa, is she the black lady? I don't want English people coming in here and looking about my kids." She seemed to be saying that Lisa was good because she was not English. I asked her why she thought Lisa was different from 'English people' (I knew that Lisa had been born and lived her whole life in England), and she told me about a time when she was living with her brother-in-law and his wife, Iulia. Iulia had just had a baby girl called Teodora and a 'social lady' had come round to the house. Cristina said that this 'social lady' was 'Pakistan'. She explained how this 'social lady' had bought a bed for Teodora because it was bad for her not to have her own bed. At first Cristina had been scared that the 'social lady' would report her, but they were not visited again.

Cristina was fearful because she had heard that another Romanian mother had two children taken into state care because they did not have their own beds. Cristina told me that the 'social' had said the mother could have her children back when she had a big enough house for them to have their own rooms and their own beds. Her previous experience with one 'social lady', presumed to be from a migrant background, had informed Cristina's perception that Lisa was not the same as 'English people' because she was 'a black lady'. It was this perception, substantiated by her previous experience and fear at the rumours surrounding children being taken into state care that persuaded her that she should ask Lisa about her legal status. Despite her fears, Cristina also saw the state as the means by which her family's future would be secured. It is this longing for the state to grant her a safe legal status within the home-land that is tangled up with apprehension when the state makes incursions into her home.

To summarise, these families had subjective perceptions and expectations of frontline workers that were entwined with their objective positions. Many could not read and write and therefore could not understand their legal status for themselves. Their complicated statuses were exacerbated by the ambiguous status of Romanians in the UK; moreover, they relied on others who also had unclear notions about their residency status. These situated positions tended towards bureaucratic encounters that were tense, complex and based on contradictory information and understandings. Furthermore, it is crucial to bear in mind that these encounters were the only site where Romanian Roma were able to learn about their statuses, and their performances required them to negotiate with frontline workers to gain formal and informal support, and ultimately to gain legal residency in the UK. Home encounters with frontline workers therefore took on great significance. Families made sense of regulations through previous experiences, including life histories marked by discrimination, unfair treatment and particular understandings of the everyday consequences of racism. While it is important to bear in mind that not every aspect of migrants' lives were shaped by discrimination (Solimene 2014; see also the Interludes throughout this book), their experiences had an indelible effect on how frontline workers were understood. For migrants whose settlement strategies depend on subjective evaluations of opportunities and dangers, these narratives provide a key source of information to assess against their own transnational experiential knowledge.

Crucially, experiences of racism affected the spaces where encounters took place. The following incident occurred when a Romanian Roma mother attended a Stay and Play[43] session at the local children's centre. In the course of my fieldwork one other mother had been invited to this children's centre but had been refused entry because she did not have a voucher (on account of having no recourse to public funds (NRPF), even though there were special vouchers given to NRPF mothers).

> It is a cold February morning in 2014. I arrive at the children's centre a little earlier because Kassia, the children's centre worker, has invited Mariela to the Stay and Play session that starts at 11 o'clock. None of Mariela's children were in school (she has seven children, ranging in age from 13 years to 7 weeks). Kassia told Mariela that all the children could come to the Stay and Play because she didn't want Mariela to leave some children alone at home. When I arrive Mariela and the children are already there. They are waiting in the reception area because Mariela doesn't know what to do and doesn't speak English. They are taking up all the available space in the small waiting room and Mariela is doing her best to make sure the children don't get in the way of other mothers and buggies who are arriving. When she sees me, she smiles and all the younger children get very excited and give me a big hug. I tell the receptionist that Kassia has asked for all the children to attend Stay and Play. The receptionist seems a bit

reticent but calls Kassia who is in her office in another part of the building. Eventually we are let through and the younger children begin playing while the other three sit together, sitting uncomfortably in the small chairs. They also help Mariela keep watch over their younger siblings. I sit next to Mariela and she begins to tell me about her house in Moldavia, close to the Moldovan border. It has eight bedrooms but no doors, windows or running water. Her husband is working so they can make the house better. She tells me how he couldn't get work in Romania after the financial crisis and all the markets closed down. He was previously a street trader.

After about 20 minutes there was some confusion with one of the other mothers who had been sitting near to us. I don't take too much notice as I am trying to follow everything Mariela is saying in a dialect of *Romanës* that is not familiar to me. Kassia comes over to me and asks if I could ask Mariela if she has seen a mobile phone. I ask Kassia the reason and she responds that one of the other mothers has lost her mobile phone and she believes Mariela or one of her children has stolen it. I try to explain the situation to Mariela because she looks confused and wants to know what is happening. She asks her children if they have seen a mobile phone and they have not. Kassia and some of the other mothers begin to check underneath the sofa cushions and around the room in case a child has taken the phone 'by mistake'. Mariela seems unconcerned but I am actively trying to hide my disbelief (and anger) at the situation. The mother who lost her phone wants to search Mariela's buggy but Kassia suggests that she check her own buggy first. She finds her phone in her own buggy and leaves. Kassia apologises to Mariela. Kassia must have also told Clare, head of the children's centre, because she comes over to Mariela to apologise as well.

This incident arose in my interview with Samantha, deputy head of the children's centre, who told me "There was that episode with the missing mobile phone – we are on to that and if that happened again we would have to do something about that. And then you start to think. Is this the experience that Roma expect?" This encounter further indicates how racialisation operates to segregate families and to strengthen particular perceptions of Romanian Roma. Stigmatisation is a powerful way of keeping Roma separate. It also foregrounds what is at stake for both mothers and children's centre workers when they state their preferences for situating encounters in the home. This incident also shows how everyday racism that Roma face in their daily lives gets explicitly translated into, and has implications for, how they encounter the state.

Final remarks

This chapter has traced the building and bordering of Romani identity through the bureaucratic label of 'Romanian Roma'. Two key points are made about labelling: it is both generative and relationally co-produced.

Romanian Roma families appeared to frontline workers through the lenses of governmentalisation of the 'vulnerable' child; subjective perceptions that were attached to the label Romanian Roma and the objective positions of the frontline workers and Romanian Roma. These lenses interweave to make families visible, and create the bureaucratic drive and licence for actors to enter the home (while also serving to exclude other forms and spaces of encounter). Through performances and technologies of enforcement, frontline workers were implicated in the reproduction of these categories and the violence of racialisation that they necessarily entailed.

At the same time, Romanian Roma brought particular positions and subjective personal histories and experiences to their encounters with frontline workers. Just as frontline workers gained particular lenses for seeing Romanian Roma (see also Chapter Two), the families also created their own perceptions and expectations of frontline workers through encounters. These perceptions were also infused with their life histories, experiences and expectations, often marked by segregation, discrimination and state violence. The information that migrants used to make sense of their situated experiences and plans for the future was primarily through word-of-mouth from family or members of the Roma church (*khangheri*). Particular understandings, fears and desires circulated within this social field that created the conditions for encounters to take place. The label of Romanian Roma led to home encounters, which created opportunities to build fragile caring relationships between frontline workers and Romanian Roma but also the potential for painful acts of exclusion.

The first three chapters of this book have examined the subjective representations and the objective positions of the different sets of actors within home encounters. This lays the ground to understand how and why frontline workers and Romanian Roma came into contact, how specific lenses, tensions and value judgements were foregrounded in these encounters, and the processes that move towards the specific frame of intimate state encounters. The latter three chapters unpack and analyse these encounters as a specific set of processes within a relationally understood and relationally reproduced state. Previous literature about state interactions tends to focus on the practices of either state agents or citizens, while holding the other contributor (the state agents or citizens) constant. This book focuses on both sides of the relationship. Moreover, it seeks to break down the binary divide between 'bureaucrat' and 'client' to provide a more nuanced account of frontline service work.

The following chapters foreground how intimate state encounters contribute to a mutual constitution of respective identities, how these identities shape how the state emerges in interactions and what the state comes to mean for those involved.

Interlude | Remembering Brussels with Georgeta

Georgeta and I are sitting in the living room of the small semi-detached house where Georgeta and her family have been staying for the last two months. There is a kitchen and living room downstairs and three bedrooms upstairs with a small bathroom. At this time there are five adults and three children living in the house: Georgeta and her husband, Rosvan, their eldest son, Emil, his wife, Denisa and their new baby, Sarah, their younger son, Vali, and me. She is worried because she doesn't have the money to pay the rent this month. She says this quietly while looking into her empty coffee cup, "I don't want these problems in my life, I want peace," (*me chi kamav problema ando viatsa – me kamav pace*). She doesn't like asking people for money and begging in the street (*me chi kamav to zhau te mangav ando strada*). She says that she thinks it is "*lazhav*" (shameful).

At this point she begins to talk to me about her background and life experiences. She says she is not a 'true Roma' (*chechi romni*) and not 'true gazhi' (*chechi gazhi*), not like her husband. Her family were from Sibiu, a city in Romania. However, they moved from Sibiu when she was very young because her uncle "went crazy with a knife, causing a scandal" and the whole family had to move very quickly. She got married when she was 17 and went to live with Rosvan's family. At that time she didn't speak any *Romanës*, but had learnt it from Rosvan. It was a difficult time for Georgeta. She explains how she didn't like living with Rosvan's family and left to live with her mother for a short time. However, she was pregnant and returned to Rosvan's family when her son, Emil, was due to be born. At this point, Georgeta makes a distinction between herself and Marina, the wife of Rosvan's brother and the mother of Denisa (who is her daughter-in-law). She complains that Marina speaks too much and is not intelligent because she has never gone to school. In contrast, Georgeta repeats to me that she had attended 10 years of school and could read Romanian very well. She often told me that she had gone to school for 10 years.

The conversation turns to her happiest memories of when she lived in Belgium. She worked and provided for everyone in the family. She had a flat with Rosvan and Emil, her first child, and was going out to work as a cleaner every day but had to stop. I ask her why she stopped and she tells me that she had to walk a long way to get to the cleaning job. She was pregnant with her second child and she lost the baby. After this incident Rosvan told her that she had to stop working.

The disjuncture between Georgeta's aspirations and her current situation emerges again a few weeks later. Within this time Rosvan's brother,

Bogdan, his wife, Catina, two sons, Dorin and Ilie, and daughter, Petronela, come to stay. The boys sleep in the same room as Rosvan, while Bogdan sleeps on one couch and Catina and Petronela sleep on the other couch downstairs. It is around 11.30 at night and I am sitting on Denisa's bed with Georgeta, Denisa, Catina and Petronela. We are waiting for the men downstairs to come to bed so we can all go to bed. Denisa is passing the time by polishing her nails. When she has finished her nails, she begins to paint mine. At this point Petronela was falling asleep, lying across her mother. This does not stop Denisa from pulling her hand to paint her nails as well.

In this quiet moment Georgeta begins to talk about Brussels again. She tells us that she used to have a Moroccan friend who painted nails. She charged between 60 and 200 euros. I ask if she had a shop but Georgeta explains that she worked in people's houses. She took everything with her in a big bag, including flowers, crystals and all the paints. Then she took pictures and put them on a website. Georgeta explains how she had looked at the website with her and all the pictures of the beautiful patterns she had painted. Georgeta describes how she had wanted to be a beautician when she was younger but her father wouldn't allow it. She would have had to travel to the next town to attend a college. She was his only daughter and he would not let her travel alone. As she was beginning to tell us more tales from Brussels we heard Rosvan and Emil coming up the stairs. Rosvan disappears to his room where the boys are already sleeping and Emil goes into the bathroom. Catina wakes Petronela and they make their way downstairs while Georgeta and I make our way to the room where we sleep. Within 10 minutes the house is silent and I am left wondering about the other stories from Brussels that Georgeta was about to share with us.

4

Intimate bureaucracy and home encounters

It is a Tuesday morning and I wake up at around eight o'clock. Dan, a Romanian Roma father, has already left to go to his construction job. I walk into the kitchen, ready to put the kettle on to make a cup of tea for me and a cup of coffee for Cristina, a Romanian Roma mother. This morning everything seems a bit different. Cristina is rushing around frantically, boiling water in the kettle and taking it upstairs to the bathroom where she is filling washing bowls (there is no running hot water in the house). I offer to help her and she asks me to get cereal ready for Lucia, her 3-year-old daughter's, breakfast. I settle down at the table in the front room next to the kitchen to have breakfast with Lucia. She is happy and full of energy as usual. She eats about half of her corn flakes and manages to put half on the table. She absentmindedly points into the kitchen: "Rat," (*shobolan* [sic]) she notices. I shut the kitchen door quickly and bang on it a few times to scare the creature away.

In the meantime, Cristina has finished rushing up and down the stairs with the hot water. Eventually she brings the babies downstairs and places them on the couch. They have been dressed in the clothes they often wear for church. Cristina has also dressed differently. She has plaited her long blonde hair that reaches to her waist, has a long satin skirt and blouse. I say that she looks very pretty (*shukar*) and she replies that Louise from the church had given her these clothes. She makes the babies' breakfast of bread and yogurt and we sit down to feed them, trying not to get breakfast all over their clean clothes.

After the babies have eaten, Cristina jumps up again to clear everything away and to sweep the floor. She runs upstairs and brings down an armful of soft toys. She places them around the babies as Lucia picks them up and throws them around. Louise, a children's centre worker, and Kay, a volunteer at the local Baptist church arrive. Cristina greets them with hugs and invites them into the house to sit among the toys and babies, offering them "a cuppa tea". The house seems suddenly calm and Cristina's demeanour has changed dramatically; from frantically running around to sitting quietly and nodding and smiling to the two women who are cradling her children. They ask her if she needs any food for the children and whether she has all the school uniform she needs for her oldest son, who is five and attending the nearest primary school. Kay asks whether she has received any letters about her child benefit appeal. Louise also questions her about how often she takes the children out to play, or to the park or the museum in the centre of town.

When they leave Cristina seems visibly tired and flops down onto the couch. I make her a cup of coffee and she tells me that her "life is very difficult" (*me viatsa si foarte pares*). Louise and Kay had talked a lot about how Cristina should be taking her children outside. She returns to this conversation and tells me that it is not safe to go out with all of them and Lucia. She knows that she should take them out more but she finds it very hard. She feels bad about not taking them outside to play but she can't help it. It is just too difficult for her. Eventually, she tells me that God is helping her and she gets up to pick up all the toys and takes them back upstairs.

This extract from my field notes introduces several main themes of this chapter. It focuses on how and why 'intimate state encounters' in the home became the dominant site of interaction between mothers and frontline workers, and what impact they had on mothers' daily lives and implications for gaining legal status in the UK. The practice of the home encounter developed from the intertwining of different individual positions, perceptions and processes; and was reproduced through these encounters. Importantly, in most cases the decision to locate encounters in the home was discretionary, rather than a matter of formal policy, and became the primary or sole space in which Romanian Roma could interact with frontline workers and negotiate their formal legal statuses (see Chapter Two).

Recalling the previous two chapters we have seen how Romanian Roma are not only perceived as passive objects of charity ('vulnerable'), rather than subjects of law, but also as active subjects who cope with their everyday life circumstances inappropriately ('undeserving'). This chapter traces how Romanian Roma come to be governed through their most intimate spaces and how some mothers were seen as morally legitimate to receive care while others slipped into invisibility. The space of the home is contingent and subject to shifting social significations rather than being a fixed place, and the pernicious ever-present spectre of the border overshadows the 'tactics'[44] that are available to Roma mothers. For example, in the extract above where Cristina brought toys downstairs when she knew frontline workers were going to visit. This sheds light on the different expectations to which mothers are subject, the tactics and performances they use, and how the presentation and arrangement of the home space can have a direct impact on the conclusions drawn from encounters and therefore the support that mothers may or may not receive.

The family has often been a target of state management efforts, and many attempts to achieve national and imperial prosperity have relied on expert interventions into individual's intimate lives (Rose 1999: 6). Chapter Two explored how those who implement state policies at the frontline worked through ideas of compassion and are also individualised and responsibilised to 'uplift an Other, who is not (yet) modern' (Jefferess 2011: 78).[45] Compassion categorises people according to their positionality and recalls the civilising mission where charity was always racially marked (Stoler 2002: 69). The politics of compassion and benevolence therefore provide the tools and possibility of these purportedly altruistic interventions. Within welfare projects and institutional practices there are, on the one hand, those entitled to perform civilising missions and, on the other hand, the 'vulnerable' who become the recipients of benevolence and care. However, as argued in Chapter Two, the line between these two positions can also be slippery as frontline workers themselves increasingly occupy precarious citizenship positions.

The significance of the family elucidates the gendered inflections of this 'civilising mission'. As described in Chapter Two, scholarly work has traced the historical underpinnings of surveillance of poor women in their homes. Ann Stoler has examined the deep genealogies that course between imperial moralising missions and contemporary humanitarian interventions (2002). While this work has focused on 'North–South' relations these dynamics resonate with current social policies that seek to govern internal Others. Compassion and sympathy are 'braided through the politics of security and the intimate violences condoned in the name of what Michel Foucault called the imperative "to defend society" from its internal and external enemies in the name of order and social peace' (Stoler 2002: xiii).

This chapter explores how the dichotomy between public and private space is utilised to govern Romanian Roma mothers as internal Others. The limits and contradictions within the notions of the public and private are revealed through the frame of the intimate state encounter. Achille Mbembe (2001: 28) argues that, for colonial governance, 'what marked violence in the colony was its miniaturization ... it does more than confuse the public and private, it depends on and reproduces that confused space'. As will be shown in this chapter and the following two chapters, the confusion and contradictions between public and private felt (in different ways) by Romanian Roma and frontline workers was part of the governing logic that led to the marginalisation of both. Different values and meanings are contested within homes that are formal and informal, public and private, juridical and affective, and fundamentally affect how Romanian Roma form relationships with frontline workers, and thus their relationships with the state.

Frontline workers had distinct ideas about appropriate private space that were shaped by their own backgrounds but also inextricably linked to notions of the 'deserving citizen' and 'good motherhood' through their training and professional roles (see Chapter Two). The home encounter represents both a site of opportunity and danger in different ways for frontline workers and for mothers. The framework of the home encounter and the attention to the mediating role of space allows the position of actors on both sides to be brought into analysis. Crucially, relationally embedding both sets of actors does not sideline unequal power relations. Rather, this perspective hopes to more fully account for the subtle workings of power through interactions, to go beyond dichotomies of care and control or repression and compassion, and fully acknowledge the conjunctions between forms of regulation and forms of resistance.

Journey to the home encounter

Except for rare cases of interventions by social services, most of the home encounters I witnessed between frontline workers and Romanian Roma did not have to take place in the home as a matter of formal policy. In dealing with different groups or individuals, the frontline workers might have meetings under the same auspices at the children's centre, at a community centre or in their own offices. It is important to understand that, though the home took on a major role as the site of these encounters and became a form of domestic 'surveillance', this was not in itself a part of the bureaucratic logic behind their interactions. Rather, the practice of home encounters developed as the dominant form of interaction through a series of processes reflecting different discretionary decisions, value judgements, perceptions and individually situated positions. But the fact that these home encounters became the only, or principal, interactions between the frontline workers and Romanian Roma took on its own driving logic.

By the time I began my fieldwork the home encounter had already become typical, and was reproduced by both sets of actors as the appropriate, best or easiest way for them to interact. These interactions in the home became entangled with many different norms, value judgements and assessments requiring different performances by all actors which came to shape how Romanian Roma negotiated their legal statuses. Before looking at the impact of the home as the location for the encounters, it is worth understanding how and why the home encounter became so dominant in these interactions.

A few encounters between frontline workers and Romanian Roma took place in the home as a matter of formal policy, but these were limited mostly to interventions by social services. On one occasion, Cristina mentioned to a Romanian teaching assistant at her eldest son's school that there were rats in her home, and this report was referred to a family liaison worker who then visited Cristina specifically to inspect the conditions in the home. On another occasion, one couple – Catalina and Radu – were faced with a home visit following reports of domestic violence. Another mother, Rodica, had a formal visit from social services to examine the conditions of her home after a referral regarding specific concerns from a health worker.

Other home visits also had a place within formal policy. Emma, early years health visitor for 'hard to reach' groups, conducted home visits for mothers of children identified as potentially 'vulnerable' during the first two years of the child's life. However, this was partly discretionary; while Emma's work generally involved home visits, she also scheduled meetings with some non-Roma mothers at the early year's clinic. When I asked Emma in a formal interview whether everyone had these meetings in their home she told me that some (non-Roma) mothers requested check-ups to take place at the clinic, but this was not routinely offered, and only accommodated when requested. Emma's approach of focusing solely on home visits with Romanian Roma mothers reflected the general practice towards them, though it was partly inscribed by her formal role.

With these partial exceptions, as far as I came to understand, the practice of visiting the home was neither standard procedure for frontline workers for non-Roma families nor inscribed as a formal part of their official duties and requirements.

In the narratives of the frontline workers, home visits emerged as being the 'best' approach to reach Romanian Roma. This was based in part on difficulties with many of the families' lack of literacy or formal understanding of state processes, meaning that on occasions when some individuals had been expected to attend meetings elsewhere, they had not shown up. In particular, there were many attempts to call Romanian Roma parents in for meetings at schools about their children's attendance, but the general experience seemed to be that this was unsuccessful and ultimately the school followed-up at their homes. It was often stated to me that Roma never manage to attend appointments. While this is sometimes the case, missing appointments was often due to not being able to read the letter, being dependent on another to give directions, or because newcomers, or those fearful of previously negative experiences in other countries, were uncomfortable visiting bureaucratic offices alone, or they genuinely did not recognise the value of attending a bureaucratic meeting. However, these causes were generally not considered and not attending meetings was assigned to a pervasive cultural logic that it was something about their 'Roma-ness' that stopped them attending meetings.

These experiences intertwined with negative perceptions of the label Romanian Roma to variously assert that these families lived chaotic lives, could not be trusted to make appointments and were hard to reach (Chapter Three). Equally, as noted in Chapter Two, frontline workers had specific targets to identify and register 'hard to reach' or 'vulnerable' families, with limited time and resources in which to achieve these targets. The consensus seemed to be that visiting Romanian Roma at home, rather than inviting them to meetings at the children's centre or at frontline workers' offices, was a more efficient and effective way of achieving these targets. On one occasion, I witnessed Samantha, deputy head of a children's centre, questioning this approach. Samantha suggested that frontline workers could work with volunteers to collect Romanian Roma and then conduct meetings at the children's centre. Also present at the meeting were Paula (equality and diversity officer for the children's services department) and Simon (pastor of the Roma church), who both responded immediately that this would not work, and that visiting Romanian Roma at home was the 'best' way to reach them.[46]

This approach was therefore applied in general to anyone perceived to be within the category of Romanian Roma.

The practice of home visits by frontline workers was further reinforced by the role of church volunteers. As discussed in Chapter Two, the limited resources available to the frontline workers and the challenges they perceived in reaching Romanian Roma as 'hard to reach' groups meant that the support of the church, and the networks especially offered by Simon (the pastor), were relied on, and became a formalised partnership in the frontline workers' approach.

Simon had met with Clare, head of a local children's centre, to discuss how he could help them to identify and register Romanian Roma families. Simon agreed to accompany one of the children's centre's family support workers, Kassia, to register families. As the Roma pastor, Simon was familiar with most of the homes and had already entered many of them to offer pastoral or spiritual support, or to hold prayer meetings. Simon's role shaped which families were introduced to Kassia, as he was selective about who he thought would benefit from these services, and limited the route to homes that were easy to walk to from the children's centre. In consequence, families' encounters with frontline workers often began in the home from the first meeting.

More broadly, the intertwining of bureaucratic and voluntary roles furthers the practice and understanding of home visits. There was a close relationship between many of the frontline workers and volunteers, especially those connected to the church. We will see in the following chapters how volunteers shaped home encounters and Romanian Roma families' legal statuses. Simon and another church volunteer, Christian, became particularly involved with several families (where there was a shared religion) and often accompanied frontline workers on visits, blurring personal and religious relationships with more formal state encounters and reinforcing the practice (and apparent ease) of visiting families at home.

Temporality of encounters: 'popping over'

As part of the practice of home visits, the idea of 'popping over', or making brief unannounced visits to the home, became key to home encounters, and for some frontline workers was the primary mode of interaction. This developed for a number of reasons and was linked to migrants being identified as Romanian Roma. First, due to many mothers' lack of English language skills as well as not being able to read or write, frontline workers expressed the notion that it was better to 'pop over' rather arrange a formal meeting in advance. Second, many mothers did not have telephones in their homes, did not have a mobile phone or did not want to give frontline workers their mobile phone numbers. They also often switched mobile numbers because they bought cheap SIM cards which deactivated if they were not topped up with a certain amount each month. In my experience it was more common for men to have mobile phones rather than women, or women would give up their mobile phones if men needed them. On one occasion, I gave Georgeta an old mobile phone in order for her to receive calls for her domestic cleaning business. However, when her eldest son's phone broke (he accidentally dropped it down the toilet) she gave him her mobile phone because, from her perspective, it was more important for him to maintain social and business contacts. Limited phone access again made it harder to pre-arrange meetings. Third, as mentioned above, by this point the possibility of inviting Romanian Roma to meetings in offices had been largely rejected because families were considered to lead 'chaotic lives'.

These perspectives on the part of frontline workers meant they chose informal means of 'popping over' as their most common tactic for interacting with mothers, interweaving with the pressures of high workloads and limited time. In particular, Louise (the head of one of the children's centres) would 'pop over' to different families' homes if she was driving near them in her car, which served to save time in meeting her targets. Another frontline worker, Lisa, used 'popping over' as a tactic when she was providing discretionary support outside her official remit, as it allowed her informal contact time for cases she could not account for in a formal environment if such meetings were scheduled during working hours at her office. Where individuals were considered to be 'deserving' the approach of 'popping over' allowed frontline workers to provide additional support.

Desiring the home encounter

Foregrounding the home encounter in state interactions was not just a consequence of the pressures and perceptions of the frontline workers, but could also be reinforced by mothers themselves, and became reproduced as both sets of actors developed a shared understanding of the home encounter as the best and primary (or only) means of interaction.

Families had a lack of information and understanding of state processes or procedures, limited experience of different forms of interactions, and unfamiliarity with other sources of information or other potential places or contexts in which they could meet or interact with frontline workers. For example, I met one mother who had been living in Luton for two years without sending her children to school or receiving support, despite the fact that she had the status of indefinite leave to remain and an entitlement to social protection. She expressed to me that she wanted support with her benefits and to register her children for school but that she believed that there was "no 'social' in Luton" (*chi socialo ando Luton*). I told her I could call Paula or the children's centre to register her and she agreed. However, prior to that meeting she had been unable to access support and did not know who to talk to or where to go. She had therefore assumed that the services she had experienced in Croydon (where she previously lived) did not exist in Luton.

Another such example of misunderstanding emerged at an NGO Christmas party. Pathways was a charity that was fully funded by the local government to provide short-term intensive support to help people enter the labour market. Lisa (Pathways support officer for Gypsy, Roma, Travellers) invited several families to the party, thinking they might benefit from understanding her work and seeing her office. In fact, very few families attended. This appeared to confirm in Lisa's mind that there was little scope to interact with Romanian Roma mothers outside of their own homes. It was unclear to me why families had not attended the party. One reason may have been that they thought they needed to pay Lisa, and they did not have the money. This confusion regarding payment became evident to me through a conversation with Dan and Cristina. They had attended the party because Simon, the pastor, had encouraged them to go. Also, I attended the party and I told them that I would be there and I offered to go with them and direct them to the office, which Dan accepted.

However, in the evening when we were eating our usual meal of baked beans, deep fried bacon pieces and white bread, Dan asked me who Lisa was and if he needed to pay her. I explained that Pathways was like a charity (*caritate*). He continued to be confused and explained that he heard her say "'This is my client, this is my client.' Why is this? I need to pay?" I came across this uncertainty about the need to pay for services in many other contexts, including a young pregnant mother asking me whether she needed to pay the hospital in the UK when she had her baby to make sure that they didn't 'cut' her, referring to a caesarean. Many of her family members had experienced this treatment in Romania. Similarly, Sebastian, a migrant father, thought that he needed to pay the health and safety officer who visited his house to check his scrap metal and asked me directly "What do I have to pay her?"

This lack of understanding could create disjuncture between frontline workers and migrants. Migrants thought that they needed to pay to receive services and information and therefore avoided them. Or families did not see the reason why they would attend a Christmas party in an office.

This was not a practice they were familiar with and they saw no value in it. In addition, many families had to prioritise the possibility of earning money in order to pay their rent over planning to attend these gatherings. Moreover, many didn't know where these offices were located because they did not read maps but rather came to know the town through walking with others. For example, I had to direct Dan to the office because he did not know where it was. However, the fact that families identified as Romanian Roma were not seen in these spaces (bureaucratic offices, libraries, community centres) reinforced the home encounter as the primary site of interaction. Frontline workers believed that these families did not want to attend meetings outside their homes and therefore they continued with the practice of home visits.

Since most Romanian Roma encountered frontline workers for the first time when they received a visit in the home (either after giving birth, when being registered through Simon, or when a referral was made and frontline workers decided to visit), this became the dominant mode of understanding how to interact with frontline workers and reinforced the expectation that this was where future encounters would take place. When talking to each other, different mothers again would relate and reproduce this understanding. If a family member needed support, they would suggest a contact to arrange a home visit, or would simply invite relatives round to their home when they were already being visited by a frontline worker.

The learned expectation that the home visit was the primary or only way Romanian Roma could gain support and negotiate with frontline workers meant, in turn, that when they wanted support they would contact a frontline worker and ask them to come to their house. Mirroring the unarranged approach of frontline workers 'popping over', mothers would sometimes call (often on other people's mobile phones) to ask frontline workers to come to their house without delay. Lisa, Pathways support officer, explained "They phone me up and say, 'Letter – you come read.'" Lisa and Paula told me that they were often called many times by the same person asking them to come round to the house to read a letter or to solve a variety of different problems. In some instances, frontline workers gave the impression they felt hounded by the number of times a mother might call in quick succession and demand that they visit her home. I also witnessed this on many occasions, including one mother who called Paula six times in one hour to ask her to visit her at home. This pattern served to reproduce and confirm the perceptions on both sides that the home visit was the 'best' way for both sides to interact.

Alongside, some Romanian Roma were able to benefit from the informal support and personal connections developed from these home encounters, further creating a drive to reinforce and replicate this pattern of home visitation (see also Chapter Two on fears and desires for the state). I witnessed one mother, Maria, meet a frontline worker in the street and call out to her "When you coming to see me?!" In front of the frontline workers, Maria also seemed also to play up to their understandings of the Romanian Roma label, expressing a big, flamboyant personality and high level of sociability and generosity in the home, and describing herself as 'crazy' (*dilli*) and 'big momma' (a reference to an Eddie Murphy movie). Maria developed close relationships with frontline workers, in particular with Lisa (see Chapter Two), who would visit her at home, and this connection was maximised to gain support for Maria and her family members. Lisa stated to me in a formal interview when she compared her experiences between Romanian Roma and Irish Travellers:

> '[F]or them [Irish Travellers] to let me into their home – they want something from me. But I think Roma want to be your friend. If you got chatting to them on the street – this is going on the Roma ladies I've met – it wouldn't matter race, creed or colour, they would say "Come for coffee, come for coffee!"'

Similarly, another family – Miron and his wife Sanda – often received visits from Christian, a church volunteer who helped Sanda apply for a national insurance number. Sanda would make Christian lunch, extending his stays and furthering the impression that he was welcome and encouraged to visit their home. These forms of hospitality can also be seen as a way of drawing on the home space as a resource that open spaces of relational labour, which allow mothers to negotiate their legal statuses on different terms.

Summary: the social location of the home encounter

As these examples have illustrated, the home encounter developed on the basis of a shared understanding that it was the 'best' approach to state interactions. This was established and reproduced by a constellation of different processes: frontline workers' perceptions of those they term Romanian Roma; their need to meet key targets and balance limited time and resources; the support of volunteers associated with the Roma church; and the limited understanding on the part of Romanian Roma of alternative approaches to engaging with state processes. As Romanian Roma learn their understanding of interactions with frontline workers through initial home encounters, they act to reproduce this approach and affirm its value through their own tactics to gain support. This, in turn, reinforces the idea for frontline workers that home encounters are the best way to engage with these families.

A key consequence of home encounters was the potential for frontline workers' roles to shift and expand. As discussed in Chapter Two, families became visible through meetings that were initiated with a child safeguarding lens, but in the process the wider context of the families' positions (especially in relation to their legal statuses) also became visible. Several children's centre support staff and educational family workers commented to me that they 'never get round to' what they really considered their job should be (such as conducting parenting classes) and were instead 'firefighting' with immigration and benefit issues. They often felt as though they were not qualified for this type of work and were constantly faced with issues that were not part of 'their job'.

As home encounters became the primary or sole form of contact between new mothers and frontline workers, they were often the only avenue for Romanian Roma to gain information regarding other bureaucratic processes. Frontline workers were asked about, and often took on the role of, assisting mothers with a wide range of issues, including appealing deportations, creating and guiding the bureaucratic identities of mothers and channelling them through formal paths in the sequential order of bureaucratic logic. Families could easily fall into bureaucratic limbo due to simultaneous national- and local-level processes that required original identity documents. This was exacerbated by complex overlapping of bureaucratic procedures that all took varying amounts of time.

For example, one family had applied for child benefit before enrolling their children in school. The Department for Education would not release their identity documents until they provided proof the children were attending school. Meanwhile, the school would not enrol the children without their original identity documents. Kassia, children's centre family support worker, tried to help this family. The case took up a large amount of her time as she spent hours calling and writing letters to the school, the local children's service department and the Department for Education to try to have the identity documents returned. From frontline workers' perspectives, providing this additional support with legal issues was always justified through their duty to support the child, and was often a discretionary decision about how far to provide additional support; but it had the potential to represent a significant expansion of their work and their roles as frontline workers. Some of the consequences of this, and the ways in which these relationships played out in Romanian Roma negotiations over their legal and residency statuses, are explored in Chapter Six.

On a few occasions I witnessed frontline workers express uncertainty about the dominance of the home encounter, but this concern was typically with regard to the time it took up and the difficulty of justifying it in their target-based 'audit culture' (see Chapter Two). Clare, head of a local children's centre, expressed caution about the level of time that home encounters could take up, saying in an interview:

> 'It [home visiting] is supposed to be low-level work. They [family support workers] go in and do home visits. But it often doesn't work out that way. Once you are in a house then it turns out that it might be a big piece of work.'

Samantha, children's centre deputy head, also commented:

> '[Children's centres] used to be tea, cake and sympathy and all the time in the world. But now you have to justify what you are doing all the time – the review and evaluation – what benefit you are bringing to that family and that child. If you are not impacting on anything then what are doing there [in the home]? You are just intruding on someone's life.'

In contrast, Louise, a children's centre family worker who was managed and part-funded by a Baptist church, had a different understanding of the home visit and seemed to be concerned about the possible implications and entanglements created with the mothers' family lives: "[Visiting the home] feels a bit weird ... you have to respect people. I have been given this job and it is a kind of privilege." However, Louise did not acknowledge the sanctioning and possible surveillance aspect of her role, stating "[P]arents get in a 'tizzy whizz' ... they just want someone to talk to." Despite her apparent concerns she often conducted home visits without warning and enacted the practice of 'popping over' (as explained earlier), creating unseen work as mothers had to be ready to receive her into their homes at any time.

While some frontline workers may have been uncomfortable or cautious about it, during my fieldwork the home encounter was largely unquestioned as their central mode of interaction with Romanian Roma families. As has been established, this was the product of a series of different processes and perceptions, but with rare exceptions was not a formal part of frontline workers' roles and responsibilities and was not necessarily general practice. The home visit as a bureaucratic practice was thus a product of processes that foreground frontline workers' discretionary behaviour and value judgements about Romanian Roma, and the reproduction of those value judgements through their interactions with Romanian Roma. This is important to bear in mind as we turn to look at how the decision to locate interactions in the home, and the particular nature of the home space, had a direct impact on the nature and form of interactions, and thereby on the broader relationships and negotiations between Romanian Roma and state processes.

The home: space, relationships and values

First, this section explores how spaces are imbued with meanings, with effects for the home encounter and the interactions that take place there. I build on previous scholarly attention to the dichotomy between public and private space. I draw on this literature to demonstrate how and why particular values and norms of behaviour have developed around the home with implications for citizenship. Second, this section shows how these values come to have specific meanings in particular situations. Third, it explores the contradictions within the public and private space that are revealed and exacerbated when frontline workers enter the home. Finally, it concludes to bring these three elements together to argue that the location of encounters in the home fundamentally affects how Romanian Roma form relationships with frontline workers and shapes the performances and negotiations that are able to take place.

The fact that interactions took place in the home brought many other aspects of migrants' lives into view. All of these aspects then became part of the encounter and affected how the label Romanian Roma developed for frontline workers and increased the number of different aspects that mothers had to negotiate to be seen as a 'good mother' (see 'Staging the home' later in this chapter). Moreover, meanings began to be formed before a frontline workers had set foot inside the house; for example, gardens were discussed to make meanings about Romanian Roma mothers (see 'Thresholds and gardens').

Relationships between support workers and mothers were shifting and contingent. The following encounters explore the fragility through which value judgements about mothering are constructed and negotiated within home spaces. In addition, the crucial importance of these relationships for navigating legal statuses in the UK are demonstrated, as well as the constrained positions that mothers are placed in because the encounters occur in 'private' space.

It is important to note the underpinning for the dichotomy between the 'public and private'. The dichotomy has multiple uses and has been deemed one of the most 'powerful signifiers of how our social worlds are ordered' (Davidoff 1999: 268). Nevertheless it must also be remembered that this division is a fiction, but a fiction that is mobilised in particular ways and has very real consequences. The private-public distinction is often used to describe the split between the state and the family. It has roots in how liberal democratic nation-states are organised. An underpinning logic of this organisation is how those living within the territory of a nation-state are turned into citizens with individual rights and responsibilities. The role of the citizen in this formulation is deeply permeated by gendered imaginations of family and personhood. Gendered expectations split the public space as a privileged space for men and the private and 'domestic' as the sphere for women (see Pateman and Phillips 1987: 119; Chapman and Hockey 1999: 10–13; Massey 2007: 237–8).

The space of the home has come to be recognised as the quintessential physical and emotional setting for intimate lives in European welfare states and in European colonial communities where notions of privacy clarified racial difference and where women became the bearers of refined colonial morality (Stoler 2002: 55). Ideas of the 'home' and 'family' were intermeshed with that of the 'child'. This process was also accompanied by an idea that childhood encompassed distinct phases of life and throughout each phase, children were seen as requiring the physical and emotional nurturing that could best be supplied 'privately' by their mothers at home. This construction of the 'private' as the family's retreat was closely linked to the definition of the woman's separate sphere, which glorified the role of the wife as a homemaker and full-time mother (see Fraser 1987: 117–18; Lister 1997: 41–2). This image of the family and the home deeply permeated frontline workers' views of 'good motherhood'. This context goes some way to explain the underlying logics within the social policies and practices that guide assessments of mothering and the social meaning that is entwined within particular spaces.

Feminist and anti-racist scholarship has been working with the notion of citizenship and care to critique how the divide between public and private space has been conceptually reproduced (Pateman and Phillips 1987; Brown 1992). On the one hand, work in the home has been deemed 'private, nothing to do with citizenship' (Pateman 1989: 12), while on the other women's reproductive activities (both biological and social), have historically been a site of considerable public anxiety and intervention (Skeggs 2004; Luibhéid 2006; Gedalof 2007; Erel 2011b; Tyler 2013),[47] and central to how the state defines and reproduces itself. The concept of kin-work has sought to contest the public/private dichotomy, which separates out and distinguishes work performed within the family/household from paid work performed in the labour market. The physical location of the workplace should not divert attention from women's economic, social and political contribution to society (Lutz 2010). Furthermore, through examining intersections of gender and race scholars have argued that poor and racialised mothers have always been open to surveillance in their homes by the state, thus revealing the conceit about privacy: it is always at stake in the inequalities between those with more or less symbolic and material resources to guard their own 'privacy' (Hurtado 1989; Humphris 2017). Crucially, this literature convincingly demonstrates that to experience home (and home-land) as a place of safety is contingent on power asymmetries (Anderson 2000; Bhattacharjee 2006).[48]

Recently the distinctions between public and private space have been contested through the notion of 'domopolitics', which traces how gendered notions of citizenship produce racialised migrant women's reproductive practices as a legitimate and necessary site of securitised state intervention, as part of a broader project constructing the national 'home' (Walters 2004; Lonergan 2018). These mechanisms have not only persisted under neoliberalism (Rose 1999; Nyers 2004; Brown 2015) but gained salience as tools of neoliberal governmentality (Lonergan 2018). While this literature is insightful in highlighting the structural power relationships at stake and the repercussions of the separation between private and public it necessarily lacks sustained empirical analysis of how the state emerges *relationally* in everyday life. My aim in the rest of this chapter is to show how the confusion between public and private, affect and formality and the way they are tangled together are part of a distinct governing logic that depends on and reproduces this confused space (Andersen 2000; Mbembe 2001; Thelen and Alber 2017). The advance to the literature made in this chapter is to bring together the anthropology of the state and the role of discretion within street-level bureaucratic work with the literature on mothers' work and black women's motherhood. The encounters below unpack how different notions of appropriate public-private space become mobilised and unsettled in encounters, and the multiple, shifting and contradictory workings of power and layered knowledges that are in process. The aim of this and the following chapters is to show the costs for the constitution of Romanian Roma and frontline workers as caring and cultural subjects within these webs of governance (Erel et al. 2018).

The complex layering of differing understandings of public and private space, power relationships and the different intentions and motivations drawn from these understandings are evident in a home encounter between Paula, equality and diversity officer for the children's services department, and a Romanian Roma family. This interaction also highlights the importance of such encounters, the growing responsibilities on both sides and the restricted room for manoeuvre.

It is past six o'clock on a dark and cold February evening when I receive a call from Paula. She is visiting a mother who has been identified as Romanian Roma with children who are not registered for school. Paula has called me because she is inside the house but Mirela, the mother she needs to interview, is not there. She thinks I might know where Mirela lives. Another family (Florina, Sebastian and their children) are present, but Mirela seems to be missing. I am sitting with Maria, Mirela's second cousin, who wants to know what the conversation is about. Maria decides that we should go to the house. We arrive at the small, terraced Victorian house and enter a dimly lit front room. The air is thick with the mixture of cigarette smoke and sweet cleaning products, intensified by the small electric heater which is on the highest setting and making a loud humming noise. Florina and Sebastian are sitting on the couch opposite Paula, who is sitting on a bed. Five children are running in and out of the small room. The conversation focuses on Sebastian's scrap metal business. Paula explains to me that she is going to get Sebastian a letter from the council to enable him to register as a scrap metal dealer. She also comments directly to me that since she arrived the door that leads to the rest of the house has been firmly shut. She remarks, "You have to laugh, don't you?" When the children come in and out of the room the door is closed tightly behind them.

Paula asks again about Mirela and her two children. Florina and Sebastian shrug and tell her they don't know who she is talking about. Sebastian keeps talking to Paula about scrap metal and what he has to do to get a national insurance number. Paula explains that she is just there to talk about the children and school and tries to bring the conversation back to Mirela. The conversation flows back and forth in this manner for around 10 minutes when four men arrive. Two of these men walk straight through the front room to the interior of the house, do not engage in any way with anyone, and shut the door closely behind them. The other two remain in the room, watching the interaction unfold. The first two men return and begin talking to the other men. Occasionally all four men watch the interaction unfold, and at other times they begin conversing with each other. Florina, Sebastian and Maria do not interact with the men or acknowledge they are there. Paula, on the other hand, is clearly distracted by their presence, particularly when some of their conversation becomes very loud. It is a very small space, filled with a couch, a bed and a small table in the gap between. There is a large TV on one wall and shelves fill the alcoves on either side of the TV. The shelves are full of plastic bags filled with boxes, a telephone and various piles of envelopes and papers. A few minutes later, two of the men leave the house by the front door. (I had visited the house on previous occasions and these men had told me that they stayed there. They described themselves as cousins, but it later emerged that three are brothers. They worked with Sebastian collecting scrap metal.)

While this is taking place, Maria, ignoring the men, talks to Paula about her daughter who has been abducted to Spain by her estranged husband. Once again, Paula tries to bring the conversation back to Mirela and her children. Sometimes she is met with silence and shrugging, at others Maria and Florina change the subject to their own children. At one point Mirela's son joins the throng in the front room from behind the door and starts punching Sebastian, and then does a mixture of dancing and boxing, moving in the small amount of floor space between the couch, the wall and the door. Paula asks Florina directly about the identity of the boy and in particular whether he is Mirela's son. Florina's four children are also coming in and out of the room, and balancing themselves on the top of the couch behind their parents or climbing over them. After a few minutes of further questions, Mirela appears and stands next to one of the men, who, it emerges later, is her husband. Paula asks her directly if she has children and Mirela shouts to her son to get the papers from her handbag upstairs. Paula is shocked that she had been told directly by Florina and Sebastian that Mirela was not there, that they had denied knowledge of Mirela and not answered a direct question regarding Mirela's son. Gradually, Paula gains the information from Mirela and begins the process of enrolling the children for school. The men leave and the children continue to run in and out of the room, the door now ajar.

In this encounter, Sebastian had tried to negotiate a scrap metal licence on behalf of his family, something that might help to secure the family's legal status in the UK. He did not know any other frontline workers or services where he might gain support. However, Paula's only focus was the mother of the children who were not attending school. She had a particular lens on the house and had entered under distinct circumstances. The timing of her visit was also indicative. Her work requirements had increased, the number of staff and resources had decreased and she was working longer hours. She often told me that she enjoyed the job but no longer felt supported by her management team, and she was anxious about the growing requirements and regulations with regard to migration status. The increasing complexity of welfare and migration legislation was exacerbated by the increasing numbers of migrants who were subject to different constellations of regulations. However, the situation within the house had seemed to make it impossible for Paula to gain any of the information she required. Her direct questions had been met with denial or, perhaps more frustratingly for her, silence, with the conversation shifting towards gaining a scrap metal licence leading to a national insurance number.

The men who entered the house did not openly acknowledge the interaction and did not absent themselves from the space. From my experience of this household, it was usual for the men to be working well into the night, particularly if they were buying or selling cars or other merchandise. On many occasions at different times of day (especially in the evening) when I was sitting talking and drinking coffee in someone's house, a family member would arrive and gather up some men if there was a deal to be done, or if they were going out driving or if they were all going to the internet café to look at cars being sold online. This also meant that men could be found sitting at home during the day, socialising with each other and 'taking' coffee and cigarettes. These behaviours did not conform to support workers' perspectives of appropriate use of the home space, which was not only gendered but linked to distinct rhythms and temporalities. Some frontline workers presumed that the men did not have jobs; however, it was more likely that they worked during the evening, either as self-employed or in shifts at the local factory or they had completed early shifts in construction work.

This example vividly shows how the home space does not neatly map onto frontline workers' conceptions of it being private, domestic and a refuge from 'work'. Similarly, time is not separated into distinct divisions for work and leisure and therefore the home does not map onto Paula's ideas of the rhythms of intimacy and domesticity. The men were still 'working' even though they were within the domestic space and it was the evening. However, for Paula, the presence of these men added

119

to her confusion about the relationships between everyone in the room, compounded by the soft rebuttals and silences to her direct questions. In this instance, the men did not seem to think that they had an effect on the interaction; they were sharing the space but, from their perspective, they were not involved in the encounter. For Paula, they infused the space with a meaning that made her feel uncomfortable. The presence and behaviour of the men added to the sense that all relationships were confusing, the house was chaotic and the children were unsafe.

The timing and trajectory of her visit was crucial. She had arrived unannounced and had no previous encounter with Mirela. She conducted the visit on her way home from the office and it was her last task for the day. She was tired from working and had given the family no forewarning that she might arrive. The behaviour of the unclaimed boy who punched everyone exacerbated the feeling that children were not being cared for. Her uncertainty and confusion about the relationships between household members was strengthened when her direct questions were met with denial or, perhaps more frustratingly for her, silence.

Crucially, despite Paula's focus on mothers, the women in the house had played a secondary role in her understandings of the encounter. The women had the responsibility to arrange for their children to go to school and to present themselves to Paula as appropriate mothers. But Mirela had little control over this space and had no opportunities to learn how Paula might 'see' her domestic space and relationships, let alone the time or attention from Paula (or any frontline worker) to begin to learn the terms in which she might have engaged with them. She was living with Florina and Sebastian, who were named on the rental agreement, and she was reliant on them for both livelihood and housing, even though her husband and Sebastian were brothers. Mirela also had little control over the men who came in and out of the house. The men were working to provide for the household and therefore Mirela might not have wanted to stop them, even had she had been able to do so. The space of the encounter had therefore placed Mirela in a hugely constrained position and her response, seemingly, had been to remain hidden in the kitchen until her husband arrived. In addition, Paula had no resources through which to offer any further assistance due to the demands on her time, increasing workloads and complicated legal situations of migrants.

The space of the encounter is important in other ways. Unlike in a bureaucratic office where one problem is defined and dealt with at a time, Paula had been bombarded by different questions by different family members: appeals for her to act, to take responsibility and ultimately to care about many others in the household. Sebastian had entreated Paula to help him look after his family through registering his business and helping him to gain a national insurance number. He referred to their previous encounters, calling on her to remember their shared history and, simultaneously, evoking future encounters where she might be faced with the same issues. Sebastian's invocations for Paula's support were intensified because Paula was the only person he knew who represented formal advice or help with his scrap metal licence. Paula was his only 'bridge' to formal processes and, effectively, was 'the state' for him. In response to his entreaties to 'make up' or embody all forms of the state, she refuted this role and endeavoured to draw the boundary around her own mandated role, stating that she only worked with children and the school. She refused Sebastian's invocation for other forms of the state to be drawn into this encounter (namely scrap metal and legal residency). By reiterating she was "only for the school" Paula closed down the boundaries of her discretion, and in doing so constrained the realms of the state which here become transformed through affective intensity into negotiations of care which she was unable or unwilling to give.

The boundaries of Paula's role were also spatial. Although she laughed about the activity behind the door, she did not get up and try to enter that space of the house. She did not, unlike a social worker, 'inspect' the house, nor ask intimate details about the residents (for example, where they slept and how they supported themselves financially). Through placing spatial and role restrictions on herself Paula defined the limits of her support, rebuffing this form of care for Sebastian's family, and in turn she delimited the state for Sebastian. Her refusal to care was also a refusal to recognise his political belonging.

This encounter demonstrates how notions of public and private are tangled between different power relationships, representations and expectations. Paula entered the space of the house and, in so doing, fundamentally changed the nature of the space. Because the encounter took place in the house, she assessed the family through her expectations of domesticity. Mirela was hugely constrained, she remained invisible and hidden. Paula had brought a notion of the state with her through her role as a frontline worker but when Sebastian tried to relate to her as such she closed down the conversation. They both negotiated over the tension of her being present in the space through the constrained ways that familial relationships need to be performed to be seen as a morally legitimate or deserving subject of discretionary care.

This section has demonstrated how actors are not only socially positioned but spatially located and how the co-constitutive nature of social relationships and space fundamentally shapes the encounters that unfold in the home. The first part of this section demonstrated how the contradictions inherent in hegemonic narratives of mothering and domestic space are revealed. Romanian Roma homes fulfil multiple functions, which do not map neatly onto frontline workers' conceptions of home, such as privacy, intimacy and domesticity, and yet this is the space where they are surveyed and governed. Mothers need to learn that frontline workers view the home as a non–market space where children and the community are nurtured along deeply entrenched and intimate symbolic meanings. Mothers need to produce and maintain this space and perform the appropriate relations in order to gain the crucial legal support from frontline workers to secure their residency status in the UK.

Thresholds and gardens

Paula mentioned to me when I was joining her on home visits that she could recognise a Romanian Roma house as she was walking down a street. She noted that all of the windows would be open and that there might be a couch outside if it were summer, or there would an unkept garden with buggies, various broken household items or discarded objects. Recalling Foucault and Miskowiec (1986: 24), the home garden represents a symbolic order that counterbalances the disorder and imperfection of the surrounding physical and social world. Unruly gardens can come to symbolise unruly or uncivilised subjects, becoming a representation of local disorder. Gardens convey important cultural ideas about the relationship between individuals and the surrounding world.

The use of the space outside the house is highlighted by the following two encounters, which illustrate different kinds of positioning and negotiating values. Both encounters take place in gardens. Two mothers, Violeta and Cristina, engage in gardening primarily as a place for their children to play. Violeta and Cristina are also keen to show and explain their garden to me, to volunteers and to frontline workers. They also represent the two families most intricately involved in the English church (*englezi khangheri*) and in my experience were most able to exchange information and negotiate performances which frontline workers found valuable.

> It is a sunny July afternoon in Luton. Lisa, Pathways floating support worker, arrives at Cristina's house where we are both in the kitchen preparing food for the evening. Cristina offered Lisa a "cuppa tea" (she tells me that she learnt this phrase from the nurses in the hospital when she gave birth) and invites her into the garden. All three of us go into the garden and Cristina explains that Dan has laid a small lawn because he had some turf left over from a gardening job a month earlier. Cristina

discusses the noisy dog from next door and then some of the problems she has been having with Dan getting a national insurance number. The discussion in the garden while looking at the grass provides space for shared values between Cristina and Lisa. Lisa understands Cristina's complaints about the noisy dog and they laugh about how he might be stopped. Cristina seems proud of the patch of grass and Lisa congratulates her on keeping the garden so well when she has five young children to look after. Lisa continues to visit Cristina in her home and liaises with Louise, children's centre worker, to make sure that they are doing everything they can to help Cristina and her family. This converging of values in the garden illustrates one of many ways mothers manage their relationships with others, drawing on many different symbolic and material resources.

Turning to the second encounter, another migrant mother, Violeta, similarly understands the importance of the garden as a space where she might be assessed or where she could work to build common values. Violeta is visited by two church volunteers at different times; Sue, who visits Violeta very rarely to drink tea and speak to her in English to improve her language ability, and Christian, who visits Violeta regularly to manage her household bills and self-employed tax records. Violeta has large patio doors that lead from her living room to the back garden. The doors are broken on one side and she has carefully balanced them so they remain in place. She tries to pre-empt any negative assessment of her garden that can be seen through the patio doors. On one occasion, she explains to Sue, the "outside" is not neat and tidy due to her "Gypsy children". "They are Gypsy boys – what can I do?" In this way she evokes what she perceives as her visitor's ideas about Gypsies, and explains her messy garden in terms she hopes her visitor will understand and also empathise with. When I visit the house with Christian, a volunteer, he often remarks on her hanging baskets with brightly coloured flowers and makes a distinction between the way she keeps her garden compared with 'other Roma mothers'.

By drawing on racialised perceptions and apologising for her children Violeta indicated to her visitors that she shared their common values regarding the outside space around the house and drew on her understanding of others' perceptions of 'Gypsy' boys as unmanageable subjects. Through this performance and understanding of space she hoped to invoke empathy for her 'unruly' boys and her position as a single mother, rather than being placed in a stigmatised category herself. The effect of managing the space outside the home was evident when I went on home visits with frontline workers. The space outside houses had become a marker to identifying Romanian Roma families. Frontline workers used the garden to tell them about the people who lived inside the house. Violeta had learned this was potentially a negative association and could have an effect on the relationships that developed with frontline workers and volunteers. Through decorating the outside of her house with hanging baskets she signalled to those who entered that she was outside their judgements of a 'usual' Romanian Roma house and this afforded her room for manoeuvre in her relationships (see Chapter Six).

Staging the home

Objects become imbued with meaning in particular spaces and contexts. The material aspects of the home were linked to child safety and 'development' and emerged as a key feature of the bureaucratic gaze in encounters. Narratives of objects emerged as a way that frontline workers expressed confusion or uncertainty about a family they identified as Romanian Roma. These narratives were often about the conspicuous presence or absence, and appropriate or inappropriate use, of objects related to children in the home. The importance of the objects can be traced to the duties bestowed on frontline workers who entered the home through the licence gained from 'safeguarding'. The statutory duty placed on frontline workers to engage with families is part of the safeguarding agenda, enshrined in the Children Act 2004. Chapter Two isolated the importance of the safeguarding agenda and how the governmentalisation of vulnerable children, coupled with the notion of early intervention, provided frontline workers with the discretionary duty to become involved in the everyday lives of families. Home visits were conducted through this perspective and therefore children's safety was at the forefront of shaping frontline workers' interactions.

All frontline workers had training in child development and the mother-child relationship. It became clear through conversations with children's centre workers and other frontline professionals, such as

Emma, early years health visitor for 'hard to reach' groups, and Paula, equality and diversity officer for the children's services department, that child development was their priority and 'playing' was central to their understanding. Frontline workers drew on mothers' choices of playthings in narratives to describe relationships and attribute value to different behaviours. Toys and the material markers of the presence of children became the signals through which understandings regarding good mothering and safety were perceived.

In addition, discussions concerning toys and parents providing 'appropriate stimuli' for children convey constellations of meanings among frontline workers at multi-agency meetings. Some behaviours are perceived and imagined as sources of concern and 'in need of corrective measures that lead to the systemisation and codification of feelings that become constitutive of formal and systematic beliefs' (Fortier 2000: 107). Toys and playthings were put to work in different ways to mobilise meanings from these interactions. 'Things' have often been insufficiently acknowledged in accounts of 'the social'. However, material objects infused the bureaucratic gaze, as can be seen through the discourses about toys that are linked to notions of children's safety or security. These perceptions of toys acted to (re)produce certain perceptions of Roma mothers, leading to negative ascriptions of value.

The significance of the home space in turn meant that migrants could affect their interactions and relationships with frontline workers by 'staging' the home as a space for encounters. This section presents examples of where mothers 'staged' the home through learning (and being able to implement) certain behaviours which frontline workers recognised as valuable. It also explores situations where this was not the case (where staging did not evoke the desired responses from frontline workers) and where mothers tried to perform in ways that they thought the frontline workers expected but in fact created further disjuncture in their relationships.

Cristina negotiated her home encounters through learning and shifting her performances following many home visits and conversations between herself, Kay, a volunteer from the church, and Louise, a children's centre worker. Cristina migrated to the UK from Moldavia in 2012 and met Kay, a retired nurse, at the English church (*englezi khangeri*). Kay described Cristina on one occasion as 'her daughter' and was encouraged by the pastor of the Roma church to take an active role in the life of the family. Kay took Cristina and her new baby to Louise's clinic at a children's centre in a Baptist church near to Kay's house. Louise later described Cristina as 'standing out' and began to make home visits with Kay.

Cristina learnt a 'bureaucratic identity' through her interactions with Kay and Louise as they presented ways of behaving appropriately as a mother and what was expected in the UK welfare system. Previous scholarly work has presented how migrants and working-class mothers negotiate the categories that are laid open to them by frontline workers (Boulton 1983; McMahon 1995; Fox 2006; Gillies 2007). Cristina had the opportunity to negotiate her encounters, to build relationships with frontline workers and learn the ways she might gain a more secure status. She was able to do this through invoking shared religious values to gain informal assistance, protect her family from being considered 'destitute' and perform her role as an 'appropriate mother'. However, despite convergences regarding notions of 'good mothering', these relationships were fragile, subject to contradictory and conflicting expectations of behaviour, and framed by the spectre of the border that threatened to emerge across the mother–child relationship.

Through the encounters between Kay, Louise and Cristina, the physical space of the house became a source of conflict and tension. At this point in my fieldwork, I was living with Cristina, her husband Dan, and their five children. Cristina mentioned to me on many occasions that she didn't want people coming in to "look at my kids". Dan and Cristina both acknowledged the house was 'dirty' (*melalo*) due to its poor condition such as holes in the roof, rats, dampness, and a broken kitchen, bathroom, doors and windows. Cristina was responsible for trying to make it as clean as possible; for visitors, because she thought a dirty house would be reason to take her kids away from her; for Dan who would sometimes complain that "you slept all day" if the house was very untidy; for herself, because she took pride in having a tidy and well-kept house and garden (see also Skeggs 2004); and to friends and family members who she believed might gossip about her for not making her house 'straight' (*nai vorta*). While all of these actors expected a straight and tidy house, they imposed different expectations of mothering on Cristina.

Dan worked in temporary jobs in construction and gardening because he was unable to enter the formal labour market due to restrictions on A2 migrants (see Introduction). He had been refused a national insurance number four times on the grounds he did not have 'genuine self-employed work'. He felt helpless to change his family's situation. Similarly to Gigi, the role of his work had been devalued and he had no access to social rights (see Chapter Five). Cristina's bureaucratic encounters therefore assumed significance as they are the only site of engaging with frontline workers. Although they offered the potential for the family to gain informal support and legal status, they also involved judgement of Cristina's caring capacity as a mother. Perceptions of good mothering often require 'intensive' resources (Hays 1998) based on normative moral behaviours and 'middle-class' family values (Gidley 2007). In the negotiation of values between Cristina and Louise, the home was where performances were judged. Louise made discretionary decisions regarding whether to refer Cristina to social services and whether to provide informal support to assist her in securing the resources to perform good mothering.

Louise and Kay usually visited the house at around 11 o'clock on Tuesday mornings. However, as noted in the previous section, Louise also 'popped in' unannounced if she was driving past in order to save herself time. Cristina had crafted a particular perception of her family life, which resonated with Louise. Cristina was aware, through rumours that spread among families, that Louise has the capacity to refer her to social services and the capability to remove her children from her. However, she was also aware that her relationship with Kay and Louise represented an opportunity to gain resources and informal support that would secure the family's position in the UK.

Tensions and subsequent negotiations are illustrated through the perceptions and expectations surrounding toys, food and relationships with others. Louise gave Cristina toys from the church, but was disappointed when they were left in a cupboard: "We have given them toys but you don't often see the toys out. It's very difficult." Thus, when she knew Louise was going to visit, Cristina very carefully tidied the house but also threw the toys on the floor. When they left we often cleared the toys away together to make the house 'straight' again. This highlights how the home must be 'staged' differently for encounters with frontline workers (as opposed to, for instance, friends or family members).

Cristina's own perceptions of mothering oscillate, although she often reminded me that I couldn't understand her feelings because I didn't have children of my own. However, on one occasion following a particularly lengthy visit from Louise, Cristina flopped onto the couch with a baby in her arms. "Why did God give me five!" she exclaimed, referring to her children. At other times she explained to me how she had always wanted a big family with lots of children around her. She seemed to eagerly maintain Dan's expectations regarding the organisation of the day, food and gender roles. However, despite the intensity of time and labour that she dedicated to her role, her room for manoeuvre was heavily circumscribed by different people's perceptions, which could be contradictory.

'Staging the home' demonstrates how important objects become to performances of relationships. Both volunteers and frontline workers mentioned instances where the presence or absence of objects in the home was detrimental and liable to break or shift a relationship. Drawing on Douglas's (1966: 36) notion of matter 'out of place', where the presence of such objects disturbs the social and spatial order of things, the difference between mothers' and frontline workers' notions of good mothering can be brought to the fore. For frontline workers, the absence of such objects disturbed the perception of social and spatial order with the private space as a place for children's development. For Cristina, they created intensive work as she tried to stage the home space for different encounters.

Throwing away objects and unruly mothering

The presence of toys all around the house did not correspond to many mothers' ideas of a 'straight' (*vorta*) house, which should be clean and with no objects on the floor or other surfaces. The idea that objects were left on the floor and surfaces around the house provoked the potential for gossip and rumours from family members who came to visit, and would be seen as 'shameful' (*lazhav*). Children's toys were not exempt from this evaluation. Cleaning the house was sometimes undertaken quickly and by different women or girls who stayed in the house. On many occasions Maria, who lived with eight others, complained that letters went missing. It was difficult for her to keep track of letters because many different women cleaned the house and, as none of them could read and write, they often threw away pieces of paper.

On one occasion I was talking to Maria in the back garden of the terraced house where she stayed with her brother's family and various others who worked for her brother. She was sorting through a large pile of different objects that had been swept and cleaned from the house. She extracted socks and a cardboard packet that contained moisturiser. She checked cigarette packets to ensure there were no cigarettes, before throwing the remaining items in the bin. It was unclear who had done the sweeping but it was evident that it was not Maria and she was annoyed, particularly because her new moisturising cream had been thrown away. There were a number of such incidents that made me aware of the likelihood that objects would be thrown away if they were left on surfaces. For example, when Maria got a letter from the hospital she told me not to leave it on the table but put it in her handbag and carried it around with her. I also saw her place letters that she wanted to keep on a high shelf in the kitchen. Similarly, Mirela, a migrant mother who also lived in a house with her husband's extended family (10 adults and six children), placed all of her identity documents in her handbag (including the children's temporary passports and the adults' ID cards).

In these cases, illiteracy and family organisation combined to create different values and behaviours related to material objects. This had particular effects for toys or material objects related to children. On one occasion I was walking along the street when I saw Radu walking back from the newsagent's with his three youngest children. They were playing with fluorescent toy guns, pretending to shoot each other and also throwing them across the pavement. They were playing with them so vigorously that by the time they got home the toys, which were made out of thin plastic, were broken and immediately put in the bin. Similarly, Georgeta had picked up a children's tea set that had been placed outside a nearby house, indicating that it could be taken if wanted by someone else. Georgeta gave the tea set to her son and his cousin to play with. After an hour or so the children got bored and began running outside in the garden, at which point Georgeta picked it up and threw it away as they no longer wanted it.

For frontline workers, throwing away material items infused with values linked to the child-mother relationship evoked the idea that children's needs were not prioritised and therefore the children might be 'at risk'. This included throwing away school jumpers, toys, books and letters from school. This also linked to an idea that these families lived such 'chaotic lives' they were unable to hold onto such things. When items of school uniform went missing, this was also infused with ideas about Roma families not valuing education. On one occasion, Paula was very frustrated when one mother requested a second school jumper. It emerged that her older daughter was visiting and had tidied the house, placing a lot of different objects in the rubbish bin, including the jumper. These feelings of frustration were heightened when budget cuts meant that Paula could no longer provide uniform vouchers for European migrants without recourse to public funds (see Introduction). This was similarly the case when a church volunteer brought books around to Margereta's house. The children were not used to books and tore the pages, throwing the paper around the room and putting the covers on their heads as hats. Instances such as this cumulatively gave the impression that children were unruly and that mothers were not providing them with the appropriate guidance to become responsible citizens.

The inappropriate use of objects and different understandings of what was required to perform appropriate mothering was evident in descriptions of mother-child relationships when frontline workers entered the home. Frontline workers noted children playing adult computer games, which was 'not appropriate'. This happened in one interaction I witnessed between Paula, equality and diversity officer for the children's services department, and Stelutza. I was in Stelutza's house when Paula came to visit because she had recently come out of prison and had a 3-year-old son. The boy had been running around but when Paula arrived she placed the boy in front of the large TV and switched on a games console for him to play with. She did not seem to look at what kind of game the boy was playing and concentrated on the interaction with Paula. However, in a multi-agency meeting Paula expressed concern he was playing with violent video games that were not appropriate for his age.

Similarly, Kassia, children's centre family support worker, noted that when she visited homes children were just "stuck in front of the TV all day". In some instances, this was an active tactic by mothers to try to keep children quiet and stop them running around during meetings with frontline workers. These actions served to worry family workers who deemed the children were given inappropriate games, there were no stimuli in the house and they were not being cared for. Such observations about children in one home seemed to become generalised and applied to all Roma mothers. For example, this concern was raised about Grigore's household; Kassia had officially noted that one boy seemed to be 'listless' and in front of the TV all day. However, I was aware that Claudia, Grigore's wife, often took the children to the park but did so when Grigore came home from work, which was impossible to plan as he was a self-employed scrap metal dealer. While these negative assessments on their own may not have had immediate harmful consequences for the mothers, they had cumulative effects in two ways. First, for an individual mother such assessments could become crucial if children were considered to be 'at risk' and social services became involved. Second, such assessments served to reproduce the negative meanings attached to the label of Romanian Roma in general, further solidifying the pejorative effects of the term. It is also important to note that these assessments became part of the discourse surrounding these families only because of the home encounter. The home encounter therefore becomes a self-fulfilling prophecy that both mothers and frontline workers are unable to evade.

Final remarks

The home is a particular kind of space that is deeply imbued with meaning through embodied, materially interwoven practices. This chapter has shown how these meanings shift depending on the people who occupy a given space at a particular moment. Anthropologists and geographers argue that space is co-constituted with social relationships, meaning that they cannot be fully understood without reference to the other (Pandya 1990; Massey 1994; Munn 1996). Indeed, 'a place' is a nexus of relations that are continually reproduced out of the interactions between people and space. The home is not simply a determinate 'place' (or set of determinate places) that has a fixed meaning, but is always shifting in relation to the movement of people and objects. Meanings are attached to the material and physical aspects of the home, as well as in bodily practices, routines or thoughts and feelings that are performed or verbally expressed. When frontline workers were in the home, they changed the space and the way that people acted and felt within it. Through these 'intimate state encounters' in the home the boundary work that is done to separate public and private spaces, and the practices that have become inscribed into different spaces, gets confused and tangled, revealing the dichotomy's inherent contradictions. These incursions do not just affect how objects are treated in the home, for example Cristina throwing soft toys around her children prior to frontline workers' visits, they affect thoughts and feelings about what 'home' is and could be.

Not only do frontline workers have this effect on the home space and the migrants who live there, at the same time they are drawing understandings from the space through their own perceptions and expectations of 'appropriate mothering' and through the lens of identifying the family as Romanian Roma. The fact that encounters take place in the home, which is deeply circumscribed as a non-market space replete with symbolic meanings that are profoundly intimate (the site of familial relationships) and yet have such wide implications (in terms of how a person is judged in their relationship to a political community), makes these encounters an extremely complex and difficult terrain for mothers to navigate. They are completely different from an interaction that happens in an office, where there are set roles, behaviours, objects and pathways. Moreover, as we learned in the previous chapters, frontline workers' roles have a significant basis in discretionary decisions and value-based judgements. Therefore the assessments that are made in this highly emotive space have a direct effect on whether frontline workers feel comfortable, which relates to whether they assess mothers as morally legitimate receivers of their discretionary care.

I have used the term 'tactics' to describe the *mētis* or 'ways of operating' of both frontline workers and Romanian Roma. This term foregrounds the constrained positions that both sets of actors have in their daily lives, but I do not want to mask the highly asymmetric balance of power, which allows frontline workers the primary role in setting the terms for different performances and negotiations (including the time of the encounter). However, the ongoing development of the encounters is nonetheless shaped by both sets of actors. We will further see in Chapter Six that, as relationships between frontline workers and different Romanian Roma mothers and families develop over time through the relational labour required by the home encounter, frontline workers' own room for manoeuvre can become limited as they take on different roles and entanglements in the families' attempts to negotiate their legal residency statuses. In some circumstances frontline workers become bound up in relations of care and kinship that change how the state is 'made up' or, in other words, where the state is 'located'. The following two chapters will explore some of the specific processes that can be seen as taking place within, and being shaped by, the home encounter. Specifically, the chapters focus on how the confusion between public and private plays out and the consequences for the constitution of mothers' as caring and cultural subjects. They explore the consequences of the various legal, moral and normative regulations and discourses, which are produced by the state and discretionally applied by frontline workers, on the frontline workers themselves and those who are subject to these judgements and meanings.

The main aim in this chapter has been to foreground the contingency within the space of the home, and how it is not a fixed place but subject to shifting social significations. The pernicious ever-present spectre of the border within the home, along with the entanglement of welfare entitlements and migration statuses, overshadows the strategies available to mothers, such that performing deserving motherhood in the home can become the determinant of a precarious presence on national soil.

Interlude | Clara's Belgian torte

I first saw Clara in a large framed picture in the front room of the house where Maria stayed. It was a wedding picture. Clara was dressed in an elaborate white dress and next to her stood Sergui in his suit, waistcoat and baby-pink tie. Clara had her hands on her hips and head slightly tilted. Sergui stood beside and slightly behind her, looking straight at the camera. I learnt later that she was 15 in this photograph and Sergui was 17 years old. Their fathers were brothers, making them first cousins or *nepotes cheches* (true cousins), which I was later told by Maria was "very important to our family". The wedding took place in the same summer as that of William and Kate, the Duke and Duchess of Cambridge. The parallel was not lost and Clara later told me her wedding was like the royal wedding. It took place in Romania and the guest list included famous Manele singers, one of whom had made Clara's dress.

When I started my fieldwork I only saw Clara in photos and sometimes online when Sergui's father would call his brother (Clara's father). However, I often saw Sergui, either in the house where Maria stayed (where he also lived) or around the town with other men his own age outside the internet café or sitting eating chicken and chips in the large square outside the cinema. She returned to live with her husband and parents-in-law (also her uncle and aunt) and her paternal grandmother. She had given birth to a boy, also called Sergui (often called Serguitso), who was now around 9 months old. I spent many hours talking to Clara in the house. She wanted to practise her English, which she spoke with a strong French accent.

During the day the house was often quiet. Her mother-in-law Ramona would watch TV in the front room of the house while looking after baby Serguitso. Her grandmother would be out in the high street begging next to the bus stop. Her father-in-law often went on long journeys with her husband to work but I was never told what this entailed. When I asked I was told that they were driving. Clara sat at the kitchen table with her sewing machine making clothes, sometimes with a big box of Maltesers next to her and an instant cappuccino (she did not drink the strong black coffee that the older woman drank). Or she was in the kitchen making large and elaborate cakes.

One of our conversations took place in May 2013. Sergui and his father had just come into the house for lunch. Ramona and Clara had made chips, fried fish and chicken nuggets. There were also two large garlic bread baguettes. They put all the food on the table and the two men ate, also encouraging me to sit down and eat with them. They teased me that

I ate like a bird and needed to get 'big' (*bari*). After the men had eaten they got up and went into the front room to watch TV. At this point Clara and Ramona sit down to eat. Sergui calls to Clara to get him coke, and she gets up and goes to the fridge to take glasses of coke to the front room before returning to her lunch.

Eventually Ramona gets up and goes into the front room, and I realise the men have left the house. Ramona is watching Indian soap dramas on the TV and looking after Serguitso. She calls to Clara to get her some 'torte'. It emerges that this is for Alin, Ramona's youngest son, and not herself. Clara goes into the kitchen and produces a huge piece of cake. There are four layers of sponge filled with chocolate spread, cream and tangerine pieces topped with more cream and desiccated coconut. I tell her it looks like it could be in a shop window. She cuts similarly huge slices for both of us and we sit down with our cake while she tells me about learning Latin at school in Brussels. She describes how "I knew that it was for medicine and I don't want to be a doctor so I changed." We talk about languages a lot and she explains how she doesn't really know Romanian because she was brought up in Brussels. "I didn't know '*mashina*' was car but thought it was a washing machine. Car is '*motoro*'." She also makes fun of me when I make mistakes in *Romanës*. For example, I call potatoes '*baribulia*', which is what Dan and Cristina in their Moldavian dialect called potatoes. Clara calls potatoes '*kolumpiray*', and thinks '*baribulia*' sounds like '*bari bul*', meaning 'big bum'.

Her father had gained refugee status in Brussels and she had entered the school system where her maths teacher helped her to read and write in French (something that her parents could not do). She won many school prizes, which her father hung up around the mantelpiece in the Brussels flat. As she tells me about her prizes she takes out her phone to show me the flat where she had grown up, with all her trophies and medals displayed.

She carries on describing her friends who are from "many, many different countries" and how "I was wearing jeans, just like you". After speaking about her school life for around five minutes she suddenly stops and says "That was two years ago – it is all gone." I ask her if she liked school and she says "I liked school but I am married. I have a baby – for me no."

5

Gender and intimate
state encounters

On 23 July 2013 it is a warm, sunny day in Luton. Simon, the
pastor, and Kassia, a children's centre family worker, are visiting
families Simon knows from the church to register them with
the children's centre. I have gone along with them. We knock
on the door of a terraced house. Simon has visited the house
before for a prayer meeting and knows at least two families
with children live there. Nicolai, a Romanian Roma father,
opens the door, recognises Simon and invites us in. We pass
the front room, which has two double beds jammed into it,
and go through to the back room, which has a table and some
mismatched chairs. I see the kitchen is beyond this room, in
an extension that looks like it might fall down at any moment.
Dinka, Nicolai's wife, is sitting in the room breastfeeding
her youngest child while her other two young children run
around the room. Nicolai has heard about national insurance
numbers from his cousin, Cezar, who also lives in the house,
and he tries to engage Simon and Kassia in conversation about
how he can apply for one. He works on Cezar's scrap metal
van and sometimes manages to get work with the other men
in the house in a meat packing factory. His wife, Dinka, a
20-year-old mother of three, does not speak English and does
not engage with either Kassia or Simon. She quietly hands
them papers from her handbag throughout the interaction and
then attends to her three small children. Nicolai continues to
ask Kassia about a national insurance number but she maintains
she is there just for the children. Kassia does not seem to want
to engage with this family more broadly, closing down areas
where she might go beyond her formal role.

As we leave, Simon tells Nicolai to call him about the national insurance number. When I ask Simon a few days later about the family, Simon responds that Nicolai was "like a stuck record" and has no chance of gaining a national insurance number as he has no documentation for the work he is doing. Simon explains that Nicolai is being paid in cash and isn't keeping any record of his income because he can't read and write.

This vignette raises a number of issues about how gender performances are shaped by expectations of being a good welfare client and deserving citizen. This chapter focuses on how mothers and fathers have different opportunities to negotiate with frontline workers, volunteers and others. For example, Dinka did not speak in this encounter and the family as far as I knew was not visited again and did not receive any support to gain legal residency. Unlike Mariela, whom we met in Chapter Two, Dinka did not receive a large amount of help and support from Kassia. Both mothers were very similar in terms of their migration experiences. However, Mariela played the part of the hostess, giving Kassia a lot of space in the house, and did not bombard her with questions or make demands. She also demonstrated gratitude through gifts of warm, freshly homemade bread. These actions can all be read as gendered performances of appropriate femininity within a welfare encounter. In these conditions Kassia recognised affinities between herself and Mariela, such as the bureaucratic loops she was caught in. She associated her own struggle with Mariela's and wanted to use her own experience to help Mariela overcome similar difficulties. In addition, Mariela's husband was working in a fruit shop during the day while Dinka's husband collected scrap metal at night, therefore Nicolai was at home when Simon and Kassia visited. When fathers were at home during the day (as will be shown later on) they contributed to a preconception that Roma men were lazy and did not work. Nicolai engaged Simon and Kassia with his concerns for the safety of his family through his own gendered role. He foregrounded his work and his desire for a scrap metal licence. As this conversation was happening in English, Dinka did not engage with Kassia apart from to smile at her and show her new baby. Kassia registered the family on the children's centre record and never returned.

The aim of this chapter is to explore how mothers and fathers had different opportunities open to them within the home encounter. These differences, notably how mothers were the main focus of frontline workers' attention, had varying effects depending on the gendered differences already in place and playing out within families and how different families perceived the state (Pantea, 2012).

This chapter's main argument is that Romanian Roma mothers were engaged in, and by, state care in two ways: as subjects of care through their mothering practices and as objects and receivers of care from frontline workers. These two facets are inextricably linked. If mothers' caring practices were legitimised by the state (as 'deserving') then they were also perceived to be potentially good receivers of care, and vice versa. Their motherhood allowed them to be redeemed from their stigmatised status as 'despicable' mothers. They could be recast as good receivers of care through performing appropriate motherhood. However, this route (or subject position) was not open to fathers. They were perceived as a legitimate subject of care if they provided for the family through work (a role that is denied to them through institutional racism and transitional controls blocking their access to legitimised work). They were not perceived to be appropriate objects of state care because they could not perform as the appropriate deserving subjects of care.[49]

This chapter elaborates on how Romanian Roma gender performances align – or not – to appropriate gender performances of being a welfare client. It also addresses how frontline workers' situated positions affect encounters. The analysis centres on unpacking the idea of 'deservingness' through a gendered lens. It also pays attention to the role of space and the further implications of why the home space matters.

The often cited understanding of gender is 'a hierarchical division between women and men embedded in social institutions and social practices. Gender is thus a social structural phenomenon but is also produced, negotiated and sustained at the level of everyday interaction' (Jackson and Scott 2002: 5). Crucially, gender relations cannot be understood in terms of binary oppositions (Gay y Blasco 1997) nor are gendered relations impervious to change (Deutsch 2007). Gender differences are always mediated through social interactions and therefore always contain the potential for change, or reinscription. Appropriate performances of femininity are crucial in home encounters as they offer the potential to be redeemed from marginalising stereotypes of motherhood. Mothers are potentially able to perform good femininity if they are trained well and this perspective is institutionalised within policies and practices of parenting (Lister, 2003).

The previous chapter reviewed the academic scholarship that has conceptualised migrant women's reproductive practices as a legitimate and necessary site of securitised state intervention and has linked social reproduction with state reproduction. The advance to the literature made in that chapter was to bring together the anthropology of the state and the role of discretion within street-level bureaucratic work with the literature on mothers' work and racialised motherhood. Much previous scholarly work on migrant parenting practices either focus on fathers *or* mothers with the majority on mothering practices (Tsolidis 2001; Gedalof 2009; Erel 2011b; Krummel 2012; Intke-Hernández and Holm 2015; Lillrank 2015; Lonergan 2015; Nordberg 2015; Reynolds et al. 2018). There is increasing literature on migrant masculinities (Charsley and Wray 2015; Griffiths 2015) and migrant fathers (Auerbach et al. 2008; Pustułka et al. 2015). This chapter advances the literature further to foreground performances of masculinities and femininities of all social actors in encounters (Romanian Roma, frontline workers, myself), how they interrelate and affect judgements of deservingness in the home space.

Through this approach this chapter argues that legitimised masculinity presupposes that fathers cannot be trained or 'domesticated' in the home (as legitimate subjects of care) and therefore are excluded from becoming receivers of care in the home-land (that is, legitimate objects of care). Men can easily be refused care, which also entails a refusal of political belonging (see Introduction), whereas mothers can be redeemed through their performances of care. The chapter also argues that the state's imaginings of appropriate gender relations and performances (and the policies, practices and interventions that legitimise these imaginings) can compound the constraints on mothers through the sidelining of fathers. Through tracing the inextricable relationship between subjects of care and objects of care this chapter further demonstrates the way the nation-state is reproduced within and through the home space.

Redeeming belonging through motherhood

The particular sets of expectations of 'good motherhood' and appropriate femininities in the home created conflicting pressures, for Romania Roma mothers. In developing different tactics and performances (more or less valued by frontline workers) to gain support from frontline workers, they took on exhausting work. Many of the encounters already featured in previous chapters have shown the different kinds of negotiations and performances mothers took on during home encounters. Mothers can potentially be 'domesticated' and that potential provides an opening to challenge and rupture hegemonic narratives on Romanian Roma motherhood. This small opening allowed mothers to create a relation with frontline workers to unsettle their dominant and views about Romanian Roma mothers. This opening is what is at stake as mothers try to square the circle of being labelled as a 'despicable' mother, but gaining political belonging through performances of motherhood. Crucially this happens in a very particular space: the home. The home space can offer increasing room for manoeuvre through the relational labour of hosting or can further narrow the potential for rupture and production. To elaborate, I take several of Cristina's experiences of home encounters to explore the different kinds of work she did in different encounters with different actors and what kind of home she achieved under these conditions.

Safe domesticity through silence, absence and prohibition

This encounter between Lisa (Pathways support officer), Simon (Roma church pastor), Cristina (mother) and me reveals the work Cristina undertook to create a balance of formality/informality or public/private. In addition, we can see the gradations of visibility and exclusion in the home, which further highlights the large material and symbolic resources needed to maintain a 'safe' home space. The encounter demonstrates the intensive work and understanding of different expectations and perceptions that Cristina had learnt and maintained so that she could uphold particular values of mothering. In return she was in the process of gaining a more secure legal status for her family.

When I arrived at Cristina's house with Simon, Lisa was already there and was sitting on the couch in the front room, talking on her mobile phone. She was trying to rearrange Cristina's council tax,[50] which she could not pay. Simon placed himself at the wooden and slightly wobbly table next to the kitchen door and the couch where Lisa and Cristina were sitting. I sat on another couch, close to Cristina. It was between five thirty and six o'clock in the evening. Lisa and Simon immediately engaged each other in deep conversation and were not acknowledging Cristina. Rather, they were focusing on the latest developments in bureaucratic requirements for Romanians to gain residency status in the UK. Cristina offered them both cups of tea, but apart from this interruption was not part of the interaction. However, her use of silence and management of the space actively shaped the encounter.

Cristina's careful management of the space was further exemplified through the absence of her children and Dinni, her husband's half-sister, who was upstairs looking after the children. Lisa's presence in the downstairs part of the house had pushed Dinni and the children to become invisible upstairs, creating a space of prohibition downstairs. Dinni only emerged when everyone left, and she went straight to the kitchen to make food for the babies. This was the case for every interaction between a frontline worker and Cristina in the house that I observed. Dinni disappeared and did not re-emerge until the support worker left. This encounter also highlights the contested nature of the home space for different actors. Dinni was being employed as a live-in nanny and was brought over from Romania by Dan, Cristina's husband. Dinni had a very different understanding and experience of this space. It was her place of work. She excluded herself from the downstairs space when there were visitors, but at night this was where she slept.

Moreover, Cristina used silence and absences through her understandings of how the home space changed when support workers were present, intersecting with the configuration of relationships in the house. Cristina was able to perform particular roles of host and deserving mother as Dinni silently looked after the children upstairs.

This instance demonstrates how Cristina was able to uphold certain conditions in home encounters and reveals the amount of work she invested in doing so. She learnt to make cups of tea and to sit silently while others used the space of her house. She drew on Dan's family connections to gain help in the house, as he had asked his half-sister to come and join them to help look after the children. Dan explained to me that Dinni had come to help Cristina so that she could look for a job, as she had gained a national insurance number, thus indicating the beginning of a shifting relationship between Dan and Cristina, which had been set in motion by her different bureaucratic status. In addition, this encounter highlights how different family circumstances and relationships shaped home encounters. Cristina was able to maintain this space, and could control its use over Dinni, who was living with them to help her. Dinni's care for the children and their absence in this encounter was instrumental in Cristina creating a space that was deemed to be an appropriate and safe space for the family. Cristina could only fulfil the high standards of mothering that are required for her to be perceived as an appropriate subject of care by employing a family member to conduct this care work for her. This was in contrast to some other mothers, such as Mirela, described in Chapter Four, who could not control the home space in such a way because she lived with her extended family and they had a shared household economy. They did not have the extra resources that would have helped them to achieve the standard of mothering that was perceived to be redeemable. These different family forms, living arrangements and economic activities affected how home encounters unfolded.

Safe domesticity through maintaining intimate, non-market space

This encounter between Louise (children's centre worker), Kay (church volunteer), Cristina and me was complicated for Cristina by the presence of another Romanian Roma couple, Mihai and Ilinca. This encounter foregrounds the complex identity work that Cristina undertook to ensure she maintained her position outside pejorative assumptions about Romanian Roma mothers, and how she upheld the home as a non-market space that was framed by intimate relations between friends rather than a space of economic exchange.

Mihai and Ilinca sometimes worked with Dan collecting scrap metal. Dan told me that he would always try to help Mihai because when Mihai had learnt that Cristina had given birth to her fifth child he had brought cooked chickens to their house. Dan believed Mihai had a 'big heart' (*barro yillo*). Mihai and Ilinca were both sitting at the kitchen table discussing when they would next go out and work on the scrap metal van when Kay and Louise 'popped round' and made an unplanned visit. Cristina immediately introduced them to Kay as Pentecostals. Kay exclaimed "Hallelujah! Praise the Lord!" and when Cristina went on to explain "They are good people, a different type of Gypsy, not here for stealing, they are here for job," Louise remarked "Hooray!" Cristina continued to refer to Pentecostalism, explaining "These are not the stealing Gypsies, they read the Bible."

This encounter serves to highlight how Cristina negotiated her position. She endeavoured to control Louise's perceptions of her relationships and family life. However, due to the encounter occurring in her home she could not plan and manage the space to suit the circumscriptions of every relationship and interaction. The house was used as a place where Dan met others to arrange work and maintain social connections. Therefore Cristina could not (and did not want to) restrict others from visiting as they were also crucial for maintaining her family's daily life. In this encounter she used Pentecostalism to reaffirm her commitment to a certain type of behaviour, invoking a common set of values between Kay, Louise, Mihai, Ilinca and herself. In the process she acted to perpetuate, legitimise and reproduce certain other perceptions and categorisations of the 'stealing Gypsy' in her efforts to move into the subject position that was open to her to maintain her relationship with Kay and Louise to secure her family's status (see Chapter Three). This encounter shows how the space of the home fulfilled multiple functions which do not map neatly onto frontline workers' conceptions of home (such as privacy, intimacy and domesticity). Cristina could not guard against all of these different uses at all times but instead sought tactics to mitigate their effects.

Safe domesticity through gratitude and respect

A final encounter between Louise, Cristina and me shows the fragility of Cristina's relationship with the state.

Louise bought food for Cristina if she had money remaining in the church budget at the end of the month. Despite asking Cristina what she liked to eat, Cristina did not specify a choice and always seemed happy, and smiled and thanked Louise when she brought the food. Louise told me that she tried to buy food that was 'nutritious and healthy' for the children, but much of it sat unused in the cupboard. I asked Cristina why she didn't cook it and she answered that she didn't know how to cook it (porridge oats) or she didn't think it was good for the children (tinned soup which she thought was *guglo* (sweet) and not as healthy as *supă* (a clear soup), or *ciorbă* (a sour soup)). However, despite not eating the food, the expectation of feeding the children 'healthy food' caused another source of tension for Cristina. Families who did not have anywhere to stay or had been evicted frequently stayed in the house. Seeing others in the house upset Kay and Louise as they thought the food they bought was not being eaten by the children, a perception that threatened their assistance. It also created an idea of family life that did not correspond to their ideals of 'good motherhood'. Louise had mentioned to me previously that she was 'despairing' because there were lots of people staying in the house and eating the food that the church had given the family. Louise felt a need to help Cristina, but was shaken when her behaviour fell outside what she considered to be 'morally legitimate' or deserving. I felt very embarrassed as I thought she was referring to me eating the food and told her I was paying rent. At this point she laughed and told me that she wasn't worried about me, but the 'other people' staying with Cristina and Dan. Louise had also voiced these concerns to Cristina, telling her when she delivered the food that it was for her and her children. Louise's reaction also highlights her situated position and her need to help Cristina, but only through very particular modes such as directly feeding her children 'healthy food'. Cristina's performances were therefore about responding to Louise's needs and how Louise constructed value for herself in performing these actions. Cristina's actions allowed Louise to gain the meanings she desired and recognised through her role as a Christian, but also as a children's centre worker whose remit was to keep children safe and healthy.

When placed within this context, Cristina's reaction to Louise seeing Mihai and Ilinca (as detailed in the previous encounter) can be more fully understood. Cristina had to justify the presence of Mihai and Ilinca, using the fact that they are religious to try to assuage Louise's fears. Cristina was constantly required to think about how she and her family were perceived by others and worked hard to counter any negative opinions that Louise and Kay might form about her. It is important to note that Louise was not concerned about me living in the house but other people whom she identified as Romanian Roma. The strong pejorative connotations linked to Romanian Roma made it difficult for Cristina to easily and simply explain her relationships with others. Louise did not know (and probably would not have imagined) that Mihai had given Dan and Cristina food, rather than the other way around.

These instances indicate the complexity and fragility of the relationships that Cristina negotiated with Louise and other frontline workers. A fundamental aspect of governing through intimate state encounters and the delicate balance between formal and informal relations was the gratitude for Louise's multiple forms of support (which included bureaucratic help to gain a secure right to reside in the UK and material assistance through buying food and school uniforms). This was because this support stems from Louise's discretion rather than any entitlement that Cristina could claim. Louise gained some understanding of Cristina's limited resources, which could prevent her from fulfilling the high standard of mothering that Louise might have hoped for. Louise seemed to think that Cristina's mothering was 'good enough' because it was assessed in light of her other personal qualities (particularly her religion) and the way that Cristina was able to present a particular type of household environment that resonated with Louise.

The work that Cristina put into these encounters to maintain these relationships has been detailed throughout the encounters. She organised her house so that it was staged to conform to ideas of 'good motherhood' for frontline workers, but immediately tidied everything away for her husband's, her own and other families' ideas of what a straight and tidy house looked like. She changed her children's clothes, her own clothes and tied her hair differently when frontline workers were likely to visit. She used the experiences that she learnt interacting with nurses and other mothers in the hospital when she had her children and re-enacted them in her house, using phrases that resonated with frontline workers such as 'cuppa tea' which made everyone smile, reaffirming her use of the phrase. She tried hard to hide the fact that the house was in a state of disrepair and was infested with rats. I noticed that she tried to hide the kitchen, closing the door behind her when she entered and left the room. On one occasion when we only had one light bulb she moved it to the front room, rather than the children's room, so that frontline workers would not be able to see that the light fitting was without a bulb. Cristina also drew on her family's wider resources, such as deciding, with Dan, that his half-sister should come and help her with the children so that she could try to find a job.

In addition, whenever she engaged with frontline workers she was grateful, quiet and undemanding. Simon described Cristina as 'saintly' in one conversation because she seemed so calm in the face of, in Simon's perceptions, intense hardship. He compared her with his wife who, he stated, "worries about everything". I only witnessed one occasion when Cristina did not maintain this demeanour. This instance provides some indication of how she chose to interact differently with frontline workers and the various ways she assessed relationships. It shows the importance of the situated position of the frontline worker and the importance of the home encounter as a discretionary form of care.

Cristina became very angry with a local government housing officer. He visited the house because Simon had helped Dan make a complaint to the local government about the landlord. He had never visited the house before and did not come to the house again as far as I was aware. When the man first entered Cristina was calm and spoke very quietly, indicating to me that I should speak. We both took the man to look at the windows on the second floor of the house which were rotting and could easily be opened. Cristina was very worried because she thought her children could easily fall out of these windows. We also showed the man the holes in the ceiling where water dripped through when it rained and the mould and damp in the kitchen. The man listened but did not write anything down and seemed in a hurry to leave.

As he was turning to leave Cristina began to shout that the landlord was a 'terrible man' and that her children could die in this 'terrible house'. The man was taken aback at Cristina's sudden change in attitude. He told her to calm down and he would speak to the landlord. He then rushed to leave while looking at his mobile phone. After he had left Cristina was very angry and shouted that the man was in shorts, which she believed indicated that he was not 'serious', and she thought that he might have been drunk. It seemed as though she had become angry because she felt that the man had not shown respect to her and her family. The fact he had been wearing shorts seemed to indicate this in her view. In this instance Cristina did not assume a relationship based on gratitude with the man. Her reaction to him provides stark contrast to the qualities that she expressed to Louise and others who she did consider to be 'serious' and who developed a relationship with her over a long period of time.

Her reaction also indicates Cristina's high moral standards and her sense of respectability that was entwined with her religiosity. These values were also upheld by Louise and might explain why Cristina put a great deal of work into showing that she was grateful, was often silent and made a point of being undemanding.

Cristina's 'saintly' demeanour was part of how she perceived her relationship with frontline workers who visited her house. The housing officer was not in her house because of discretion but because he had to be there – it was the location of his job and therefore this was not a relationship of hospitality or relational labour. He was not interested in Cristina's broader life circumstances or negotiating to help her with her legal status. There was no space for her to receive discretionary support from this man. However, through her shouting and getting angry the housing officer did nothing to help her with the landlord.

Cristina was successful in negotiating support through enacting gratitude, never asking or demanding assistance and through using silence conforming to particular ideas of gendered behaviour that was similarly upheld by the frontline workers who entered her house. However, through these practices she also placed herself beyond automatic entitlement. Gratitude speaks to powerlessness, an inclusion by exception rather than expectation. It is highly individualised and contingent (see Chapter Two for discussion of this move towards individual and moral decisions at the frontline). This was the position through which Cristina was able to gain support, because of particular relationships with frontline workers and because these encounters happened in her home. These encounters indicate the contingent and shifting nature of relationships between frontline workers and mothers, which were highly spatialised, and the fragility through which value around mothering was constructed and negotiated.

Through using Pentecostalism as a shared value and drawing a contrast between herself and racialised notions of 'Roma', Cristina was able to uphold her relationships with Kay and Louise. They continued to visit her, providing informal support and assistance, granting the resources to perform appropriate mothering for them and other frontline workers who entered the house, such as family support workers from the local primary school. Her access to formal state-mandated social protection and belonging (through appealing against the refusal of a right to reside) closely relied on the relationships she maintained and her everyday practices of belonging, such as performing 'appropriate motherhood'.

These encounters foreground the work done by mothers during the home encounter. As has been established elsewhere through feminist critiques of the welfare state and liberal citizenship, labour in the home has been undervalued, despite its constitutive contribution to social welfare (Fraser 1987; Pateman 1989; Brown 1992; see also Chapters Two and Four). The work done by mothers during home encounters should be understood as enacting citizenship (Isin and Nielsen 2008) in the sense that it is constitutive to social welfare, but perhaps more importantly mothers are also actively negotiating their families' formal legal membership through mothering practices. Mothers' practices challenge hegemonic narratives of racialised citizenship and our understanding of the places and spaces where political belonging is negotiated and under what terms (Nordberg 2015; Erel et al. 2017).

The distinction between public and private space is blurred by the gendered incursions into the home. As mothers work to contest their citizenship in (and through) the home space through the optics of frontline workers who themselves occupy precarious positions within citizenship hierarchies, the home can best be understood as a space of indeterminacy where situated actors are continually negotiating the balance between public and private, affective and formal (see Chapter Two). This balance can be reconfigured at different moments and lead to moral justifications, either to offer discretionary support or acts of refusal to care (see Chapter Four). This section has elaborated on the terms on which Romanian Roma mothers were able to make a home and feel at home through gendered performances of motherhood and domesticity that could redeem them from their stigmatised position as a Romanian Roma mother (Chapter Three) and move to being seen as a legitimate receiver of care. This section has also laid out the kinds of home conditions that mothers work to achieve to fit into the appropriate performances of the feminine welfare client.

Unredeemable masculinities: closing down spaces of political membership

Having looked at the different gendered performances available and the work taken on by mothers in managing their interactions with frontline workers through the home encounter, I now turn to explore the differential experiences of Romanian Roma fathers.

The significance of child safeguarding as the route to 'visibility' for these families, and frontline workers' understanding of their roles with regard to the position of children and mothers (Chapter Two), served to directly exclude fathers from home encounters although they were indirectly implicated as will be shown below. From the start of my fieldwork I noted that, in most cases, men would actively remove themselves from the home during these encounters; or if they were in the home, they did not interact with the frontline workers at all (even when they were in the same room). As home encounters were typically the primary, or only, interaction between the families and frontline workers of any kind, this further worked to exclude most men from any relationship with frontline workers or ways of accessing state resources.

A case in point is Mihai, a Romanian Roma man whose children had grown up, got married and had children of their own. He moved to the UK without them. In consequence, he remained largely 'invisible' to frontline workers and had little or no relationship with the state in any form. He had no access to healthcare; lived in housing registered under a different family; received no state services or support; did not have a national insurance number and worked only by going out on other people's scrap metal vans or performing informal services for others; and was never subject to home visitations. On one occasion, he received a parking ticket on his car, and he was told by one of the other men in the household that this was important and he needed to pay it. Mihai could not read; he did not understand what the parking ticket was, did not understand what to do, did not have access to any information about how to resolve the parking ticket, and subsequently became very distressed. He mentioned this to me, and I took him to the town hall (which he was previously unaware of), and I accompanied him throughout the short process which took around fifteen minutes to resolve. He was also very worried about the cost, as he had little income, and I explained that he could arrange an instalment plan to make payments. I presented this to the cashier at the town hall and she quickly processed the request. In this situation I believe I became like a frontline worker, or at least a mediator, for Mihai and he treated me in a similar way to Cristina's treated Louise, by expressing extreme gratitude. However, as a man with different resources, this gratitude was expressed through offering to drive me around in his car. Mihai's position, without any children who would provide any interactions with, or understanding of, frontline workers or services, illustrates an extreme case of how men could be entirely excluded from a relationship with (or any understanding of) state forms and how gratitude circulates within this affective field but is expressed in differing and gendered ways.

In addition to the processes and understandings that exclude fathers from developing a relationship with frontline workers, the situated position of male Romanian Roma experiences made forming relationships with frontline workers problematic. In particular, the networks and shared experiences between mothers provided different resources, information and understandings about interactions with frontline workers that men did not engage in as far as I observed. Their lack of these resources created heightened tensions and fears for fathers about possible bureaucratic encounters.

The following encounter between Sanda (a Romanian Roma mother) and Christian (a church volunteer) demonstrates how the home space can exacerbate the perception of Romanian Roma fathers as 'failed citizens', while providing mothers with space to perform appropriate care and therefore also become legitimate receivers and objects of care. Here, Christian's gendered perspective serves both to focus his support on mothers and to place strain on his relationship with Sanda because of his perceptions of her husband's behaviour. It also allows Christian to perform his own good citizenship as a caring person and a good Christian.

Sanda was a mother of three who attended the Roma church (*khangheri*). I met her at the church early in 2013. She was a small woman and had a round open and smiling face. She seemed quick to laugh or find a joke in any situation. Sanda found a small amount of domestic cleaning work by walking around the streets where she lived, knocking on doors and asking whether anyone wanted their house cleaned. Sanda was well aware of how Christian had helped Violeta gain a national insurance number through cleaning work. Through conversations at the Roma church she persuaded Christian, who was also keen to ensure that she was working legally, to visit her at her house to help her apply for a national insurance number. Christian bought her an invoice book, organised her cleaning product receipts as expenses and kept her accounts (Sanda could not read or write). Christian began to visit Sanda every Wednesday and considered this to be part of his 'missionary' work. He successfully helped Sanda gain a national insurance number. He wanted to apply for child benefit and then housing benefit for her; however she persuaded him that it would be best to apply for them all at the same time.

Christian's relationship with Sanda highlights the focus on mothers' work that is shared between volunteers and frontline workers. For example, Sanda's husband Miron bought and sold second-hand cars. Christian never mentioned the possibility of registering Miron's business to help him gain self-employed status. Miron also showed no interest in this and did not talk to Christian about his work. Not only did Christian not mention the possibility of registering Miron's second-hand car business, but he seemed perplexed about the number of men he saw sitting in Sanda's house. He mentioned to me that he did not know who all the different men were.

I visited Sanda's house with Christian on one Wednesday and it seemed as though they had a routine. We arrived at around midday and sat on the couch in the small front room. Sanda made us both coffee, handed Christian a pile of papers and envelopes, and set about preparing lunch in the adjacent kitchen. On this occasion, five men were also sitting in the house as well as three women and Sanda's youngest daughter, who was not yet old enough to go to school. When we arrived there were four men, including Miron, who variously sat at the kitchen table or went outside or upstairs. They were talking, watching TV or smoking cigarettes. Christian read letters for Sanda and either threw them away, filed them in a large ring binder that he bought for her or set them aside for further action. Sanda then served pasta with ham and cheese sauce to both Christian and me; she then served the men but did not eat herself. She sat down opposite us and watched us eat, asking whether it was good and encouraging us to eat more. She asked Christian whether she should serve this in her restaurant. It seemed that opening a restaurant was Sanda's dream and a common topic of conversation between Christian and her.

Following the meal, Christian began dealing with Sanda's letters, which included an electricity bill that she needed to pay. We begin to prepare to leave when her youngest daughter became upset, crying and throwing herself on the floor. Christian said to me later when he was driving back to his house that he thought it was 'sad' that Miron did not seem to recognise that his daughter was upset nor did he comfort her. He also seemed to be frustrated that he drove Sanda to different appointments at the doctor or the school when Miron had a car and could do this. He seemed particularly annoyed about this when appointments took longer than he had originally planned and made him late for other engagements. His relationship with Sanda was affected by seeing Miron seemingly not working during the day and sitting in the house smoking cigarettes. This placed strain on his relationship with Sanda, especially when he was busy and he thought Miron could help. However, due to Sanda's continued commitment to the Roma church and her hospitality they maintained their contact and he continued to visit her.

Christian and Sanda's interactions demonstrate the subtle ways different gendered understandings shaped their encounters. Christian did not engage with Miron and did not engage with, or gain any understanding of, Miron's work. At the same time his perception of him as lazy, along with his confusion about the role of the other men in the home, placed strain on Sanda. Miron was seen as the 'failed' male citizen who, according to Christian, did not seem to work or help Sanda, for example when looking after her daughter. These encounters were also layered with the individual situations of the actors, as the convergence of Christian and Sanda's religious values formed the basis for sustaining their encounters. Miron did not attend the church; this was therefore another perspective Christian could not share with him. Through focusing solely on Sanda, whom he saw as redeemable through her hosting, her religiosity and her care of her children, he excluded Miron at the same time. This exclusion placed strain on Christian's relationship with Sanda.

Christian's situated position is also important. He described how he wanted to provide support for those who were trying to work but disadvantaged through no fault of their own, such as Sanda's illiteracy because of segregated and inadequate schooling in Romania. Much like Cristina and Louise above, Sanda provided the appropriate conditions for Christian to feel as though he was gaining what he expected from their encounters; he therefore continued their relationship despite his reservations about Miron.

This encounter has shown the very different performances and spaces that are open to mothers and fathers, and the implications of home encounters which closed down opportunities for fathers, but provided the potential for mothers to perform appropriate femininity. Through these caring performances mothers were seen as appropriate objects and receivers of state care.

Processes of male exclusion could also intersect with other subjectivities, as in the case of the only Romanian Roma father I came across who did have success in navigating his position in the eyes of the state – Grigore. Grigore was able to gain a form of secure legal residency specifically because of his position within the Roma church. He was considered by Simon, the pastor, to be a devout member of the congregation and had experience of being a pastor in a church in Moldavia. Simon often expressed the hope that Grigore might one day take over as pastor, and they developed a close relationship on these terms. Simon actively guided Grigore through state bureaucracy, encouraging him to establish a formal legal position and supporting Grigore in these interactions. Again, the position Grigore found himself in was directly related to the situated position of Simon. Simon opened an opportunity for Grigore to perform the role of the appropriate masculine welfare client. He bought him a van so he could register as a scrap metal dealer and delivery driver. Simon also helped Grigore pay for a heavy goods vehicle licence so that he could gain a regular and legitimised form of income. Grigore successfully gained a national insurance number and housing benefit, and became his family's primary negotiator with state bureaucracy assisted by Simon.

Furthermore, as a man with a national insurance number Grigore was quickly able to gain one for his wife (conversely, if mothers gained national insurance numbers their husbands were not given one, highlighting how the male breadwinner model underpins bureaucratic systems). In contrast to most families, Grigore's strong position and the differential treatment between male and female partners and their ability to gain a national insurance number meant that his wife had limited interactions with frontline workers and was not subject to home visitations. This was also notable as Simon was male (most of the frontline workers directly negotiating with families were female) and he served to mediate Grigore's relationship with state processes. While, in general, the processes of home encounters excluded fathers, Grigore's case foregrounds the complex layering of individual situations in differentiating gendered experiences of state processes. The church can be seen to provide a different 'entry point' to negotiations that were within men's access to power, though this was a rare exception.

Gendered marginalisation within families

The following encounter further examines the implications of gendered performances and how they insect with welfare clients' perceived appropriate masculinities and femininities in the home space. This is one encounter of many I was involved in, where state encounters in the home were shut down because fathers had more control over who entered the house and their activities were usually seen as more important than mothers' activities.

I was walking along the high street when I met Doru (a Romanian Roma man I had met previously in a different family's house) smoking outside the Sunshine internet café run by Somali refugees. Doru stopped me and asked "*So kheres rakli? Kai zhas?*" ("What's going on young [non-Roma] lady? Where are you going?"). We began a conversation and he was telling me about how he loved living in Madrid but that there was nothing there now when his oldest son, Puju, emerged from the internet café. He was followed by one of the Somalis who worked there. Referring to Doru, the man from the cafe said "This guy is a good man – he comes into my shop all the time. Spanish man – you should come too. He is good customer." They began speaking in Spanish to each other before he went back into the shop. As the café owner left, Doru invited me for coffee to meet his wife Lenuţa.

Puju drove us to the house and when we entered the small front room I immediately recognised Doru's daughter-in-law, Bianca, who was married to Doru's second son. Bianca told me she used to have '*socialo*' (child benefit) but it had stopped and she didn't know why. She had also given birth three weeks ago to a baby girl, Catina. I offered to tell Paula, as she already had a connection with Bianca and might be able to help her regain her child benefit.

At this point Puju came into the room and sat next to me on the couch. He told me he had three children and his wife had left the UK to live in Spain with another man. He had lived in Luton for 10 months, trying to find work but he hadn't been able to find anything. He was trying to buy and sell second-hand cars that he found on the internet to support his family. His three sons ran around the room while Lenuţa, Puju's mother, made me coffee and tried to put it down somewhere where the three boys wouldn't knock into it. I recognised Lenuţa because she begged outside the local doctor's surgery when it wasn't raining. Neither of us acknowledged that we had seen each other many times in that context. I held the coffee in my hands and thanked her before she took a seat at the other end of the room to watch the conversation with her son unfold. Filip was 7, Versace was 5 and Marco was 2 years old. The oldest two boys had been born in Spain and had never attended school. I asked Puju whether he wanted to register the children in school but he refused. He said sharply that he didn't want anyone coming to the house but he did want to know how he could get 'socialo' to help pay for the children. He explained that he couldn't pay for the clothes and the food in the school. He told me he must have socialo first, and then the children could go to school.

Puju seemed aware that becoming visible to frontline workers had concomitant responsibilities. He did not seem to consider that engaging with frontline workers might be a pathway to gaining his rights and entitlements, but rather as entering into (potentially dangerous) negotiations that he may not be able to effectively manage. He did not have the resources to fulfil these negotiations and seemed to fear revealing his family to surveillance. His concerns closed down the opportunity for Bianca to have home visits to help her gain support for her children, which she was entitled to receive as she had gained indefinite leave to remain as a child. However, the reticence of Puju seemed to affect her and she told me that she also didn't want me to call Paula about her new baby and her child benefit.

Puju's reaction draws attention to how complex legal statuses of different family members and the gendered positions within the house intertwine with home encounters to impede access to entitlements. This interaction also highlights the importance of mothers' conversations about their interactions with different frontline workers and the spaces that they open for each other, and the effects of the absence of the details of these conversations and actions between men. For example, in the previous chapter I presented how Georgeta was happy for Lisa, the support worker for Pathways, to come to her house to talk about gaining a national insurance number. She had heard from her sister-in-law Violeta that a cleaning job had enabled her to gain a national insurance number. Not only had she been told this, but she had visited Violeta's house and was aware of the better condition of her house and, as Georgeta described it "She slept well, ate well and drank well," meaning that she had few worries. Romanian Roma mothers exchanged this information through conversations on mobile phones (when they had credit) or at the Roma church. Although information was exchanged in different ways depending on the relationship between mothers (and could therefore sometimes include misinformation), the processes of engaging with frontline workers with regard to children was not discussed among fathers in my experience of living my everyday life with families. Not only did mothers discuss interactions with frontline workers, but they also introduced mothers to frontline workers. For example, when Paula, the diversity and equality education officer, visited Margereta, she called Denisa, who was living around the corner, to come round and ask Paula a question about moving her son to school that was closer to her house. Mothers could be introduced to a frontline worker in a different house before they encountered them in their own home, creating some understanding and familiarity in their relationship before they entered their home (the importance of the trajectory entering the home for how relationships unfold was established in Chapter Three).

The foregrounding of mothers in interactions in state processes alludes to an important nuance in the way gender roles are negotiated. Mothers take on these roles as a reflection of their assessment of how men and women are perceived by frontline workers and others. The frontline workers they encounter are mostly interested in mothers and their children and their focus is directed towards them. Frontline workers are also women and therefore mothers can draw on their shared experiences (such as being mothers or wives or daughters). For example, the relationship between Maria and Lisa was underpinned by their shared experience of being single mothers as described in Chapter Two, which allowed them to laugh and joke with each other about finding a new partner.

To return to Puju, although he potentially had a pathway to engage with frontline workers, and was aware of examples where particular frontline workers had been very helpful to other members of his extended family, he was very reticent to engage with actors himself. He did not have the networks, resources or previous experiences that may have made him more likely to engage with frontline workers. He had been excluded from a subject position where he would be able to perform the appropriate welfare client as a single man without a job.

Puju's experience as a single father excluded him from conversations that might have helped him to understand the roles of different frontline workers (and the performances required to engage them). His wider family experience of negative interactions with local frontline workers seemed to shape his decisions to evade all further interactions, even when they may have been open (and potentially beneficial) to him. In this way, fathers can be seen to have a different situated position and experience from mothers, which could limit both fathers' and mothers' access to the information and resources that could help them negotiate their own relationship with forms of the state.

The salience of home encounters, particularly when mothers gained state resources through their performances within the home, disrupted and unsettled gendered relationships. This is particularly clear in the case of Cristina, a migrant mother who (as documented earlier) was highly successful in negotiating her relationship with a variety of frontline workers through home encounters. As Cristina's home encounters became more regular, and she was able to use them to gain access to resources and information, the changing family dynamics caused strain on her relationship with her husband, Dan.

As Dan came to perceive Cristina's apparent skill at negotiating with frontline workers, he began asking her to interact with people on his behalf. On one occasion, he asked me to show him how to get to the tax office and, when I accompanied him, he took Cristina along and told her to speak to speak to HMRC services (on the telephone) on his behalf. Cristina was very uncomfortable about this request and she became very shy and told me that she didn't want to speak on the phone because she was embarrassed about her English. On another occasion, she had gained support from a church volunteer to teach her English. The volunteer visited Cristina at her home on Fridays. Cristina had organised to teach her how to make *sarmalay* (stuffed cabbages) which was a dish reserved for special occasions such as Christmas or Easter. I was also in the house at this time and joined in the activity. The cooking took much longer than we had expected because Cristina could not afford mince so we chopped off-cuts of pork finely by hand (with very blunt knives), which took around two hours. Dan (who had been coming and going throughout the morning) returned home, expecting Cristina to come with him to sell vegetable peelers on the street. They had to time the sales carefully as they didn't have a permit. Cristina wanted to continue cooking and as the delay in leaving continued, Dan became increasingly agitated and angry with Cristina. Cristina wanted to finish cooking the *sarmarlay,* as we learned when we had finished that she had planned to give the volunteer half the food to take away with her as a gift in exchange for coming to visit her.

At that moment this seemed to alter the balance in her willingness to leave the house and work with Dan, or for Dan to control the timings of activities. By this time, Cristina had gained a national insurance number and had strong independent relationships with frontline workers through her successful negotiation of home encounters. This caused particular strain on their relationship. Cristina criticised Dan for what he spent money on. She told me one day that she kept asking Dan to put credit on her phone but he hadn't. He was happy that he could ring her, but didn't want her ringing anyone else. However, the SIM card expired and that number was on all of her documents for benefits and for the hospital. She explained that it was a cheap SIM card so the numbers couldn't be retrieved. She was angry at him because it had all of her numbers on it and it was the number that frontline workers used to contact her. She continued to complain that Dan had changed their car three times and that this was very expensive but she had had to sell her clothes just to buy medicated olive oil for the children's ears (they all had an ear infection because the house was very damp).

On a different occasion Dan had had a particularly hard day at work on the construction site where his boss had told him that he had to do 'very hard work' by himself. Cristina began quizzing him about a 'yellow card' (a work permit). She was worried that he needed one because she heard from a 'gazho' (a non-Roma man) that the rules had changed and now to get a national insurance number, a yellow card was required. Dan retorted that he was going to break his back by working and then she would be pushing him 'in a wheel chair' because his work was so hard. He continued that he was going to leave her and go back to Romania and relax, "no children or nothing". He said to me, "She is the boss – no? The big boss but just a cleaner," referring to her successful national insurance number application through her self-employed cleaning business. Cristina began to swear at him and he replied "Thank you darling – thank you for saying things so nicely to me," and then stated that he was not going to work tomorrow. At one point Cristina considered leaving Dan because of the strain on their relationship throughout this process. The trajectory of her home encounters (from which Dan was excluded) created shifts in Cristina's relationships, resources and understandings, all of which interwove with her position to deeply unsettle their family and gender relationships.

Dan had been excluded from gaining a national insurance number because his self-employed work doing gardening and other small construction jobs had not been considered to be 'genuine' because he was not paid enough money to support his family. In contrast, Cristina's self-employed cleaning business, although she had earned less than Dan, had been deemed 'genuine' and she had gained a national insurance number. In addition, as mentioned throughout the book, home encounters gave

Cristina (constrained) opportunities to build relationships with church volunteers as she took on the role of negotiating on behalf of her family. Cristina's access to power in the form of performing appropriate mothering created strain in her relationship with Dan, which was exacerbated by their uncertain status in the UK and the state's refusal to legitimise Dan's work.

Gendered marginalisation between family and state

So far this chapter has demonstrated how mothers had positions open to them through performing appropriate care and how a similar subject position was not open to fathers as appropriate masculine welfare clients. It has reviewed how the home space exacerbated men's positions as they were viewed as lazy and unwilling to work, and how fathers' exclusion from legitimised subject positions constrained mothers. It has also detailed how the space of the house and the particular conditions that form the home encounter (see Chapter Four) constrained mothers when they were unable to reconcile their many different roles.

A case in point is the relationship between church volunteer Christian, migrant mother Violeta, and Violeta's sister-in-law, Georgeta. The following encounter serves to bring together a number of different strands that have been developed in this book: the opportunities and constraints opened by welfare encounters taking place in the home (Chapter Four); the implications of the shifting faces of the state in enacting welfare (Chapter Two); the effects of basing welfare decisions on charity and compassion rather than rights (Chapter Two); and the gendered expectations of welfare clients that take on particular salience under these conditions (this chapter).

Violeta had become isolated from her wider family when her husband died and, later, when she was baptised. However, this had begun to change in 2013 and she happily told me that on Christmas Day Georgeta and her brother's family had come to her house to celebrate. She particularly emphasised that it was the first time they had all come to the house as a family, which seemed very meaningful to her as a marker of better relations. Around this time Violeta began to refuse offers of help from Christian, a church volunteer who had previously provided her with regular support. One afternoon, Christian, Violeta and I were driving in Christian's car when Christian decided he was going to drop off something for Georgeta. At this point Violeta became agitated and asked to be let out. She did not want Georgeta to know that she had been in the car with Christian. She insisted forcefully and Christian let her out of the car; following our visit to Georgeta, we picked her up to take her home. Christian had also offered to teach Violeta English but she had refused.

I was living with Violeta at this time. A week or so after the incident in the car, Violeta told me that she and Georgeta had lived together in Rome where they had had a big argument about a local NGO worker. He had helped Violeta gain a job in a local primary school as a teaching assistant, but had been unable to find a similar position for Georgeta. Violeta also told me that she had been in an intimate relationship with this NGO worker, which had upset Georgeta because she felt Violeta had received preferential treatment. Violeta seemed fearful of jeopardising her reconciliation with some family members on account of being seen with Christian and Georgeta's knowledge about her previous relationship with the NGO worker in Italy.

Concurrently, Christian had been supporting Georgeta but had tried to disengage when she had asked him for help to pay the rent. Georgeta blamed Violeta for Christian's reticence to visit the house. Georgeta felt that Violeta was taking up too much of Christian's time and therefore he couldn't help her, a situation she believed had happened before in Rome. There were also rumours that Christian and Violeta were having an intimate relationship. This made Violeta uncomfortable. She stated to me that "God knows my heart" (*o del genel murro yillo*). Mindful of the rumours, Violeta rebuffed Christian's offer to teach her English in order to dispel gossip and to maintain valuable family ties. The gendered perceptions of Violeta's home encounters with Christian acted to destabilise their relationship and to cut off future encounters that might have benefited Violeta (such as improving her English).

In this way, disjunctures in different actors' information and understandings interweave with individually situated positions and complex life histories, which are layered on top of gendered performances within encounters. Frontline workers and volunteers are often not aware of these histories but (in this example combined with the power of rumours, see Chapter Three) they fundamentally alter relationships and shift performances. For Romanian Roma, engaging with volunteers as 'faces of the state' can therefore directly shape their parameters of performances. The encounter has also illustrated how Romanian Roma families tried to create their own boundaries regarding home encounters, many of which were not linked to gaining rights and entitlements but rather family histories, social position and gendered expectations.

Final remarks

Notions of the 'deserving' welfare client as a morally legitimate receiver of care are highly gendered. This chapter has drawn out the gendered performances within, and their implications for, home encounters. It has demonstrated how home encounters open up spaces for mothers to perform appropriate femininity through being appropriate subjects of care. Romanian Roma mothers who learn to give the right amount of space, silence, gratitude and respect create the conditions for situated frontline workers to recognise them as appropriate caring subjects. Crucially, these performances must also create the space for frontline workers to feel as though they themselves are appropriate caring subjects. This is a significant intervention in the literature on the politics of care through situating all social actors, their manifold caring positions (as subjects and objects of care) and how these affect the politics of belonging.

Fathers are excluded from these constellations of caring relationships. Their work is deemed as 'not genuine' by the state (see Chapter Two for discussing of 'not genuine self-employed work'). Unlike mothers, fathers have no subject position to be seen as an appropriate receiver of state care, thereby creating further strain for mothers. In some circumstances, mothers portray themselves as 'single' because their husbands' non-legitimate work threatens to sully and undermine the careful performances required to maintain these highly contingent relationships with frontline workers. Home encounters make this more difficult because intimate relations are revealed to frontline workers.

This chapter adds to the literature on migrant mothers' citizenship by examining their wider networks of relationships and how these create increasing 'work' for mothers. Erel and colleagues (2018: 69) have highlighted the emotional costs of migrant women's relegation to low-paid jobs in the reproductive sector and the repercussions this has for their constitution as caring and cultural subjects. This chapter extends the literature to examine the interrelated costs for families, frontline workers and volunteers. The exclusion of fathers from the labour market creates manifold consequences for their families. These particularly affect mothers, both in terms of the amount of work they undertake in managing their own performances and because men's exclusion acts to further jeopardise their work in trying to maintain 'good motherhood'. When men are deemed 'lazy' it sullies their families' reputations.

In addition, they also create costs for (female) frontline workers who are also subjects of state care. It is vital to remember the situated positions of the frontline workers (and the volunteers they work with), whose own gendered situated position brings specific perspectives to the home encounter. Frontline workers are also subject to additional, often unrecognised, work, as they attempt to balance complex pressures and targets in their roles (Chapter Two). As has been traced in earlier descriptions of encounters, many frontline workers are also mothers, and bring their own values about gender and family roles to their interactions. For instance, Lisa (Pathways support worker) formed a particular bond with Maria, and viewed Maria as 'deserving', based in part on a shared narrative of their experiences as single parents. Kay (church volunteer) often cited her personal experience of her son's divorce and separation from his child as framing her positive feelings towards what she perceived as Cristina's strong family values. Paula also brought her own experience as a mother to bear, at one point commenting on the perceived lack of stimulation provided to the Romanian Roma children that "My kids were playing with building blocks from 4 months [old]." The wider lens of the safeguarding agenda, in which all the frontline workers have been trained, both added to and reproduced these perceptions of the importance of providing 'good motherhood' as it was understood from the perspective of the UK welfare state. At the same time, the gendered dynamics of the home encounter (typically comprising interactions between women) foregrounds how many men were differentially included and how men could act to facilitate or hinder encounters.

The gendered nature of the home encounter is interwoven with different, individually situated positions, entangling racialised identities, social statuses, previous experiences, religion and family expectations. These different layers all act to create complex and often contradictory processes with the potential to unsettle gender dynamics within families, foregrounding the contradictory aims of the frontline workers who, through their focus solely on mothers, act to constrain them further.

Home encounters not only have implications for families' legal statuses and life chances in the UK, but have deep consequences for relationships within families. The fact of encounters taking place in the home opens up a wider range of actions, expectations and perspectives through which assessments can be based. Encounters in the home can create tensions, such as engaging with male volunteers in 'private' space (which would not happen if encounters took place in a community centre or church) and therefore have to be carefully managed by Romanian Roma mothers. Chapter Four explored how the presence of frontline workers shifted understandings of the home space and the kinds of performances that could take place. This chapter has focused on how these encounters have direct implications for families' intimate relationships and how these affect families' negotiations of political belonging.

The home encounter is the site where access to state resources is negotiated and where state forms are reproduced. Norms and forms of social reproduction are judged within this space and directly affect whether mothers are able to realise their rights and secure residency statuses for their families. The judgement of their practices of social reproduction directly affects state reproduction and the terms on which they can be conceived as belonging. The politics of care and the politics of belonging are deeply entwined for these families who are subject to the intense surveillance of their everyday practices in their homes.

Interlude | Losing Sophia and Angela

I meet Sophia walking down the street with Armando, who is now 13 months old. She is pushing a buggy which is also laden with shopping bags hanging over the handle bars. The buggy looks old and one of the wheels isn't working properly. It seems to be taking all of her energy to push it through the residential backstreets. She tells me to come with her because she has moved to a different house. I offer to push the buggy but after I try and am completely unable to steer it along the pavement, I take the shopping bags and walk along beside her. She tells me she has been refused child benefit for the second time in London. She has indefinite leave to remain and has a national insurance number but she has been refused and she doesn't know why. We arrive at the house and it seems very different from the other houses I have previously visited. It is not a small Victorian terrace but a bungalow. When we enter it has many different rooms with locks on the doors, separated by small dark corridors. There is a large kitchen and living room that are almost entirely empty and bare apart from three couches which look as though they have been made for an office waiting room. They have grey plastic cushions and wooden frames. There are large glass doors that open out to a large grassy back garden. There are two men at the bottom of the garden looking into cages full of dogs. Sophia tells me that this is the landlord who is breeding dogs. Armando has fallen asleep so Sophia takes me to her room and places Armando in a drawer on the floor that she is using for a cot. We return to the kitchen where she begins to unpack the shopping she has just bought and begins to make chips out of a large bag of potatoes.

Another young woman comes into the room. She introduces herself as Angela and switches from *Romanës* to English when she hears my English accent. I tell her that her English is excellent and she replies that she first came to England when she was 12 years old to get married and she learnt to speak by communicating in shops in London. Over the course of next two weeks I visit Sophia and Angela in this house. It emerges that there are no intergenerational families living there, only young couples or single men and women. No one seems to be related although they all speak *Romanës*. I gradually learn from Angela that she came to England with her father in a car when she was 12. She says that at this time she was "illegal" because it was "before Europe". As she tells me this story she kicks off her sandals and curls her legs up under herself at one end of the grey plastic couch. She was living in East Croydon and got married at 13 and had a baby. Her son will be 9 years old next month. She explains that she "played with the Home Office" because she didn't have any documents, hadn't applied for asylum and lived without seeing anyone apart from her family and people she met in the shops.

She lived with her husband's family, looking after her son and the other children and cleaning and tidying the house. However, when she had her second baby in the hospital everything changed and there was a "big problem". When she got home from the hospital the police came to the house and were asking for her by her name. "They come to the house and ask my name. Then they put me on plane back to Romania." She returned to her parents' house in central Romania. However, her son and her new baby stayed with their father and family in East Croydon. She doesn't have a birth certificate for either of them or any documents and isn't sure if they are still in East Croydon. She said that she was happy to "run away" from her husband's family but that she wants her children but doesn't know how to start to look for them.

I tried to continue visiting Angela and Sophia but when I returned after one week they had moved away and I didn't see either of them again.

6

Borders and intimate state encounters

'You need to know where they have come from, who they are married to or not, whether children are in school, whether there is domestic abuse. You have to ask the right questions, and give the right information, because if you have a lack of understanding about what the legalities are you could easily be responsible for someone being deported...'

This extract is taken from an interview I conducted in 2013 with Clare, head of a children's centre in Luton, UK. She clearly expressed her confusion about UK migration policies and the unwanted responsibility and life-changing decision-making power that had recently befallen her and her employees. In the same interview Clare described the large budget cuts the children's centre had to make in the previous three years. It would be a familiar story for anyone working in public services in the UK. She had no 'core funding' for her centre. Instead, all of her budget was ring-fenced and targeted for particular projects, such as parenting classes. One of her main concerns was to register and engage with 'vulnerable' mothers in her local area.

As we have already seen, locating encounters with the state in the home changes the nature of any negotiations with frontline workers (Chapter Four) and has gendered effects on the intimate everyday lives of Romanian Roma families (Chapter Five). This chapter will show how home encounters go to the heart of negotiations over access to state resources and contestations of migrants' belonging and explores how these intractable issues are reconciled by individual, low-level frontline workers or volunteers who have wide areas of discretion, increasing responsibilities and decreasing resources. In order to make sense of their roles they draw on their own life experiences, professional training and relationships within the network of frontline workers. It is also worth reiterating here that the patterns that emerge through home encounters are shaped by the UK policy context of the hostile environment and the restructuring of the local authority (Chapter Two), which directly affect the life chances of migrants and our understanding of the governance of marginalisation in the UK (Humphris 2018a).

The home encounter opens spaces for some mothers to develop long-term, personal connections with frontline workers that blur formal bureaucratic roles with informal relationships. These intimate state encounters are both forms of hyper-surveillance and spaces of constrained opportunities to gain a more secure legal status in the UK (Chapter Four). This chapter explores how practices of social reproduction (Laslett and Brenner 1989) and the politics of care (Tronto, 2013) are fundamental to decisions regarding formal legal residency statuses, state reproduction and the politics of belonging (Yuval Davis 1997).

Governing through intimate state encounters means that personal entanglements, frustrations, confusions, comforts and pleasures become part of how negotiations of political belonging take place. Crucially, only those who are judged as 'deserving' and therefore 'morally legitimate' are considered for additional informal support and the receipt of care needed to begin formal processes of securing rights in the UK. Those who are not deemed as 'deserving' experience painful acts of exclusion through refusals to care (Ticktin 2011; Muehlebach 2012; Chauvin and Garcés-Mascareñas 2014). This chapter extends the literature to argue through shifting focus from 'acts' to 'encounters' we can see frontline workers' decisions are inextricably linked to the situated positions of all social actors. In particular, migrant mothers need to create the conditions for frontline workers to perceive they are fulfilling the caring role they set out for themselves; thus adherence to particular forms and norms of behaviour in intimate and domestic space, rather than rights or entitlements, is the basis on which Romanian Roma migrants' belonging to the nation-state is based.

The chapter is structured as follows. First, through exploring three relationships in greater depth I trace how care and belonging are interrelated through intimate state encounters. The relationship between Ecaterina and Rosemary demonstrates the disjuncture of values that led to families (re)becoming 'invisible' to state processes and how governing through intimate state encounters provided frontline workers with moral justification for marginalising Romanian Roma. The second and third relationships explore how families were able to gain a formal residency status through strong intimate bonds where frontline workers are 'kinned' and become like family members. The ethnographic examples in this section demonstrate the crucial role where one person mediates (or not) the relationship between migrants and their political membership. Frontline workers draw heavily on their own experiences to make sense of their decisions within these contexts. I argue that rather than 'state acts' these home visits are 'intimate state encounters', which reflect the processual and relationally co-produced nature of these encounters (while acknowledging asymmetries of power).

Second, this chapter addresses the stakes that are involved in these encounters, as frontline actors act as gatekeepers not only to the welfare state but also to the territory of the nation-state. I demonstrate how bordering mechanisms become 'activated' across the mother-child relationship through the home encounter. Frontline workers become not only moral guardians over state resources but border guards over the state territory. Families have to choose between whether to lose their children or move. These processes give rise to the 'silent sorting' of Romanian Roma across local or national boundaries.[51]

Un/Domesticating the state: care and refusal in intimate state encounters

The process of entering the home makes families' wider circumstances visible to frontline workers, so that relationships, family organisation, objects in the home, routines and all manner of activities that take place are laid bare to frontline workers, particularly when they 'pop in' unannounced at all times of day and early evening. All of these aspects are folded into the encounter and exacerbate the already devalued label of Romanian Roma, constraining mothers' room for manoeuvre (Chapter Four). The different trajectories and relationships that develop between differently situated actors then interact with the substantial discretionary scope in frontline workers' roles, by which they 'interpret rules and programs following their own preferences or prejudices' (Dubois 2014b: 39). In some cases, these roles remain narrow, as frontline workers can act to reinforce their specific understanding of the responsibilities to the children (as opposed to the wider family) and draw boundaries around their roles. In others, frontline workers' situated understandings and values around 'deservingness', and the ways that the home encounter widens their lenses to encompass the broader situations of the families, serves to expand their roles. Over time, these understandings are relationally reproduced in repeated interactions between the same frontline workers and families, creating trajectories that further widen frontline workers' involvement with myriad aspects of Romanian Roma relationships with different state forms. Recalling Chapter Two, these encounters relationally 'make up' the state for Romanian Roma (Painter 1995; Mitchell 2001; Mountz 2003). The following examples will look at some of the ways in which Romanian Roma were able to negotiate this access through, and because of, the home encounter.

Throughout this book, as we have looked deeper at home encounters, we have seen how volunteers (particularly though the church) are entwined with frontline workers and in some cases undertake work for them. I argue that the interactions with these 'non-state' actors can still take on the form of a 'state act' in the sense Dubois understands, because they can equally determine access to (public) resources. However, the crucial difference is that volunteers do not procedurally have to try to treat everyone equally (see Chapter Two). Their decisions to engage with Romanian Roma are not through the guidelines of their employment but through adherence to shared values (Humphris 2018a). As will be shown below, this involvement of volunteers to conduct 'state acts' increases the salience of performances of particular kinds of values (which may also be contradictory). This individualisation and diffusion of discretionary state power also allows Romanian Roma to become further marginalised and slip into 'invisibility', despite being eligible for, or having legal status, in the UK and recourse to public funds. The hyper-surveillance of the home therefore also widens the scope for further marginalisation of Romanian Roma families.

As detailed in previous chapters, the pressures on frontline workers and the limited resources available led to the church being 'co-opted' as part of a shifting and informal bureaucratic strategy to reach these families. Frontline workers often conducted home visits together with (church) volunteers, who would be recommended to the families as being able to help them access resources. Recalling Chapter Two, volunteers became a key part of how Romanian Roma experienced state processes, and took on 'faces of the state'. The ways in which different Romanian Roma experienced state forms were also situated according to their individual positions and relationships with the church. The ethnographic examples that follow demonstrate the complex ways in which individually situated positions and the intertwining roles of frontline workers and (church) volunteers as 'faces of the state' acted to reform and continually expand the role of the home visit to become more than a singular 'state act' but a form of processual and relationally co-produced intimate state encounters. This has substantial implications for our understanding of the nature of these specifically located 'intimate state encounters', as well as implications for the very real differences in how individuals are able to negotiate their roles as potential citizens.

The home encounter created, and was the site for, different processes through which frontline workers' perceptions of 'deservingness' and scope for discretionary decisions broadened their understanding of their roles. Home encounters had practical implications in facilitating political belonging for those families who were able to build relationships with local frontline workers. This was in contrast to a number of encounters, where the differential expectations and understandings of home encounters served to 'gatekeep' access to the welfare state through individual families' relationships with frontline workers, allowing them to become further marginalised. In part, this marginalisation was due to the nature of governing through intimate state encounters, which were highly individualised and widened areas of discretionary decision making.

Rosemary and Ecaterina

A case in point is Rosemary (church volunteer) who initially worked to support Ecaterina but whose perception of her changed over a series of encounters over three months before coming to regard Ecaterina as a chaotic, ungrateful and therefore 'undeserving' mother. Rosemary decided to stop visiting Ecaterina and stopped helping her liaise with the school for her children and apply for housing and child benefit (even though Cezar, Ecaterina's husband, had a national insurance number and was therefore eligible for them).

The following ethnographic encounters build on this understanding of how 'success' and 'failure' (as perceived by frontline workers) in home encounters came to constitute a specific form of intimate state encounter. These encounters illustrate the complex interweaving of different perceptions and values regarding children, families, the label of Romanian Roma, and the roles of the frontline workers and the church in the home encounter.

Rosemary was an English volunteer at the Roma church (*khangheri*). She had previously been involved in teaching the children of one family from Bucharest who were waiting to be enrolled in school. She had also been a missionary in Bangladesh and had taught English to children of recently arrived migrants for two decades. This encounter involves Rosemary's encounters with Romanian Roma couple Cezar and Ecaterina and their three children, who arrived in Luton having previously lived in Blackburn and Tottenham. The father of the children, Cezar, gained a national insurance number from his scrap metal business. They had moved to a small terraced house with another family with three children. There were also many different single men who stayed in the house for varying amounts of time, ranging from a couple of days to a few months. Cezar could speak and write English but Ecaterina, his wife, could do neither. As Cezar was often absent for long periods of time working with cousins in London, Ecaterina could not understand or act on any letters or documents sent to the house. Ecaterina became 'visible' to frontline workers initially when Simon (the pastor) and Kassia (children's centre family support worker) conducted home visits together to register families. Again, Rosemary's experiences illustrate how volunteers became a 'face of the state' through relationships that developed through the home encounter. Following registration, Simon referred Rosemary to help Ecaterina and suggested that she made home visits. Rosemary took on a role similar to that of a children's centre family support worker. She also acted as a liaison between the family and the local school, where she had been a governor. Ecaterina asked Rosemary to look at various documents when she visited. Rosemary, who felt that this would help her gain a better relationship with the family and would ultimately help the children, began to take on more of these tasks and further expanded this role.

On one occasion, Rosemary and I were drinking tea in a café and talking about her experiences, when she described how Ecaterina's family reminded her of the Bangladeshi families she used to teach. These resonances were placed in terms of the material aspects of the house, which she used to evaluate the relationships between Ecaterina and her children: "If I took around pencil and paper then they would be on the top shelf out of the way – the children would not be able to reach them." She explained fondly that there was one boy from Sylhet whom she began teaching at 7 years old. His parents were illiterate and the school had asked for Rosemary to 'take charge of this child'. She explained that she had worked with him for a long time and now he was a family worker in a school. "He is married and has a 1 year old. I went round to his house and there were books and toys all over the place. I almost said – this is like a normal house!" She continued, "It probably won't work with the women, but I can put in the time with the children and this is what will pay off, if they are going to stay here." A certain constellation of understandings of childhood and value is played out through Rosemary's narrative. Rosemary justified her volunteering and investment of time through the parenting of the next generation of children. Her comment 'this is like a normal house' confirms that her efforts created a value she recognised that was identified through material objects related to children (Chapter Four). She had invested in the future of the child, which she felt had been reciprocated by how her former student acted as a parent towards his own children.

Her narrative also highlights a feature that was considered to be a 'Roma' trait, foregrounding the figure of the racialised migrant mother. She explained that she thought the family wouldn't stay in Luton and therefore her efforts would not be reciprocated in the same way. Her assessment can be attributed to an essentialised view of 'Roma-ness' based on nomadic roots and seemingly confirmed by the nature of this household, with many different men coming and going. In fact, from my experience, Roma men moved quickly due to the irregularity and informal nature of their work, typically in construction, factories, seasonal agricultural work or manual labour.

Similar essentialised views emerged in another aspect of the way that Rosemary tried to consolidate and make sense of her experience with this family and her previous experience of teaching English. In one instance, she became dismayed by Ecaterina and couldn't understand her behaviour. This was infused with certain views regarding the correct behaviour of children and parenting. She explained:

'I went round and took colouring [materials] and two balls. Horia took the ball and then refused to give it back. The parents have no desire to help them behave differently. Ecaterina just let him do it – did not help to educate him. I keep reminding myself that they are coming from a completely different culture and that is why they are like this. They want to keep everything but they don't keep it. I spend a long time making and laminating things but then we only use them for two seconds and then they nab them and put them in their pocket and then I never see them again. It is like living in a wagon isn't it? If your whole family is living in one room then you don't keep things do you?'

Rosemary became particularly annoyed that Ecaterina was in the kitchen cooking and playing loud music when she was trying to teach the children. The behaviour of Ecaterina and her perceived disregard of the materials that Rosemary created to teach the children made Rosemary feel as though she wasn't valued. On one occasion, Ecaterina left the house and the children in Rosemary's care. Ecaterina told me that it was good to have the children in the house while she went to look for scrap metal. Rosemary was assisting the economy of the family but she didn't recognise it. Rather, after this incident Rosemary complained to me that Ecaterina had just left her with the children and was therefore taking her for granted. Rosemary also rationalised the family's behaviour as being linked with mobility and movement: "I wouldn't be surprised if they suddenly disappear." Ideas linked to itinerant lifestyles are how she understood the act of throwing out material things on which she has placed time, effort and value, and resonate with particular stigmatised views of Gypsies along with long-standing historical tropes about the poor being feckless and shiftless through vagrancy and are therefore not 'hard working'.

Rosemary found it increasingly difficult to understand Ecaterina's behaviour and eventually stopped going to her house. In particular, the incident of throwing out toys clashed with Rosemary's values of what constituted good mothering, and it derailed the relationship. She also stopped filling in Ecaterina's forms and managing her bureaucratic identity. Cezar and Ecaterina did not claim any social assistance because, although Cezar had a national insurance number, child benefit had been refused because he did not have a right to reside. Without the assistance from Rosemary, who had been compiling the documents to appeal this decision, the family withdrew from all bureaucratic processes despite their entitlements.

Ecaterina's relationship with frontline workers thus began from an initial home encounter with both a frontline worker and a church volunteer, which led in turn to a series of home encounters with another church volunteer, in the course of which support was initially provided in a very similar form to that of a frontline worker (and had the same understanding in Ecaterina's experience). Rosemary's assessment of these encounters was linked to racialised perceptions and disjuncture in different understandings of the arrangement and performance of the home space. Rosemary also felt consistently both unwanted and taken for granted. Ecaterina was not creating the environment for Rosemary to perform the role that she wanted to fulfil in the house. Rosemary had encouraged the children to call her Baba (grandmother) and wanted to feel useful and needed. She was an older woman who had never had children and had no family close by. She seemed to be undertaking volunteering because it resonated with her Baptist faith but also to find the comfort of a large family and the desire to the needed. She also drew on her previous experience of being an English teacher to a family from Sylhet and contrasted this experience with Ecaterina's family. The differences did not resonate with Rosemary and therefore she retreated from the relationship. Once more Ecaterina became 'invisible' and without access to categories or resources she might otherwise have gained.

This illustrates the complex ways that different processes and roles interweave through the home encounter, 'gatekeeping' access to the welfare state and foregrounding the role of the home encounter as a specifically located intimate state encounter. Intimate state encounters are based on depoliticised forms of sympathetic action and are how Romanian

Roma experience the state and how they must negotiate access to state resources.

The dissolution of Rosemary and Ecaterina's relationship was linked to racialised perceptions and ideas linked to hard-working families and moral discourses of parenting, but also the situated position of Rosemary and her desire to fulfil a particular role within the family. This example illustrates that when volunteers assume gatekeeping roles (often unwillingly) their own moral judgements shape their support and also justify their withdrawal. In a hostile and austere context these conflicts of values determined whether families were able to gain legal residency. This example shows how performances of behaviours – here, the performances of motherhood and care – effectively became the border that new migrants must cross.

Christian and Violeta

The trajectory of Violeta represents the same process of highly moralised and individualised forms of state care but with the contrasting result. The aim of expanding on this relationship is to show the contingency on which some families were able to gain a form of political belonging through appropriate practices of belonging. Crucially these practices must resonate with the frontline workers' gendered perceptions of the 'good citizen' *and also* their own perceptions of themselves as good citizens within the welfare state apparatus. The relationship between Christian and Violeta explores the wide-ranging support that can stem from the different processes related to the home encounter, the interweaving of state and church actors, and the variations of forms and norms of belonging that are forged through contingent care. Violeta had six children whom she supported alone because her husband had died in Italy two years previously. Her oldest daughter was married and she lived with her remaining five children who ranged from 16 to 5 years old. When Violeta first moved to the UK she stayed with her brother and his family, who had migrated earlier and gained indefinite leave to remain. Paula (who had a good relationship with Violeta's sister-in-law, Margereta) had met Violeta and her children and registered them in school. Violeta had an argument with Margereta and moved to a small privately rented terraced house in a slum-like condition.

Violeta told me she refused to beg (*me chi zhav te mangav*) and sold roses at night outside the local cinema to provide for her children. When I was living with Violeta we had many conversations about this difficult time when she first moved to the UK. In particular she told me that she didn't like Paula because she had visited her in her small terraced house shortly after she had moved in. She described her worry (*ingrisimay*) because the house was in a very bad condition but it was all she could afford from selling roses (and she was already getting into debt). When Paula visited her house she made her feel "not good" (*chi lasho*). A teacher from Violeta's son's primary school had also accompanied Paula. This teacher told Paula that Violeta's children always came to school and that they were well behaved. Violeta felt protected by the teacher and described how she was '*indiano*' and wore a headscarf like Violeta. From that point forward, Violeta avoided contact with Paula.

Simon, who was to become the pastor of the Roma church, had also begun to visit Violeta frequently during this time. Violeta had become very religious about a year earlier when she made 'a promise' with God following the recovery of her eldest son from meningitis. She promised to stop smoking and live a 'straight life for Jesus'. The frequency of Simon's visits during this time and the help he provided often changed in Violeta's narratives to me over the course of the four months that I was living with her and having conversations about her life. Simon invited Violeta and her children to his church on Sunday mornings and picked her up in his car and took her home. Simon also related how at times Violeta became angry when he spent time with other families. She stated that families with many male members didn't need Simon's help, asserting: "I am alone" (*me som korkorro*). Violeta often repeated her commitment to God, saying "I don't have a boss [husband], my boss is above" (*nai man bosso, murre bosso si opre*). Violeta began to invite families (women and children) to her house to talk about the role Jesus had played in her life. The numbers of people at these meetings grew as increasing numbers of relatives moved to Luton, and the meetings become a social event for mothers (men did not attend). At this time, Simon met a Methodist minister, Leslie, conducting outreach work in the area. The local population had become predominantly Muslim, and the two churches located in the area had dwindling congregations. Simon's suggestion to begin a service in the 'Romani language' was agreed and services began on Wednesday evenings. Simon also organised the hire of a minibus to pick up those who wanted to attend. Women did not drive and although many men drove, they very rarely attended and did not drive their relatives to the church. Simon's congregation became the 'Roma church' (*khangheri*).

As mentioned above, Violeta also attended the 'English church' (*englezi khangheri*). As well as attending the service she made tea and washed and cleaned the kitchen after the service. Through attending the English church Violeta met Christian who was new to the church at that time, recently divorced and wanted to undertake missionary work. Simon suggested that Christian undertake missionary work with Violeta. Christian mentioned to me that he thought that this was in line with his values because the Bible suggests that followers of Jesus help widows, which Violeta was. In addition, Christian foregrounded in his descriptions of Violeta that she never begged for money, but sold roses instead. Christian began visiting Violeta in her small terraced house every week. Christian and Violeta told me different stories about these initial meetings (and they changed their stories depending on how their current relationship was playing out). It seemed that Violeta was very intent on decorating the house with the limited resources that she had. At some times she told me that she painted and scrubbed the whole house herself, while at others she told me that Christian had helped her. Christian also told me that he had helped buy paints and fixed things if he could.

Christian also bought Violeta food for her whole family. He described how he took her to Asda, a local supermarket, and bought her food. He also gave his advice about what food her children should be eating. For example, when I moved in to Violeta's house in November 2013 she made porridge for her youngest son and daughter every morning, telling me that Christian had shown her how to make it. Christian had recently divorced and had two grown up children and Violeta often told me that she thought it was bad for him to alone. Violeta seemed happy to see Christian but was also aware that she was helping him by letting him be involved in her family life. Similarly, Christian felt as though he was helping Violeta. They celebrated birthdays together and he bought gifts for her children. Violeta would also buy Christian lunch. On one occasion she also invited me to her lunch with Christian. When I offered to pay Christian stopped me and said it was important that if Violeta had offered to pay then she should. Through this understanding of each other and the reciprocity it engendered their relationship developed through a long history of home encounters. They developed a deep knowledge of each other's lives but predominantly within Violeta's home among her family. Christian acted in various ways to shape her life in the UK. For example, he would visit her house and then drive all the family to church on a Sunday. He would also visit the house on Wednesday afternoons (which he always took off work and told me this was his missionary time), reading all of her bills, letters and documents.

Through the relationship that had developed in Violeta's home, Christian also worked to support Violeta in activities that resonated with his beliefs. As mentioned above, Violeta refused to beg and Christian helped her find a job cleaning a night club in the early hours of the morning. To enable her to do this job, he drove her there and back. He also mentioned to me on many occasions that Violeta's desire to do this kind of work made her 'different' from other Romanian Roma mothers, signalling how Christian also held ideas that were linked to racialised views of Romanian Roma migrants. Simon also arranged a cleaning job for Violeta in a local Christian education charity, and through this job and Christian's help to arrange her documents and keep her accounts Violeta gained a national insurance number.

Moreover, through Christian's meticulous account keeping and presentation of Violeta's case to the local government, Violeta was granted temporary accommodation provided by the local government. It became a source of amazement between Christian, Simon and Romanian Roma families that Violeta had gained this house, particularly because A2 migrants were not strictly eligible for such housing. In the first instance it was meant to be temporary accommodation but the landlord thought that Violeta had kept the house and garden so well he did not want her to move and allowed her to stay in the house with the agreement of the local government. Christian had helped Violeta navigate all of these interactions and was able to present her case very clearly because he had developed such a deep knowledge about her family and all of her bureaucratic affairs through continued engagement with her within her home. Throughout my fieldwork he continued to visit her and kept all of her accounts, checked her utility bills to make sure that she was not being overcharged and provided management of her bureaucratic identity.

Christian in this way took on the role of a 'face of the state' for Violeta, and her 'success' was based largely on his support that had been dependent on him visiting her in her house over many months and getting to know her children and the routines of her day. Her situated position within the church and apparent convergence of values with Christian was the basis of his support. Violeta strongly performed her Christian values, constantly and loudly playing Robert Kwiek (a famous Pentecostal Roma singer), often referring to God and her religion in everyday conversations and helping at the church whenever she could. She stopped smoking and drinking (although she kept alcohol at the back of her cupboard). Through Christian's commitment to visiting her, she was able to gain resources and also different state categories, accessing aspects of the welfare state beyond her apparent legal status.

Both Christian and Violeta worked to maintain their relationship through home encounters. However their relationship also provoked rumours. Violeta had to balance the assistance she needed from Christian with potential (re)ostracisation from her wider family (Chapter Five). Moreover, Violeta was often placed in conflict between her different identities. She had been ostracised by her family when she was baptised or, as she described it, went into the water (*gelem ando pai*). There was gentle teasing from younger women about how she wore dark coloured

174

skirts with no patterns and cut them straight rather than billowing (almost all women made their own clothes); or her oldest daughter would joke about her becoming 'English' because she drank tea out of a large mug rather than a cup of strong black sweet coffee. At other times I heard family members say that Violeta was like a dog because she went to bed early (as opposed to visiting other families in the evening) and woke up early.

Violeta also came into direct conflict with her immediate family. For example her brother and sons wanted to perform a *pomană* ceremony on the anniversary of her husband's death. She wanted to honour her husband, but *pomană* was not condoned by her Pentecostal religion and (perhaps more importantly for Violeta) it would involve inviting large numbers of her extended family to her house to eat a feast in the garden. She was very worried about the neighbours and losing her temporary accommodation. Eventually they performed the ceremony at her brother's house but she lost respect within her family who already had stopped inviting her to Christmas events (see later). However, Violeta maintained her house with the support of Christian through the church, which provided her with all the measures of being a morally legitimate receiver of care including waged employment, children regularly attending school and living as a nuclear family in a house. She also gave money to charity for "children in Africa". Violeta was very constrained and only shopped in particular shops that knew her because some shops didn't like "Gypsies". She also told me that she could only attend Simon's church because she was worried other churches would identify her as a Romanian Roma woman and she would suffer abuse. The emotional costs of maintaining this life were clear when it was discussed that she might lose her house and she began to become physically unwell and told me that she was suffering from palpitations and feeling dizzy. This demonstrates the fragility of her situation, both in the wider context of Luton and within her home and managing her various relationships and identities. She heavily relied on Christian's individual assessment of her as a morally legitimate receiver and object of his care, which was inextricably bound up with her ability to create the space for Christian to perform his idea of himself as a 'good citizen', Christian missionary and subject of care.

Paula and Margereta

The third and final encounter in this section explores Paula's relationship with Margereta to further extend the argument that deservingness decisions are linked to the alignment between frontline workers perceptions of their caring roles and mothers' abilities to fulfil these expectations. Intimate state encounters are not only about performances of behaviours but also how frontline workers come to view their roles within each family. The relationship between Paula and Margereta demonstrates the care and intensity of emotions on both sides of the home encounter but again foregrounds the delicate balance that Romanian Roma mothers have to maintain to ensure bordering processes do not encroach on their everyday lives. In the course of Paula and Margereta's relationship, developed through home encounters, Paula expanded her role across a large range of responsibilities and family members, extensively managing and negotiating their bureaucratic identities, citizenship statuses and the actualisation of their rights and entitlements.

Paula was introduced to Margereta because she was an asylum seeker. The family therefore received support from the local British Red Cross office who alerted Paula that Margereta had four school-age children who needed to be registered in school. Paula told me about the relationship that developed with Margereta over a period of four years. She had attended Manele[52] concerts with them in London, was invited to weddings and witnessed the births and deaths of family members. When Margereta's cousin Lazar had a problem with his benefit payments she referred him to an old friend, Mary, who had previously worked in the Traveller education service. Mary had then begun to visit Margereta's house to help Lazar fill in his benefit forms to prove that he was 'genuinely looking for work' – a new requirement in order to receive social security benefit. In addition, Mary had found Lazar work in a factory a short distance away from his house. I went with Lazar and Mary when she took him to his induction. On the way back they discovered a shared a love of horses and he told her how he missed having horses in Romania. Mary began to also take Lazar to her two horses a short distance away in her car and used these occasions to fill in Lazar's social benefit forms.

In addition to referring family members to friends for extra help, Paula negotiated on behalf of this family on many different occasions. One of the most influential negotiations was when Margereta's son Gheorghe was convicted of stealing mobile phones. He had been allegedly pickpocketing wallets and mobile phones for some time and he was in contact with youth offending services. Paula was heavily in involved in negotiating on behalf of Gheorghe. This was crucial because those with criminal records were liable to be deported from prison. She described him to me as a 'kleptomaniac'. She also noted to me how he did not have any good role models, building a very sympathetic picture of the young man. With Paula's help Gheorghe received intensive support and training. Simon was also involved in helping to support Gheorghe and I went with him to visit the headmaster of the school where Gheorghe was receiving this help. The focus of the meeting was to find Gheorghe positive role models, an action that Paula had suggested. Through her support of the family, Gheorghe was supported and accepted in a school that specialised in rehabilitation, rather than being intensively managed by youth offending services or gaining a criminal record.

Perhaps the most crucial discretionary support that Paula provided was for Margereta's daughter-in-law, Roxana. She had her first baby, and when it was born they called the baby after Paula to mark the help and support that she had given the family in developing powerful personal ties. However, the baby was not properly checked before Roxana was discharged from hospital and later the baby died because she had a blocked bowel. Paula related this story to me in a café one afternoon. This incident had occurred more than a year previously, but as she told the story Paula (and I) began to cry. We both had to stop talking about it several times because it was very upsetting. However, Paula continued to tell me how she had helped Roxana receive compensation from the hospital for negligence.

When Roxana became pregnant again and attended the same hospital Paula went with her to all of her appointments. Through Paula's negotiation they find that this unborn baby also has the same issue with her bowel. Roxana was placed on a monitoring programme and received special support from the hospital, which meant she attended the hospital more regularly for scans. At this time, Roxana's sister was getting married in Romania and all the family, including Roxana, left to attend the wedding. Paula explained to me how she received calls from the hospital because Roxana had missed her appointments. Paula knew about the wedding from Margereta and called Roxana to tell her that she needed to come back to the UK. However, because of Paula's long relationship with Margereta and her family, she understood Roxana's position and the importance of being part of her sister's wedding. Paula also understood that Roxana would not travel alone and had to wait until the end of the celebrations to return with her family. Paula explained the situation to the hospital and managed Roxana's appointment so she could receive the scans when she returned.

When another of Margereta's daughters, Bianca, had a baby she was sent a bill and notification that she had been referred to the overseas patients department, which would be taking her case to the Home Office as she did not have a right to reside in the UK. Margereta was distraught and phoned Paula who immediately came to the house with a copy of Bianca's confirmation of indefinite leave to remain. Paula drafted a letter and sent it to the hospital which dropped all proceedings against Bianca and her family. Despite having indefinite leave to remain, Margereta and her family were in a continual position of having to defend their legal statuses and residency in the UK. This was possible through Margereta's continued relationship with Paula. Similarly to Christian and Violeta, both sides become attuned to the other through a different register of relationship that is based on personal intimate details of everyday life rather than state service provision. However, these relationships remain shaped by sharp asymmetries of power. Romanian Roma mothers are not free from the spectre of the border or the disciplining state even though their work in building relationships with frontline workers has given the state a more friendly face.

To understand how the trajectories of home encounters serve to 'gatekeep' the welfare state and create differential experiences among families it is important to bear in mind that in many other situations with other families Paula continued to fall back on saying her only job was to register children for school, and she would avoid any entanglement in their lives (see Chapter Four). The complex trajectory of Paula's relationship with Margereta through the home encounter, and the care and intensity of emotions on both sides, thus served to radically alter Margereta's opportunities to negotiate access to different state resources and categories for her family. Her interactions with Paula take on huge significance as a 'state encounter', which created caring relationships over time.

Margereta's relationship with Paula was also a resource that she could broker to help but also to sully the reputation of other mothers, further demonstrating the highly situated, contextual and repetitive nature of intimate state encounters. For example Margereta's sister in law, Violeta, was sure that Margereta had turned Paula against her. Margereta did not like Violeta, ever since she had become Pentecostal after her husband had died (Margereta's husband's brother). Violeta told me about an encounter with Paula (where I was not present) that had made her feel as though Paula was not helping her and looking "badly" at her children. Violeta therefore feared Paula coming to visit and did not make appeals to her to become more involved in her daily life. Violeta also avoided Paula in the street and established relationships with the church instead to assist with her bureaucratic entanglements. Tracing the trajectories of relationships through encounters opens up kinship relationships and how they intricately entwine with how these families were able to negotiate their relationship with the state.

Although the home encounter is a defined moment, migrants and frontline workers draw on previous histories of encounters and open up future encounters in a multiplicity of modalities to serve differing ends. Paying attention to the way the state is appealed to, negotiated, contested or avoided provides a more nuanced perspective on how frontline workers and Romanian Roma came to understand their positions and what the state meant in their daily lives. Moreover, relationships between frontline workers and Romanian Roma demonstrate how identities are also forged in relation to one another. The stakes involved in these struggles has been alluded to and is the sole focus of the following section.

Border work through care

We have seen how some families were able to use the constrained opportunities provided by home encounters to build relationships with frontline workers and volunteers. However, these families all had a particular position that allowed them build these relationships, such as shared religious values, or being recognised as a refugee where there was a clear (albeit troubled and contested) path towards a secure legal status. Other families were not able to negotiate on these terms. Home encounters also became more dangerous for mothers as restrictive immigration controls and the duty to enforce them were pushed onto frontline workers. These immigration controls were entwined with welfare regulations, creating very complex legal situations. If frontline workers made a mistake (as Clare, the head of a children's centre, was well aware) they could be responsible for someone being deported. This section foregrounds how the border emerged in home encounters, effectively placing mothers in the position where they had to choose between losing their children and moving from the area.

To understand their position, a brief review of Romanian nationals' legal status is required. As previously detailed, Romania acceded to the EU in January 2007. A2 migrants were subject to transitional controls until January 2014 and were required to hold a qualifying status in order to live in the UK for more than three months. If they could not achieve a qualifying status within three months, they became 'deportable'. During my fieldwork, I witnessed two occasions of when Romanian Roma were issued deportation orders in this way. The issuing of a deportation order required a migrant not only to lack a qualifying status but also to become 'visible' to frontline workers. In these instances, the Romanian Roma became visible when one woman gave birth at the hospital and when one man spent time in prison.[53]

To achieve a qualifying status and therefore a secure legal right to reside in the UK, A2 migrants were required to be at least one of the following: a worker under a specific scheme; ('genuinely') self-employed; economically inactive and self-sufficient; a student and self-sufficient; a family member accompanying or joining an EU national who satisfies one of the other statuses; or a pensioner. In practice, the Romanian Roma families in this book were only able to pursue a qualifying status through the self-employment route. Those achieving ('genuine') self-employed status as assessed by the job centre[54] were issued with national insurance numbers. In addition to gaining a national insurance number, migrants also had to prove they were 'habitually resident' and had a 'right to reside' in the UK before being eligible for social protection.

We have already seen that the process of gaining support from a frontline worker or volunteer to apply for a national insurance number was crucial for many Romanian Roma. Many could not read or write, and had a limited understanding of what was required – and crucially, how to present this information and themselves – in order to successfully gain a national insurance number. Without support, many of them would not even try to apply, or would have little to no chance of succeeding. Again, frontline workers taking on this work were not trained, nor expected within their formal roles, to help with national insurance number applications, but came to do so because of the optics of the home encounter and the understandings and values produced from their interactions with families. As Dubois (2014a: 138) observes, 'by definition bureaucratic criteria poorly account for the unstable and confused reality of social and economic precariousness'. When frontline workers discretionarily expanded their roles in the home encounter to include supporting Romanian Roma with their national insurance number applications, they therefore took on a broader state form in those interactions. These discretionary choices were based on the situated positions of all actors' and families' performances with the frontline workers during home encounters.

For example Lisa, Pathways support family worker, and Kassia, a children's centre family support worker, helped some mothers apply for national insurance numbers, and appealed decisions if they were refused. Again, these interactions were complicated by the differing values and perceptions of church volunteers with whom the frontline workers became entangled. Christian, a church volunteer, was sent by Lisa to support some mothers because of his specific experience and expertise in accounting and bureaucratic engagement with HMRC. Christian helped some women with getting national insurance numbers, such as Violeta and Sanda, both mothers who regularly visited the church and self-identified as Pentecostal. Similarly, Grigore obtained a wide range of support from Simon, the church pastor, based on their shared religious values. In contrast, some encounters detailed throughout the book demonstrate how the processes around the home encounter could lead to support being unavailable or withdrawn, as in the case when Christian refused to support Maria's mother in her application for a national insurance number, or when Lisa refused support to Georgeta, or when Rosemary stopped visiting

Ecaterina. Without assistance in securing a national insurance number, these individuals found themselves in highly precarious positions in relation to their official residency status in the UK, potentially open to having their children removed from them or deportation.

As has been detailed, frontline workers and volunteers used discretion in deciding how much support to offer, often based on perceptions of 'deservingness', their understandings of their roles and understandings of the Romanian Roma label. These perceptions and the ways in which different performances played out with individual values and norms are central to understanding the salience of the home encounter as the location of, and framework for, these interactions. Many mothers worked to stage the home and perform appropriate use of the domestic space, in order to gain support (see Chapter Four). Thus the discretionary decisions made by frontline workers and volunteers to help with national insurance number applications (or not), and therefore secure the right (or not) for some families to live in the UK, can be seen as having a bordering effect in the processes of filtering families. These sorting processes can operate at different scales, indicating the variegated micro-geographies of 'everyday bordering' (Yuval Davis et al. 2018) where Romanian Roma may move to a different local government jurisdiction or to a different nation-state. This bordering effect must be understood as a part of the intimate state encounter.

The potential for these encounters to have a bordering effect can be further understood through the particular bureaucratic gaze on child welfare and the ways in which it interweaved with migration controls, with the potential to 'activate' bordering for some families. Indeed, as we have seen, childless women and men assumed the role of a tolerated precarious worker and were able to live and work without being affected by state processes making incursions into their lives. In contrast, there was a specific bureaucratic drive that placed attention on situated understandings of child safeguarding, and parents had no choice over whether to engage with frontline workers (see Chapter Two).

Within this lens, parents must be perceived as providing 'appropriate' care of their children, even when they are excluded from social support that could help them perform this care. If parents are not perceived to be appropriately caring for children, a child may be taken from the family. Alternatively, if the family perceived this to be a possibility or 'threat' the family had the choice to move elsewhere. While most families were not subject to formal immigration controls such as deportation orders, what could be considered a 'silent sorting' occurred when they were faced with the possibility of children being taken from the family. In this situation they might perceive the choice as either move with children or face the prospect of losing them.

This situation had particular salience because of the limits on different forms of state support that may be offered to EU national families (see Chapter Two). A mother in this position would be unable to receive support to continue in her caring capacity. When children were deemed 'vulnerable' (as all Romanian Roma children were in these instances) mothers had to rely on performances of 'appropriate' motherhood in the perceptions of frontline workers. As I have shown in the previous chapters these performances are highly fragile, contradictory and contingent. If a migrant mother was not seen to be 'appropriately' caring for her children (such as not being able to afford accommodation so each child could have their own bed), and she was not eligible for public funds to help provide 'appropriate' care, she would then be confronted with the choice between losing her children or being forced to move. This choice was experienced directly by one of the families I spent time with and will be explored in detail later.

The mother-child relationship thus has the potential to become the site for bordering processes to be activated due to the interweaving of particular legal statuses and child welfare regulations. Assessments of mothering therefore have a bordering effect. As Mezzadra and Neilson (2013: 64) have argued, 'borders, far from serving to block or obstruct global flows, have become essential devices for their articulation'. Their approach points to being attentive to 'fields of relation', whereby borders operate through 'different kinds of folding and filtering' (2013: 59). The ethnographic encounters that follow in this chapter illustrate how child welfare encounters act to filter families, preventing presence on national territory and creating a new channel of flows.

The shared understanding of the perceived 'threat' of children being taken away became clear in a story that was told to me by many different frontline workers and also by Romanian Roma mothers. The story was told with some variations. In the version told to me at one multi-agency meeting it was referred to because it was clear that the children's centre did not want a similar occurrence to happen again. At the time they were discussing a migrant mother called Georgina, who had eight children and social services had just begun to be aware of her and her family situation. The story was also referenced in my interview with Samantha, deputy head of the children's centre. Kassia also mentioned it to me even though she did not work at the children's centre when the events unfolded.

Simon told me one version of the story after a multi-agency children's centre meeting. He related that he had known about one Romanian Roma migrant mother who had seven children. Her husband had been convicted of stealing and selling stolen goods and she had been left in the house with no way to support herself. The children had been seen by a neighbour running around outside the house without shoes in the middle of the day and the youngest child had no clothes on. The neighbour reported the family to social services. At the same time the school that was linked to the children's centre became involved. The head teacher wanted to help the children and provided school uniform for free; she also tried to arrange for different teachers to pick the children up from their home to bring them to school, as she was aware that the number of children would make it almost impossible for the mother to walk them all to the school at the same time. The children's centre had also become involved to help support the migrant mother with the younger children who were not yet school age. However, as they were arranging support for the mother, social services conducted home visits and decided that the children needed to be taken into state care. The seven children could not be placed with one foster carer and were moved to several different areas across the UK. Moreover, the children under 5 years old were immediately put into adoption proceedings and therefore would not be returned to the family.

All frontline workers who were involved in the multi-agency meetings about Romanian Roma mothers were aware of this case and expressed disappointment and sadness at the outcome. They believed that they could have supported the mother so that her children were not taken into care by social services. It had become an infamous case linked directly to understandings of Romanian Roma mothering and was perceived by frontline workers as a 'failure'. One of the key reasons they expressed sadness over this case was the worsening relations with some women, as the story of this instance spread as a rumour through the Roma church and in conversations between women in the area and beyond.

The repercussions of this case were explained by Lisa in my formal interview with her at the end of my field work in March 2014: "I have had to reassure people that I am not a social worker and clarify what my role is – you know, 'I am not here to take your children.'" This danger was also expressed to me by many mothers throughout my fieldwork and emerged in different conversations. For example when I visited the GP surgery with Maria, a family entered whom I had not met before. I heard them speaking *Romanës* and I asked her if she knew them. She said,

> 'Don't talk to those people about social [welfare benefits]. Do nothing. You just tell them you [Romanian Roma family] have to get one flat by yourself. You have to take a flat. No flat, it's too dangerous [to engage in the welfare benefit process].

> The kids can be taken and then that would be very bad for
> you with Romanian people.'

The possibility that children might be taken away was ever-present in the understandings of both Romanian Roma mothers and frontline workers in their interactions. The pressure of home visits, and the potency of rumours that circulated about children being taken away from families, had displacing effects in several cases. For example, one Romanian Roma mother, Georgeta, moved away from the area when a relative, Claudia, left prison and began living in the same house. Claudia had many visits from probation to check on her and her new baby, which had been born in prison. Georgeta had not been able to gain a secure residency status despite her attempts to find cleaning work and apply for a national insurance number. The continuing visits from frontline workers and Georgeta's uncertain residency status served to provide the reasons for her and her family to move away from the area. This was difficult for her because her 7-year-old son had begun going to school for the first time and he didn't want to move. However, the continuing visits, rumours and tension in the house with Claudia living there made the situation too difficult, despite Georgeta gaining networks in the local area, such as those developed with Christian and other members of the Roma church and the cleaning clients she had gained in the local area. Georgeta and her family decided to move, losing these networks and potential resources.

Another mother, Ghizela, and her family also decided to move out of the area when the education attendance officer began to visit the house more often because her son and daughter were missing a lot of school. Ghizela lived with her husband, Emil, their three children, and her husband's mother, father, brother and sister. Her husband's brother was also married and had two children. The number of people living in the household could vary as Ghizela's husband and brother-in-law were in and out of prison at various times throughout the course of my fieldwork, but there could be up to 12 people living in the small two-bedroomed terraced house, which was in very poor condition. Ghizela's mother-in-law often begged in the town-centre. Ghizela's sister-in-law had recently had her son taken away from her in Ireland. Emil's father was very blonde and some of her children were also blonde. Ghizela's sister-in-law therefore became more fearful of frontline workers coming to the house, seeing her blonde children and taking them away so she decided to leave the area to avoid all contact with frontline workers. The potency of rumours about children taken into care did not operate along national boundaries but through families. Therefore although this incident happened in Ireland, it spread through families and seemed more relevant than other cases that happened in Luton (see Chapter Three for the role of rumours).

Frontline workers did not know where these families had moved to and could not communicate with the local government in those places, therefore the families effectively disappeared. I later learned that Georgeta, after a brief stay in Manchester, had moved with her family to Romania. Ghizela moved to Birmingham. This form of displacement can be seen as micro-geographies of bordering where 'flows' of people are activated by the potentiality of children being removed from the family. This displacement can be more explicitly seen through the story of Rodica, a 17-year-old migrant mother. Her experience reveals how borders emerge within the national territory through the intertwining of welfare and migration regulations. Crucially, I do not argue that these processes are creating new 'borders', defined as fundamental schisms and mutations in the nation-state, but rather the border of the nation-state can be said to have shifted and is becoming more diffuse and pervasive, stretching both beyond and within national territory (see Balibar 2004).

Rodica and the silent sorting of Romanian Roma

The creation of a territorial 'bordering effect' can be seen through the case of Rodica. Toma, Rodica's husband, had moved to the UK in 2011 to live nearby to Toma's mother and brother. Their asylum applications were in process when Romania acceded to the UK in 2007 and so they had gained indefinite leave to remain. However, Toma arrived in 2011 and therefore was subject to transitional controls as an A2 migrant. He married his fourth wife, 17-year-old Rodica, in 2012. When I met them in June 2013, they had a 5-month-old baby girl, Ionela. Neither Toma nor Rodica could read or write but Toma could speak English. Despite working collecting scrap metal with his brother Toma had never applied for a national insurance number and had no recourse to public funds. He had also been convicted for small crimes of theft and had spent time in prison. When I met them, Toma was on probation with a curfew and they were living with an older married couple, Mihai and Ilinca, in a small two-bedroom terraced house.

The house was in a very poor, slum-like condition with broken doors and a broken window at the rear of the house that was boarded up. There was very little furniture apart from one small table, two chairs, a large TV and an electric heater, which Toma complained that Rodica kept turned on all day, making the room too hot. Ionela had a push-chair where she slept and when awake she was held by either her mother or father. Mihai and Ilinca were not relatives but had previously lived with Toma's uncle. They all spoke *Romanës* to each other in the house. Mihai and Ilinca worked in a hand car-wash when they were needed. If they weren't called in the morning to go to the car-wash, they tried to find work with others to collect scrap metal as they didn't have a vehicle of their own. Some of this scrap metal was stored in the back garden.

In August 2013 Toma broke his probation conditions and was sent back to prison. Rodica told me that the lady who "comes for the baby" had sent different people to come and see her in her house. She explained that she didn't know who they were but they asked her lots of questions. She was aware of the rumours regarding other mothers who had had their children taken away, and in particular she told me about a relative of Toma's who had recently had eight children taken into care. This was the same story, mentioned earlier, that became a defining incident for frontline workers. In addition, the increased home encounters with frontline workers seemed to be straining Rodica's relationship with Mihai and Ilinca. When I visited they seemed not be talking to each other anymore. Rodica did not have a qualifying status or right to reside and therefore did not have access to social support, such as child benefit. In addition, as an EEA national she was denied support provided to migrants with children at risk of destitution, under Section 17 Children Act 1989 and Section 21 National Assistance Act 1948.

Rodica was faced with a decision. She believed the increasing home visitations meant that her baby could be taken into care if she stayed in the UK. The only alternative she saw was to leave the country. The bureaucratic processes in place for the care of children, through the pressures of the home encounter and Rodica's apparent failure to negotiate the required performances, instigated a border effect because of her particular migrant status. She was not seen to have the capacity to perform the 'appropriate mothering' required and frontline workers had no formal means to grant her social assistance. She could not stay in the national territory and keep her baby with her, and was forced to change either her social role as a mother or her physical location in the UK. Due to the processes linked with the appropriate care of children, infused with ideas surrounding Romanian Roma mothers, complex legal entitlements and her own situated experience, these bordering processes were activated for Rodica through her relationship to her child.

When I returned to the house in late August, Ilinca told me Rodica had joined her parents, who were living in Italy, with her baby. Rodica was at the nexus point between the lack of rights afforded to precarious workers and the values infused into perceptions of mothering. Rodica was put in an impossible position where, as a 17-year-old new mother, she was faced with losing her baby or moving from the country. The house where she was living had become increasingly hostile for her as Ilinca and Mihai were worried about people coming to the house and looking around where they lived. This decision was made even more difficult for Rodica as her husband was in prison and she was not sure when he would return and whether he would join her in Italy. For Rodica, these highly personal and intimate relationships were laid bare to frontline workers as they made assessments as to whether she was able to appropriately care for her daughter. She experienced the border as exclusion from the welfare state where she felt as though she had no other option than to move from the country to her family in Italy.

Home encounters are unique discretionary acts that Romanian Roma mothers found difficult to avoid. They act to 'silently' remove a mother and child, separating them from the UK where the father remained. For Rodica, migration and welfare restrictions, entwined with the legal duty to protect children, represented a shift from negotiations of boundaries at the territorial border to the domestic space. She had to negotiate her legal status through whether she could persuade social workers that she could look after her daughter. The border therefore emerged for her in interactions with social workers because it would force her to choose between being a mother and being in the UK. She faced these decisions in the small downstairs room of a terraced house that she shared with two others who were not speaking to her because of these interactions. Her husband was in prison and her own family were far away. Without support and faced with the prospect of losing her daughter she left the country.

For those identified as Romanian Roma they are subject to discretionary home encounters which widen the scope of state surveillance and normative expectations for the whole family and their intimate spaces. In addition, these families are excluded from the social support that would help them perform this care. If parents are not perceived to be caring for their children they may be taken from the family. Alternatively, they have the choice to move elsewhere. Most families do not receive deportation orders; however, a 'silent sorting' occurs when faced with the decision to move with children or continue to reside in the UK without them. This is a bordering effect where families are caught in different forms of filtering through their social relationships; in this case, through the social role of motherhood.

Final remarks

Intimate state encounters fundamentally shape how Romanian Roma negotiate the boundaries of citizenship in the UK. This chapter has argued that the social relationship between mothers and children becomes the site of bordering processes. It also illustrates how, through the negotiation of values between mothers and frontline workers, the home is where these performances are judged and assessments regarding access to state resources, leading to the stratified reproduction of the state in home encounters. EU transitional controls and the increasingly strict definition of 'work' placed significance on mothers' bureaucratic encounters. Post-welfare frontline workers enter homes based on particular expectations and perceptions shaped by the historical genesis of their roles, the values that underpin the policies they enact, their own desire to fulfil a particular notion of a caring 'good citizen' and often their own experiences as women with migration or 'minority' backgrounds. Frontline workers are subject to a distinct governing logic that places them, often unwillingly, in positions of confusion where they have wide areas of discretion over how to support families that can have life-changing consequences.

Mothers are required to undertake intensive work to challenge racialised representations and exclusionary migration regimes, to present themselves as deserving to gain informal assistance and as capable to perform 'appropriate mothering'. Relationships with frontline workers are pivotal for mothers to learn the bureaucratic spaces that are open to them and to gain the informal support that enable them to perform the intensive mothering required. Without this support mothers like Rodica were confronted with the choice between loss of motherhood or movement from the area. The fragility of relationships with frontline workers and the removal of assistance, or a child, was a constant spectre that frames encounters.

The bordering effects that emerged in these interactions between mothers and frontline workers resonate with Balibar's observation that Europe itself is a borderland, a zone of transition and mobility without territorial fixity. He argues (1998: 220) 'borders are being both multiplied and reduced in their localization and their function ... the quantitative relation between "border" and "territory" is being inverted'. Following Bigo (2005: 77), who conceptualises borders as moving, disconnecting and reconnecting, and Butler and Spivak (2007: 5) and De Genova (2002: 439), who observe the creation of 'deportable' populations within the national territory, borders can shift, (re)appear and disappear within everyday life as people move through vectors of space and time.[55]

Individuals belonging to different social groups experience the borders of exclusion in different ways, and borders simultaneously perform 'several functions of demarcation and territorialisation ... between distinct social exchanges or flows, between distinct rights ...' (Balibar and Williams 2002: 79).[56] The boundaries between the dynamics of filtering, subordination and labour market discrimination that once occurred at the international border now take place within the bounded spaces of national societies. One crucial mechanism that has brought 'the border' inside the nation state is the fusing of welfare regulations and migration controls. The UK now has 'internal borders' where migrants are asked to prove their entitlement before they are granted services, such as healthcare or children's centres.

Through the home encounter there is an interweaving of immigration, employment and (child) welfare controls. This builds on Yuval-Davis's (2011) argument that 'everyday bordering' can be understood as 'closely linked to particular political projects of belonging' in which Roma are constructed and reconstructed as Other. The particular advance I make is not only that these racialised processes of 'Othering' can be understood as forms of everyday bordering in themselves, but also that the intertwining of racialised perceptions of Romanian Roma with (child) welfare controls create informal processes which act to have a 'bordering effect' by creating flows of people at different scales, such as outside the local government and outside the national territory. This can be understood specifically through the relational interactions between situated individuals in the home encounter as an intimate state encounter that is based on a new politics, which functions through conspicuous affective practice and individualised moral actors.

Frontline workers and volunteers take on the work of border policing through discursive framing and the material management of spaces. It is through these spaces that they came to recognise their political relationships to Others. However, as McNevin (2011: 149) elaborates 'borders literally give shape to hierarchies of belonging that buttress sovereign power, but the spatial dimensions of borders (and sovereign power) are also dynamic'. Each encounter occurred within the home, a spatial setting. This might seem like a banal point – yet the preceding chapter has foregrounded the importance of the spatial context and reminds us of the dynamism of each encounter.

Focusing on the details of encounters also reveals how the state can be created as 'somewhere elsewhere' in these affective relationships and then becomes entwined into the actions that take place within the home. Previous scholarly work has examined how everyday private lives of state officials affect the way in which states operate (Chapter Two). However, the focus on encounters shifts ideas away from mutually exclusive public and private formations into the realm of how the state emerges and is negotiated. This fundamentally challenges the assumption that frontline workers must necessarily abstract themselves from the realm of the private in order to properly function but rather foregrounds how care is mobilised when negotiating claims on the state.

In addition, we are also reminded that each encounter also has the potential to change the associations we make about that space – its history and its future, who belongs in that space, who moves through it, and on what terms. All these ideas 'make up' that space insofar as space is the product of social interaction and collective experience. The home encounter renders the space as ambivalent and a site of indeterminacy, confusion and struggle that cannot be reduced to a coherent set of claims that works on any one socio-spatial level.

Women are actively contesting the boundary of their home and gatekeeping the border of the home-land. Therefore through these encounters between women (almost all mothers) the different scales that mark this difference between formal and informal, home-land and home, public and private collapses. In all these encounters we can witness how contestations over the right to belong within the home-land directly plays out within the home. The domestic ordering within the home directly relates to the national ordering of the home-land.

CONCLUSION

Homemade state: intimate state encounters at the margins

This book has explored what is at stake when negotiations of political belonging occur directly through everyday practices of belonging in homes. It is based on a relational understanding of the state where the state emerges through the contestation and struggle of differentially positioned and socially situated actors. It has linked state reproduction (processes of political belonging) with social reproduction (the discursive ideology and practices of care necessary to maintain and reproduce human life), paying particular attention to the role of space.

This book has introduced and elaborated on the notion of 'intimate state encounters'. Three main contributions arise from this notion. The first contribution is the movement from 'state acts' to 'state encounters'. Encounters foreground how the dichotomy between 'state' and 'community' needs to be unpacked and not assumed. This processual approach reveals the relational production of identities for all social actors engaged in the encounter. In particular, this lens makes a contribution to theory on street-level bureaucracy because it opens analysis to include the complexity of frontline work, avoiding explanations that rely on assuming roles and relationships and resorting to problematic dichotomies of 'personal' and 'professional' identities or 'front-' and 'back-'stage performances. This perspective is crucial as frontline workers' roles are increasingly blurred (see Chapter Two).

The second contribution is the importance of spatial effects, context and intersectional analysis, in this case the productive space of the home. Through focusing on the home space, and the situated positions of social actors in that space, many different literatures can be brought together, including debates on public and private space, gendered critiques of the state, the politics of care, housing studies and urban marginalisation, social work theory, and the anthropological literature on spatialised, relational and affective states. Attention to spatial effects reveals the potential for relational labour through hosting and intimacy. Hosting allows ostensibly dependent or devalued populations to purchase some sort of social belonging, and opens the potential for political belonging. Attention to intersectional analysis reveals frontline workers' processes of care for Romanian Roma at a moment when their own citizenship rights and duties are being reconfigured in profound ways. Intimate state encounters make an intervention into literature on migrants' 'deservingness', the politics of care and compassion, and neoliberal restructuring of welfare states (see later).

Third, the notion of intimate state encounters opens a new area of study to the topics of citizenship, belonging and liberal democratic welfare states. The home and 'private space' are often bracketed out in discussions around welfare state encounters. In addition, the home is seen as a limit of 'mixing' in the experiences of negotiating 'lived differences' in diverse urban areas (see Introduction). By seeing the home as a space of (enforced) mixing this book reveals how diversity discourses depoliticise the home space and the work that families (often mothers) undertake. This absence of scholarly attention on the home also reinforces stereotypes that 'Roma' do not 'mix' with others, placing the blame on them for their segregation and marginalisation. The notion of intimate state encounters reveals new sites of negotiation across difference while paying attention to the inherent power asymmetries that are already in place and playing out. The rest of this concluding chapter is dedicated to elaborating on these three contributions and how they advance our knowledge of citizenship, conceptions of care and belonging.

Street-level bureaucracy, home and the relational state

Focusing on encounters as the main methodological and analytical device, this book has started from the tensions, ambiguities and affects within different roles and practices, rather than assuming that frontline workers are those that 'govern' and Romanian Roma are always those 'governed'. This perspective allows us to trace how and when the state is drawn into or disavowed in the encounter, in what form, and why. Frontline workers do not simply embody the state but rather the state emerges as social actors with different relationships to the state come together and negotiate their different roles, positions and understandings under certain conditions. The book has developed an approach in line with Hansen and Stepputat's (2001: 25) call not to examine how relations are organised and negotiated across boundaries of 'state' and 'community', but rather to trace how those boundaries are defined and the work that is put in to maintain and reconcile their contradictions, how they are mobilised and how they reproduce hierarchies. In other words, through analysing intimate encounters we can 'locate' the state.

Intimate state encounters are more than acts of 'subversive citizenship' where service providers and their clients resist policies that they deem to be unfair (Barnes and Prior 2009). Rather, identities are shaped in these encounters and so too are understandings of what 'the state' is, different social actors' relationships to it, and evaluations of their own desires for state affordances (what they want the state to be and their role within it).

A further advantage of this perspective is it captures the agency of all those involved, while also remaining attentive to the structures that have created the encounters and how they operate to constrain and shape the possibilities for different forms of relations. Those who seemingly represent the state may also have precarious legal statuses or uncertain belongings and are also drawing and acting on their (sometimes very recent) experiences of migration (as Kassia does in Chapter Two). Their experiences of the UK migration system or settling in the UK (including everyday racism) also shape how they relate to newer migrants (such as Lisa in Chapter Two). Rather than just focusing on how securitised or marginalised subjects are victims deprived of agency (Isin 2002; Nyers 2004) or theorising how groups with precarious statuses are able to express agency and enact citizenship, even if they are not, or not fully, included in prevailing regimes of citizenship (Lippert and Rehaag 2012; Nyers and Rygiel 2012; Isin and Saward 2013), the perspective of encounters makes the situated positions of *all* social actors visible without privileging one side. In essence, encounters bring relational struggles into focus. This also resonates with critical feminist analytics, which argue that we must start from the actions and experiences of those marginalised, rather than institutional perspectives (Andrijasvic 2013).

An implication of this approach is to foreground the racialised and gendered dimensions of state encounters. Restricting access to the welfare state and placing more responsibility for guarding the borders of the nation-state onto the frontline contributes to the 'advanced marginalisation' of differentially positioned gendered, racialised and classed subjects. They are called on to discipline and govern members of 'groups' that they are 'proximate' to or 'affiliated' with. State reproduction at the margins has a double meaning in this book. Women reproduce the state not only through their capacity as mothers but also in their roles as the frontline workers who make daily 'bordering' decisions about who is able to gain the support that will allow them to continue to reside in the nation-state. The state is reproduced along racialised and classed lines, and those who undertake this state labour are women, often from a migration or minority background. Bridget Anderson (2000) insightfully argued that in societies marked by neoliberalism, globalisation and migration, 'minority' women are left 'doing the dirty work' in paid and unpaid labour in the home. New forms of governing migration have created new kinds of work in the home for marginalised and poor women and they are left, once again, to do the 'dirty work' of border control. New spaces of negotiating access to state resources and political belonging have emerged through the intertwining of welfare conditionality and the hostile environment with distinct racialised, classed and gendered implications. These implications not only affect the objects of these policies but also those tasked to implement them. Citizenship and legal status are negotiated by marginalised women on both sides of the encounter. As argued in the Introduction, these intimate state encounters bring relational struggles into focus, break down the distinction between 'us' and 'them' and reveal the often unseen and hidden work, costs and injuries on all sides that take place in the margins.

This book argues that state encounters are a relational process, where the identities and positions of all social actors are forged through interactions with each other. Political belonging is situated and embodied for those claiming, as well as those on whom the claim is being made. These frontline workers actively 'make up' the state for (other) migrant mothers (Chapter Two). They draw on their own experiences of state encounters and mix these with their current perceptions and relations and their own (shifting) identities.

Citizenship, belonging and the politics of care

As stated in the Introduction, citizenship entangles both formal legal rights and everyday feelings of belonging. Previous scholarly literature has long since established that those who are formally outside society achieve feelings of belonging that do not depend on formal citizenship.[57] In contrast, this book has focused on how feelings and practices of belonging actively shaped formal citizenship. For example Cristina, through her links with church volunteer Kay and children's centre worker Louise, gained an individualised and contingent form of social protection and a strong sense of belonging. These relationships helped Cristina with her formal legal status as Louise advocated on her behalf to appeal the refusals of social protection. These encounters engendered relations of care that were not one-sided. Cristina crafted her relationship with Louise to ensure that she felt comfortable and welcomed in her home. She often expressed concern for Louise working too hard and offered Louise comfort regarding her worries about Louise's daughter not being able to find a job. However, Cristina was also aware that Louise could refer her to social services or could withdraw her assistance entirely, leading Cristina towards a path of destitution, child removal or removal from the UK. Louise also 'made up' the state for Cristina within her home. The discretionary care of delivering food, school uniforms, paying utility bills and appealing refusals of welfare benefits became how Cristina related to and understood 'the state', and constituted her family's political belonging in ways inextricably entwined with Cristina's practices of belonging through motherhood.

Similarly, through the help of Christian, a church volunteer, Violeta was able to read letters, pay bills and manage all aspects of her 'bureaucratic identity'. Violeta gained access to state resources and a form of political belonging that was beyond her entitlements as an A2 migrant through her practices of belonging to the church. Her practices of belonging opened up opportunities for reciprocal relations of care with one individual who became her 'face of the state'. Again, these relationships were based on long-term reciprocal relations, where Violeta saw Christian as lonely and in need of a family and Christian saw Violeta as a widow that he had been 'called' by the church to support.

Mothers gained forms of political belonging because of practices within their homes. What is important is not just that the state is made up relationally but *where* these relational state encounters take place. The intimate state encounters that are at the heart of this book operate in particular ways because they take place in the home. Romanian Roma did not have similar encounters with the police or with medical staff in a hospital. There was no potential in those encounters to establish longer-term relations. They did not open spaces of reciprocity in the form of hosting. Frontline workers and volunteers also enact social belonging through their relations with migrant families. They make sense of their actions, drawing on their own feelings about their citizenship rights and duties.

However, while there were opportunities for some mothers to develop long-term, caring, personal connections with frontline workers, the home space also became the site of painful acts of exclusion. The space of the home also made deeply held assumptions about Romanian Roma extremely difficult to unsettle, where mothers' intimate social lives were revealed and read against pre-formed ideas about 'despicable' Romanian Roma motherhood (Chapter Three). These intimate state encounters are both forms of hyper-surveillance and also spaces of constrained opportunities to gain informal support through discretionary care and a more secure legal status in the UK. It is only those who manage to perform manifold and sometimes conflicting modes of care who can maintain these fragile and contingent relationships.

The relationships between mothers (both frontline workers and Romanian Roma) – made salient through intimate state encounters in the home – are based on affect, compassion and emotion that bind people together through intense affective localised belonging. This is in contrast to definitions of social citizenship that are based on an awareness of the generalisation of interdependence which links 'all members within a national collectivity, coupled with a sense of responsibility which does not impel to personal action but which instead required the poor to be cared for by the state and out of public tax funds' (de Swaan 1988: 11). Muehlebach has charted this shift and argues that social citizenship is being rivalled by a new form of citizenship under neoliberal conditions, which she calls ethical citizenship. Ethical citizenship may thus be defined:

> Instead of a universal agreement spanning classes and generations in a national society, ethical citizenship encloses citizens within the intimate space of the 'welfare society' but the meaning of 'society' has been radically recast. It is relationally produced by participatory citizens rather than an a priori domain into which the state interjects. Citizens are aligned not with the national frameworks that we have come to associate with twentieth century modernity but with a new localised politics of intimacy and immediacy. (Muehlebach 2012: 43)

In this formulation, citizens are bound together by moral and affective ties, rather than social and political ones, and primarily through duties rather than rights. Throughout the book I have noted how frontline workers justified decisions based on gratitude and behaviours rather than in terms of entitlements or a broader politics of social justice. Mothers who gained a form of political belonging all negotiated within webs of gratitude. Again, the emphasis on gratitude highlights the individualised affective relationships that these mothers were required to engage in, rather than any recourse to their rights. These actions move them beyond automatic entitlement and, in de Genova's words, represent a 'form of exclusion through inclusion' (De Genova 2013: 1185). The involvement of volunteers heightened and exacerbated the idea of behaviours and affiliations as being key to gaining formal legal residency, often causing contradictory and conflicting demands on mothers, for example regarding contraception and abortion, and through the marginalisation of fathers (see Chapter Five).

A hallmark of this new form of citizenship is the notion of 'deservingness' that has gained salience in political and academic debates. Deservingness signals a shift from a discourse based on rights to pre-welfare moral categories (Applebaum 2001; van Oorschot 2006; Yoo 2008; Chauvin and Garcés-Mascareñas 2014). Mothers who gained a degree of secure legal status were those who placed themselves outside entitlement and negotiated in the realms of favours, care and shared values, even when those shared values were pejorative and discriminatory images of Gypsies and Roma (see Chapter Three). However, to negotiate on these terms required multiple forms of knowledge and skills such as language, understandings of norms and forms of behaviour and often a home space that could, in some way, be managed and appropriately staged. The space of state encounters as a site to establish 'deservingness' is fundamental to the outcome and therefore state reproduction.

Migrant mothers had to negotiate manifold modes of care within home encounters. Previous scholarly work has identified that caring subjects are engaged in acts of care in a Foucauldian sense – a care of the self that entails specific forms of self-knowledge and self-detachment 'whereby one's innermost feelings become objects of scrutiny and then articulation' (Foucault 1997: 223) and 'the acquisition of certain attitudes with the goal of self-transformation are central to becoming an ethical being' (1997: 225). Muehlebach (2012: 8), drawing on Foucault, argues that a caring subject performs two kinds of labours of care at once: it feels (cares about) and acts (cares for others) at the same time. I argue that migrant mothers are both caring subjects (in the two aspects that Muehlebach describes) and also objects of care. As objects of care, mothers' performances are judged depending on frontline workers' perceptions of themselves as caring subjects (for example as a missionary, as a grandmother, as a frontline worker who is guided by safeguarding principles or gender equality, as a support worker who has just gained legal status). Romanian Roma mothers have to understand the expectations of the person providing care. They must ensure that frontline workers feel as though they are providing care in a manner that resonates with their notions of their own caring selves. These notions are drawn from the context of citizenship within a post-welfare state. Being a good subject and object of care are inextricably linked through the bureaucratic gaze of the intimate state encounter. Political belonging rests on these multiple performances of care within a context marked by neoliberal restructuring at the frontline (see Chapter Two). This is a crucial intervention into the literature on the politics of migrant deservingness, political belonging and critical conceptions of care. I argue that separating the two facets of care (subject and object) reveals the conflict that Romanian Roma mothers' performances try to reconcile. Conceptualising Romanian Roma mothers as situated simultaneous subjects/objects of care for frontline workers who are themselves situated subjects/objects of care provides a new entry point to debates on migrant deservingness and a way forward to critically analyse how neoliberal restructuring affects 'compassionate' action and who is seen as a legitimate receiver of care, state resources and political belonging.

Politics of intimacy and reproduction of uncertainty

What emerges from focusing on intimate state encounters is a story not of governance through control but of the proliferation of spaces of indeterminacy and their effects. The home is rendered as an ambivalent space that is rife with conflicting affects: at once professional and pastoral relationships that are framed by threat, care, need and affection. Intimate state encounters were not cases of distinct racism or 'resistance' (Barnes and Prior 2009: 30) or liminal spaces whose contradictions could be ritually resolved (Ferguson 2018), but complex and continual strategies of accommodation, negotiation and contestation that played out within, and were shaped by, the home space.

Women in frontline service roles (bearing in mind that they are socially situated actors) took on increasing labour in order to balance the demands of their jobs with their often strong ethical motivations and moral standpoints. For frontline workers, home encounters could raise intractable questions, placing them in positions of confusion about the life-changing decisions they had to make. This book has detailed how various legal, moral and normative regulations and discourses were discretionally applied by local frontline workers, resulting in diverse tactics that could allocate, classify, formalise, normalise and ultimately govern through endeavouring to reconcile these conflicts and uncertainties. The strategies they developed could leave them feeling exhausted, frustrated and deeply troubled.

One way to assuage these pressures for frontline workers was to co-opt volunteers to take over some of their work with mothers, particularly the work that involved legal documents and residency rights because they did not see this as part of their immediate remit (which was that of parenting and safeguarding children). This diffusion of power could also be easily justified in a context where the implementation of legal regulations seemed to result in contradictory and perverse decisions so that in-depth 'on the ground' experience was seen as the best kind of qualification to undertake this work. Often, volunteers from churches took on this role of managing mothers 'bureaucratic identities' long after they had begun visiting them in their homes or meeting them in the church. Therefore not only did frontline workers have the potential to be both caring and sanctioning, but for Romanian Roma, a person who previously had been a friend from the church could suddenly become a border guard in their home. These volunteers made decisions based on their own moral convictions, and drew on understandings about migrants that had been built through entirely different relationships.

In this context, the state becomes a contradictory and confusing system for Romanian Roma where a series of tactics are employed in order to attain a sense of safety and security (Solimene 2014; see also Chapter Three). Romanian Roma did not experience the state or those who represented its functions as coherent. This perception of the state as conflicting and shifting encouraged Romanian Roma to desire home visits and individualised relationships as the ideal mode of negotiating their legal status. Bargaining at the margins sometimes opened spaces where they could unsettle the dominant racialised frame that shaped their interactions with frontline workers, but were highly contingent, localised and fragile. The confusion between public and private, affect and formality and the way they are tangled together can be seen as part of a distinct governing logic (Anderson 2000; Mbembe 2001; Thelen and Alber 2017). Governing political belonging through the home space does more than confuse the public and private; it depends on and reproduces that confused space in order to ensure the continual reproduction of marginalisation. While it opened potential spaces of negotiation for Romanian Roma mothers through hosting, it also had costs for the constitution of Romanian Roma and frontline workers as caring and cultural subjects (Erel et al. 2018).

Romanian Roma families desired the state in their lives because it was an opportunity to gain the promise of safety and security (Chapter Three). The state also held a promise for frontline workers. They believed that their engagement would give Romanian Roma children a better life (Chapter Two). It is within this potential and desire for a certain kind of state involvement that governance through the home took place (Jansen 2014). Without this desire for the state and the belief in these promises repeated home encounters would not have taken the same form. The care of children created and opened these fraught and contingent spaces that were always concurrently bound together with the potential of falling into invisibility or engaging the full disciplining arm of the state (through children being taken into care or deportation).

It is through understanding this desire and promise of the state that the costs of engaging in these relationships can also be understood. As described above, the move from social to ethical citizenship has replaced 'the sovereign state' with 'the caring acts of the sovereign individual'. The public is flooded with a proliferation of private emotion and compassion becomes part of everyday bureaucratic work. Intimate state encounters are based on depoliticised forms of sympathetic action which become how Romanian Roma experience the state and how they must negotiate belonging. This is exacerbated by the increasing use of volunteers to fill the gaps in a shrinking welfare state. When frontline workers or volunteers govern through compassion, Romanian Roma are called on to meet them through these registers. For Romanian Roma the costs of these arrangements fall on mothers most directly, but also implicate (and exclude) fathers (Chapter Five). Some of the costs for Romanian Roma families are detailed in Chapter Four and include mobilising pejorative stereotypes about Gypsies, moral dilemmas from conflicting subject-positions, shifting gender and family relationships, losing children into state care and being deported. Romanian Roma are often left to reconcile the contradictions and confusion they face through ideas about 'luck' (*baxt*) (Chapter Three).

The costs for frontline workers involve the consistent reckoning with the realities of their role that juxtapose with their expectations. However, the spaces of indeterminacy that intimate state encounters create, affords frontline workers the possibility of maintaining a coherent moral standpoint while enacting painful acts of exclusion. For example, Paula and Lisa (Chapter Four) reconciled their refusals to care through ideas that Romanian Roma were claiming benefits when they should be waiting until January (unlike their Romanian-not-Roma co-nationals) (Chapter Three, p 81). Frontline workers could maintain some belief in the promise of the state that those who 'do things properly' will gain social protection and security. Governance through intimacy allows sentiment to overtake rights and creates deep uncertainties for frontline workers who justify their roles in ways that ease their dilemmas but ultimately depoliticises their refusal to care.

This governance of marginality through uncertainty and intimacy, or the 'privatisation of state acts', has repercussions at different scales, not just at the level of 'home' but also in terms of 'home-land'. When thinking about these different scales I want to pose another question: what are the implications of encountering the Other in your home, or your home-land? Bhattacharjee's (2006: 351) insight is useful to emphasise the inherent 'privateness of the national public'. The criteria on which people are judged to belong within the 'nation' are not rights and entitlements but personal qualities and whether or not they 'fit'. These criteria are racially inflected and are linked to who is considered to be a good enough citizen and good enough to reproduce new citizens. This is a key contribution of this book: intimate state encounters make visible the link between everyday practices of belonging and formal politics of belonging. Who is allowed to be a member rests on the most intimate practices within homes. These have become the criteria through which formal political belonging is based. The national home-land is reproduced within the mundane, messy and material space of the home. This book has shown how these two scales are inextricably linked, while elucidating the effects for all social actors involved in these forms of governance.

To conclude, this book has shown how the dynamics of filtering, subordination and labour-market discrimination that once occurred at the national border now take place not just within the territory, but also in domestic spaces, placing significance on mothers' encounters with local frontline workers in the home. These negotiations illustrate how the process of social reproduction reflect a historically specific and layered configuration of state, labour-market and family relations that ensures the continuation of community based on social divisions and hierarchies. The migrant family is placed at the intersection of three processes, namely systems of differential inclusion, racialised labelling and stratified reproduction. Proving 'moral worth' through practices of belonging becomes the grounds on which migrants can gain a form of political belonging and access to state resources. Mothers are required to perform contradictory expectations of 'good motherhood' to secure their families' positions and become 'morally legitimate receivers of care' (Chapter Two). These performances do not end with formal legal status, but need to be continually reproduced, sometimes on rapidly shifting and contradictory terms (see Chapter Six).

By analysing home encounters as 'intimate state encounters' through situated actors, embedded relations and the role of space this book has focused on how state forms are reproduced along gendered and racialised hierarchies. In particular, these spatial effects have deep impacts on social relations and how migrants are able to make, and feel, at home. Social reproduction is intimately entwined with state reproduction in these encounters. The domestic ordering within the home directly relates to the national ordering of the home-land. This book has revealed the emotional costs to undertaking reproductive work. These costs, as outlined above, have repercussions (albeit unequally) for all actors' constitutions as caring and cultural subjects. Intimate state encounters should be understood as creating uncertainty because they reveal the fiction of 'public' and 'private' and are therefore unresolvable and in constant tension. The result is not governance through control but through uncertainty where subjects are either expelled or depoliticised, pacified, divided and, in varying ways, 'domesticated' within a fragile home and home-land.

Notes

1 A distinct musical style in Romania that draws on Turkish, Greek, Arabic, Bulgarian and Serbian folk music and uses modern electronic instruments.

2 Romania acceded to the EU on 1 January 2007. Prior to this date, they were subject to the same migration controls as all third-country (non-EU) migrants. Between 1 January 2007 and 1 January 2014, Romanian nationals (henceforth 'A2 migrants') had new but limited rights, subject to transitional controls. After 1 January 2014, Romanian nationals had the same legal status as other EU migrants, though later that year new laws came into place restricting the old EU rights-based conditions such as earnings and residency requirements. In addition, specific entitlements at different times were linked to definitions of 'worker', 'genuine self-employed work', and 'Genuine Prospect of Work', for the purposes of rights related to employment. In 2014, a European Court of Justice case ruled that EU nationals were only able to reside within the UK national territory if they are 'self-sufficient' and do not constitute 'an unreasonable burden on the social assistance system' (ECJ Case C-333/13). All of these terms remained ill-defined and open to different interpretations and legal challenges throughout the duration of my fieldwork.

3 The book pays attention to how categorisations operate and shape the relationship-building process from the perspectives of migrants and those they encounter. Rather than using Romanian Roma as a category of description or analysis, I explore how the label emerges in Luton between 2013 and 2014, how it is brought to bear on certain individuals, and what is at stake by being identified as such and how labels develop and are appropriated or subverted.

4 To clarify, 'home encounter' is used as a descriptive term throughout this book whereas 'intimate state encounter' is an analytical term.

5 Goldberg posits two traditions of thinking about racial states. The first, naturalism, fixes racially conceived 'natives' as premodern, naturally incapable of progress. The second tradition, historicism, elevates Europeans over primitive or underdeveloped Others as a victory of progress (Goldberg 2002: 43).

6 McGarry (2017: 164) reviews how in the Austro-Hungarian Empire Roma children were taken away and given to non-Roma families to learn to be obedient and respectable.

7 The Crown as parens patriae ['parent of the country'] is empowered and obliged 'to protect the person and property of … those unable to look after themselves, including infants.' The powers of the Crown as parens patriae are exercised by the [courts] (Kennedy 2010: 42).

8 Section 17 of the Children Act 1989 (s17) outlines the duty of local authorities in England and Wales to safeguard and promote the welfare of children in their area

who are 'in need'; and to promote the upbringing of these children within their families. S17 has a broad scope and can include the provision of accommodation and financial support if families with dependent children are destitute. The support is administered by children's services departments within local authorities.

Prior to 2002 there were no restrictions for families accessing s17 of the Children Act 1989 (apart from asylum seekers under s122 of the Immigration and Asylum Act 1999). This meant that any family excluded from public funds could access s17 if they became destitute. However, in 2002 restrictions were introduced utilising Schedule 3 of the Nationality, Immigration and Asylum Act 2002. Four categories were restricted: nationals of EU countries, people with refugee status granted in other EU countries, refused asylum seekers who have failed to comply with removal directions, and people unlawfully in the UK. Therefore nationals of EU countries are not eligible for support through the Children Act 1989.

In policy, there is another avenue through which nationals of EU countries could gain social support. Local authorities are able to conduct a human rights assessment. Where the family are EU nationals, it must be established whether any member of that family is exercising Community Treaty rights in the UK and whether the provision of s17 support is necessary to prevent a breach of that right. These are rights as workers, jobseekers, self-employed persons, self-sufficient persons or students. Therefore the discretion regarding 'genuine self-employed work' re-emerges for A2 migrant families. In addition, the local authority must be satisfied, through the information available to them, that the child would be 'in need' on return to their country of nationality, and that there would be a breach of the European Convention on Human Rights if s17 support were not provided. If these conditions are not met, it can conclude in the human rights assessment that there is no s17 duty in the UK. Children of EU national parents who are considered 'destitute' therefore hold an ambiguous position in relation to law and policy in the UK.

[9] See Clarke et al. (2014) for overview.

[10] These two elements are also supplemented with other dimensions such as political engagement (Bloemraad et al. 2008: 154).

[11] Weber's (1947) conception of state bureaucracies, Gramsci's (1971) notion of hegemony, Althusser's (2006) discussion of state apparatus and Foucault's (1991) work on governmentality all approach the notion of the state in terms of the way people work within them.

[12] While there has been work on the home's materiality and its affects (Pink et al. 2015) this has not looked at governance within the home.

[13] Feminist scholars have argued that care should be the basis of social rights and entitlements, thus establishing care as an analytical concept (see Sainsbury 2013: 314–21 for overview). Tronto (2013) has argued from an ethics of care perspective that this work should be understood as a practice of citizenship that takes place in the private space (see also Chapter Four).

[14] Social workers' class dynamics have been analysed by Keane (2003), Pemberton and Mason (2008) and McNay (2009).

[15] I am indebted to Deborah James for these insights.

[16] 'Pathways' is a pseudonym.

[17] Since 2010, justified by the economic recession, austerity has become the UK's dominant fiscal policy (Timms 2010). Austerity has taken the form of deep spending

cuts with comparatively small increases in taxes (Johnson 2013). The policy has decreased welfare services in the UK, with particular effects for migrants (Gateley 2014; Keskinen et al. 2016).

[18] In attempting to understand and explain what influences street-level bureaucrats' behaviour, many scholars have examined the organisational-level dynamics, such as the role of managers (Brehm and Gates 1999; Riccucci 2005; Evans 2016) or the effect of organisational culture (Brodkin 2012; Alpes and Spire 2014; DuBois 2014b; Eule 2014). Others have stressed the significance of bureaucrats' own preferences (Brehm and Gates 1999) or their personal level of agreement with the political message a certain policy aims to promote (May and Winter 2007).

[19] As explained by Pupavac, the Children's Rights framework (as laid down by the United Nations Convention on the Rights of the Child, 1989) stems from 'the separation of the rights-holder and the moral agent, who is empowered to act by the institutionalisation of children's rights. Although the child is treated as a rights-holder under the convention, the child is not regarded as the moral agent who determines those rights' (Pupavac 2001: 99). Children seem to have rights, but they are not in a position to assert those rights, and therefore representatives of the state take over responsibility to determine a child's 'best interests'. Inherent in children's rights is the need for advocacy on behalf of the child. However, rather than parents or guardians representing the interests of children, the international children's rights regime treats children as rights-holders separate from their parents or guardians. Not only does this challenge the capacity of the family to represent their children's interests, it implicitly alludes to a mistrust of the family because of the possibility of abuse. This can be clearly seen through the 'safeguarding' and risk prevention agenda that has infused all UK welfare provision (Parton 2011). Children's rights are not only treated as separate but in conflict with those of their parents or guardians. The overall impact of the international children's rights agenda is to empower outside professionals to represent the interests of the child, displacing the child's family as advocates of the child's interests. Thus the child rights approach places children's best interests at the forefront of the policy response, but it leaves largely open what the best interest is and how it should be determined.

[20] Reeves (2014: 6) defines border work as 'the messy, contested, and often intensely social business of making territory "integral"'.

[21] Sobotka (2003) shows that there are very strong similarities between Roma and non-Roma migrants' sociodemographic profiles.

[22] The European Court of Justice has challenged this practice arguing that it constitutes discrimination against EU citizens who are disentitled by the UK government to their legitimate social rights (European Commission 2013).

[23] The Free Movement of Citizens Directive (2004/38/EC) brought together two regulations and nine directives with the aim of simplifying the legislation on the right of entry and residence for citizens of EU member states. It established that EU workers have the same rights as nationals (and those who have been resident in a member state for a minimum of five years). It also established that member states could withhold social assistance for the first three months if an EU migrant citizen was 'inactive' or did not fulfil the residence requirements. Those who wish to stay for longer than three months must hold a qualifying status. These include being a jobseeker, worker, self-employed, economically inactive and self-sufficient, student and self-sufficient, a family member accompanying or joining an EU national who satisfies one of the other statuses, or a pensioner.

24 To continue this approach following the removal of the controls, the UK government again enacted the right to reside mechanism in the Immigration Act 2014. This legislation gave EU nationals looking for work in the UK access to Universal Credit (which is gradually replacing a range of welfare benefits) for three months.

25 Following the expiry of transitional controls in January 2014, there have been a number of measures aimed at restricting EU migrants' access to social assistance. Although these changes came into force at the end of my fieldwork, they provide an indication of the policy direction towards EU migrants and the formal and informal barriers facing migrants to accessing state resources (Oliver and Jayaweera 2013). A key change was the introduction of a statutory presumption that entitlement to income-based Jobseeker's Allowance (JSA) would be limited to a period of three months unless the jobseeker could pass a Genuine Prospect of Work assessment. In addition, on 1 March 2014 the UK government introduced a minimum weekly income of £153 to define the status of 'workers', which was equivalent to between 23 and 24 hours at the UK national minimum wage of £6.50 per hour. If at the end of three months' unemployment the jobseeker does not have 'compelling evidence' to show they have a 'genuine prospect of work' their JSA will end.

26 The most salient is the Dano case. The European Court of Justice ruled in favour of the German authorities who restricted welfare benefits (Hartz IV benefit) to a Romanian national, Ms Dano, and her child who was also a Romanian national. Her lack of qualifications, language ability and work experience in Romania and Germany were considered important criteria for refusal. The ruling stated that the various regulations 'do not preclude the national legislature from choosing to exclude nationals of other Member States from entitlement to a special non-contributory cash benefit on the basis of a general criterion, such as the reason for entering the territory of the host Member State, which is capable of demonstrating the absence of a genuine link with that State, in order to prevent an unreasonable burden on its social assistance system' (ECJ Case C-333/13).

27 Freedom of movement of workers was one of the four freedoms expressed in the Treaty of Rome in 1957 (also including goods, services and capital). However, although all EU nationals can exercise free movement rights, only certain categories of persons have, under European law, certain guaranteed rights attached to their residence in the host country. The 1958 Coordination Requirements stipulated any discrimination against nationals of other Member States was illegal; and the 1992 Maastricht Treaty formally integrated a concept of EU citizenship into the Treaty. The 2009 Lisbon Treaty and Charter of Fundamental Rights further embedded this concept in Articles 15 and 34).

28 A2 nationals were unable to gain National Insurance Numbers without proving that they were workers or were self-employed. They were not permitted to gain a National Insurance Number as a jobseeker or to be employed unless specified by worker authorisation documents (as previous accession migrants had been permitted to do).

29 As Muehlebach (2012: 133) has argued, the 'postwelfarist public has replaced the Durkheimian ethic of solidarity with an Adam Smithian ethic of fellow feeling; an a priori social that pre-exists human volition and intuition with a much more fickle and frail "social cohesion" that must be incrementally built by caring individuals themselves'.

[30] Stay and Play sessions are daytime events organised and hosted by children's centres in the UK for parents and their babies or toddlers to play together and, crucially, with other families. A key aim of the sessions is for parents to 'learn how they can support their children's learning through everyday activities'. The focus of the sessions is on child development while 'practitioners have a relaxed, low-key approach using a variety of strategies to actively encourage parents to interact with their children both during session and at home'. http://directory.luton.gov.uk/kb5/luton/directory/service.page?id=psXzEduoh8g

[31] Katherine Smith (2012) provides a detailed analysis on the links between fairness and belonging.

[32] Sure Start Children's Centres are funded by the UK government's Early Intervention Grant (EIG), which is paid to local authorities under section 31 of the Local Government Act 2003. EIG is not ring-fenced. Local authorities have the freedom to determine how to fund their networks of children's centres to best meet local needs and priorities and statutory duties. Sufficient children's centre provision is a statutory duty on local authorities under section 5A of the Childcare Act 2006, as amended by section 198 of the Apprenticeships, Skills, Children and Learning Act 2009. The latest data from the Department for Education shows that overall investment in children's centres reduced by about 40% from £1.4 billion per year in 2010–11 to £0.8 billion in 2016–17. Recent research has shown that the biggest cuts to children's centres have occurred in the most disadvantaged local authorities, including Luton, where the need is greatest (*BMJ* 2017).

[33] Healthy Start is a UK-wide government scheme to improve the health of low-income pregnant women and families on benefits and tax credits (www.gov.uk/healthy-start).

[34] In November 2014, Iain Duncan Smith, then-Secretary of State for Work and Pensions, foregrounded the issue in a speech in Berlin. He said "A good example of that is *The Big Issue*, a magazine which is a brilliant idea by a brilliant individual who himself was homeless. It is wonderful. But actually what is happening progressively, more and more, is people mostly from southern and eastern Europe have actually ended up being *Big Issue* sellers and they claim, as self-employed, immediately, tax credits" (*The Independent* 2014). On 6 April 2017, a judge ruled that *The Big Issue* did not fulfil the conditions of 'genuine self-employment' https://assets.publishing.service.gov.uk/media/58ff2e4ee5274a06b00001e8/CSF_251_2016.pdf

[35] There have been long-standing academic debates regarding the term Roma as the category and boundaries of the term have always been contested (Acton 1997; Matras 2000; Hancock 2002).

[36] The construction of the Roma as a recognisable ethnic group, or 'ethnogenesis', has been considered an attempt on the part of the Roma intelligentsia, non-Roma scholars and international advocacy networks to meet the conditions set by the European official rhetoric for the recognition of the right to difference (Solimene 2014). From this perspective, the term Roma is a 'political identity' (Kovats 2002) that utilises the 'ethnological reason' (Amselle 1990) of the non-Roma as a force for political struggles. The construction of Roma identity has confronted opposition from a number of directions, not least from many of those individuals who have been identified as falling under this label (Okely 1983; Guy 2001; Kovats 2002; Gay y Blasco 2011; Acton and Ryder 2013). Solimene (2014) argues that the diversity that can be seen within Roma groups (Grill 2012; Tesăr 2012; Vidra 2013) presents a radical challenge to previous conceptions of ethnic groups.

37 The label 'migrant' has become highly depoliticised, ending up indexing allegedly neutral bureaucratic knowledge rather than questioning the boundaries of citizenship and showing the vacuity of much of Western democratic rules (Pécoud 2015).

38 The process of racialisation is a discourse and practice that constructs immutable boundaries between collectivities, which is used to naturalise fixed hierarchical power relations (Anthias 1992; Solomos and Back 1996; Goldberg 2009). Barth (1969) and others following him have argued that it is the existence of ethnic (and racial) boundaries, rather than of any specific 'essence' around which these boundaries are constructed that is crucial in processes of ethnicisation and racialisation. Any physical or social signifier can be used to construct the boundaries.

39 It is important to note that I am using Scott's conception of labelling for purposes of state knowledge. Other frameworks on labelling include Brubaker and colleagues' (2004) formulation, which conceptualises ethnicity as cognition; or a Bourdieusian perspective which would focus on performativity and the authority of the individual doing the asserting (Bourdieu 1991). However, there are also overlaps in these theories, in that all see labelling as generative and co-produced in as much as they are processual and contextual. I am grateful to Jon Fox for these comments.

40 This process is identified by Hacking (2004: 279) as the 'looping effect', describing the process through which 'people respond to the way they are classified, how that changes behaviour, what kind of subjects it creates, how frontline workers respond to this and try to make sense using their own personalities, histories, experience'.

41 Regardless of the different academic debates regarding the term Roma it cannot be denied that since the collapse of the Soviet Union and the increasing involvement of the EU in countries in Eastern and Central Europe we have seen a growing movement of self-determination encompassing many different groups, at least nominally, in the EU and the United Nations (Feys 1997; Klímová-Alexander 2007) under the umbrella term of Roma. Special funds and policies aimed at 'integrating' and improving the welfare of Roma have been developed, but at the same time there has been no significant change in the social processes locating them as 'Other'.

42 My thoughts on visibility have been developed with Nando Sigona, to whom I am very grateful.

43 See Note 29.

44 De Certeau (1984: xix) distinguishes tactics from strategies. A tactic, he argues,

> 'belongs to the other. A tactic insinuates itself into the other's place, fragmentarily, without taking it over in its entirety, without being able to keep it at a distance. It has at its disposal no base where it case capitalize on its advantages, prepare its expansions, and secure independence with respect to circumstances. The "proper" is a victory space over time ... a tactic depends on time – it is always on the watch for opportunities that must be seized "on the wing". Whatever it wins, it does not keep. It must constantly manipulate events in order to turn them into "opportunities". The weak must continually turn to their own ends and forces alien to them.'

In contrast, strategies 'conceal beneath objective calculations their connection with the power that sustains them from within the stronghold of its own "proper" place or institution' (de Certeau 1984: xix).

[45] Invoking colonial power relations, European colonial women were to uplift colonial subjects through educational and domestic management and attend to the family environment. This was part of white women's imperial duties that celebrated motherhood and domesticity.

[46] These actions draw attention to two issues. First, this situation resonates with other cases where NGOs and social workers 'colonise' needs interpretations on behalf of Roma (Trehan 2001; Timmer 2010; Matras et al. 2015). Second, it reveals the absence of Roma in any positions where they might have voiced opinions about their own needs and remedies.

[47] This has prompted researchers and policy makers to debate the ways in which migrant mothers' cultural orientation aids or hinders their children's integration (Tsolidis 2001; Ganga 2007; Gedalof 2009; Erel 2011b).

[48] There is an interesting parallel in coloniser communities where the fear of transgressions of social space were levied at colonised men who were charged with attempted rapes when they were discovered in the vicinity of white residences (Stoler 2002: 59). One of remedies was increased surveillance of colonised men and the demarcation of new spaces that were made racially off limits. However, white women were also as closely surveyed at this time as colonised men.

[49] I am hugely indebted to Umut Erel for this crucial insight and for her careful reading of a previous version of this chapter. All errors remain my own.

[50] Council tax is a tax levied on households by local government in the UK, based on the estimated value of a property and the number of people living in it. The funds raised by council tax are used to pay for local services such as collecting waste and repairing roads, among many other things.

[51] Border studies over the last two decades has been characterised by two key developmental avenues: theoretical developments, which have increasingly come to frame them as complex processes rather than static lines at the edge of nation-states (Brambilla 2015); and shifting political and policy agendas, which have moved border controls away from geographical borders and into the everyday life of communities within these states (Balibar 2002). Consequently, scholars have been responding to a growing need to understand both their proliferating forms and practices (Green 2013) and the ways in which they have become embedded in everyday life (Johnson et al. 2011; Johnson and Jones 2016). For the UK, this has led to an increase in legislation since the mid-1990s, which has multiplied state-sponsored bordering practices within society. In this everyday context, ordinary people have become involved in 'border work' (Rumford 2006) as agents of the state or, as Vaughan-Williams (2008) argues, in the role of the 'citizen-detective'. In the UK, such roles are enforced by punitive regimes, including fines levied against employers, landlords, and health and educational institutions.

[52] See Note 1.

[53] Subsequent to the research detailed in this book, I also conducted fieldwork with homeless Romanian Roma in London after the transitional controls had been lifted, when far more deportations orders were being issued (Allen et al. 2018).

[54] The Job Centre or Jobcentre Plus is the part of the Department for Work and Pensions which provides working-age support service in the UK. During my fieldwork the Job Centre called applicants for national insurance numbers to the local office to assess claims of self-employment.

55 This has different effects depending on the model of citizenship that has developed within a national territory (Anderson 2013).

56 In the UK, institutions and practices developed through the idea of nation-states with fixed boundaries, marking those who belonged by the jus soli ('law of the soil') model of citizenship. Developing notions of social citizenship, Marshall (1950) gave ideological support to the identification of rights with membership of a nation. The notion of citizenship therefore implies social rights, but also implies exclusion of those deemed as not belonging (Gonzales and Sigona 2017).

57 Those who are placed in marginalised citizenship positions have been theorised in many different ways, such as 'denizens' (Hammer 1990); mezzanine space of citizenship (Nyers 2003); fuzzy boundaries between 'legal' and 'illegal' (Bosniak 2006); 'legal liminality' (Menjívar 2006); a spectrum of grey spaces (Goldring et al. 2009). All these theories of citizenship should themselves be contextualised (Clarke et al. 2014).

References

Abu-lughod, L. 1993. *Writing Women's Worlds: Bedouin Stories*. Berkeley, CA: University of California Press

Achim, V. 2004. *The Roma in Romanian History*. Central European University Press

Acton, T.A. 1997. *Gypsy Politics and Traveller Identity*. Hatfield: University of Hertfordshire Press

Acton, T. and Ryder, A. 2013. Roma Civil Society: Deliberative Democracy for Change in Europe. Discussion Paper. Birmingham: University of Birmingham

Ahmed, S. 2000. *Strange Encounters: Embodied Others in Post-Coloniality*. London: Psychology Press

Aldridge, J., Shute, J., Ralphs, R. and Medina, J. 2011. Blame the Parents? Challenges for Parent-Focused Programmes for Families of Gang-Involved Young People. *Children and Society*, 25, 371–81

Allen, C. 2010. Fear and Loathing: The Political Discourse in Relation to Muslims and Islam in the British Contemporary Setting. *Politics and Religion*, 2, 221–36

Allen, W., Anderson, B., van Hear, N., Sumption, M., Düvell, F., Hough, J., Rose, L., Humphris, R. and Walker, S. 2018. Who Counts in Crises? The New Geopolitics of International Migration and Refugee Governance. *Geopolitics*, 23, 217–43

Alpes, M.J. and Spire, A. 2014. Dealing with Law in Migration Control: The Powers of Street-Level Bureaucrats at French Consulates. *Social and Legal Studies*, 23, 261–74

Althusser, L. 2006. Ideology and Ideological State Apparatuses (Notes Towards An Investigation). In Sharma, A. and Gupta, A. (Eds) *The Anthropology of the State: A Reader*. New Jersey: John Wiley & Sons

Amselle, J.–L. 1990. *Logiques Métisses*. Paris: Payot

Anderson, B. 1983. *Imagined Communities. Reflections on the Origin and Spread of Nationalism*. London: Verson

Anderson, B. 1991. *Imagined Communities: Reflections on the Origin and Spread of Nationalism*. Conneticut: Tantor Media

Anderson, B. 2000. *Doing the Dirty Work? The Global Politics of Domestic Labour*. London: Palgrave Macmillan

Anderson, B. 2013. *Us and Them? The Dangerous Politics of Immigration Control*, Oxford: Oxford University Press

Andrijasevic, R. 2013. Acts of Citizenship as Methodology. In Isin, E. F. and Saward, M. (Eds) *Enacting European Citizenship*. Cambridge: Cambridge University Press

Anthias, F. 1992. *Ethnicity, Class, Gender, and Migration: Greek Cypriots in Britain*. Avebury: Ashgate Publishing

Appadurai, A. 1988. Introduction: Place and Voice in Anthropological Theory. *Cultural Anthropology*, 3, 16–20

Applebaum, L.D. 2001. The Influence of Perceived Deservingness on Policy Decisions Regarding Aid to the Poor. *Political Psychology*, 22, 419–42

Asad, T. 1973. *Anthropology and the Colonial Encounter*. Ithaca: Cornell University Press

Auerbach, C.F., Bachmeier, J.D., Berry, J.W., Chao, R., Coltrane, S., Cookston, J., De Anda, R.M., Denton, N.A., Gielen, U. and Hernandez, D.J. 2008. *On New Shores: Understanding Immigrant Fathers in North America*, Boston: Lexington Books

Balibar, E. 1998. The Borders of Europe. *Cultural Politics*, 14, 216–32

Balibar, E. 2004. *We, the People of Europe? Reflections on Transnational Citizenship*. New Jersey: Princeton University Press

Balibar, E. 2009. Europe as Borderland. *Environment and Planning D: Society and Space*, 27, 190–215

Balibar, E. and Williams, E.M. 2002. World Borders, Political Borders. *Publications of the Modern Language Association*, 117, 71–8

Banks, M. 1996. *Ethnicity: Anthropological Constructions*. London: Psychology Press

Barnes, J. 2008. *Nurse-Family Partnership Programme: First Year Pilot Site Implementation in England: Pregnancy and the Post-Partum Period*. London: Department for Children, Schools and Families

Barnes, J.A. 1963. Some Ethical Problems in Modern Fieldwork. *The British Journal of Sociology*, 14, 118–34

Barnes, M. and Prior, D. 2009. *Subversive Citizens: Power, Agency and Resistance in Public Services*. Bristol: Policy Press

Barth, F. 1969. *Ethnic Groups and Boundaries: The Social Organization of Cultural Difference*. Boston: Little Brown

Batty, E. and Flint, J. 2012. Conceptualising the Contexts, Mechanisms and Outcomes of Intensive Family Intervention Projects. *Social Policy and Society*, 11, 345–58

Bauman, Z. 2001. *The Individualized Society*. Cambridge: Polity

Beck, S. 1989. The Origins of Gypsy Slavery in Romania. *Dialectical Anthropology*, 14, 53–61

Berg, M.L. and Sigona, N. 2013. Ethnography, Diversity and Urban Space. *Identities*, 20, 347–60

Besnier, N. 2009. *Gossip and the Everyday Production of Politics*. Honolulu: University of Hawaii Press

Bhattacharjee, A. 2006. The Public/Private Mirage: Mapping Homes and Undomesticating Violence Work in the South Asian Immigrant Community. In Sharma, A. and Gupta, A. (Eds) *The Anthropology of the State: A Reader*. Oxford: Blackwell

Bhattacharyya, G. 2015. *Crisis, Austerity and Everyday Life: Living in a Time of Diminished Expectations*. Basingstoke: Palgrave Macmillan

Bigo, D. 2005. Frontier Controls in the European Union: Who Is in Control? In Guild, E. (Ed.) *Controlling Frontiers: Free Movement Into and Within Europe*. Aldershot: Ashgate

Bloemraad, I., Korteweg, A. and Yurdakul, G. 2008. Citizenship and Immigration: Multiculturalism, Assimilation, and Challenges to the Nation-State. *Annual Review of Sociology*, 34, 153–79

Blunt, A. 2005. *Domicile and Diaspora: Anglo-Indian Women and the Spatial Politics of Home*. John Wiley & Sons

BMJ (*British Medical Journal*) 2017. Public Spending Cuts are Linked to 120 000 Excess Deaths in England, Study Suggests, News, 16 November. www.Bmj.Com/Content/359/Bmj.J5332/Rr

Bosniak, L. 2006. *The Citizen and the Alien: Dilemmas of Contemporary Membership*. Princeton University Press

Boulton, M. G. 1983. *On Being a Mother: A Study of Women with Pre-School Children*. London: Tavistock Press

Bourdieu, P. 1991. *Language and Symbolic Power*. Boston: Harvard University Press

Bowlby, S., Gregory, S. and Mckie, L. 1997. 'Doing Home': Patriarchy, Caring, and Space. *Women's Studies International Forum*, 20, 343–50

Brambilla, C. 2015. Exploring the Critical Potential of the Borderscapes Concept. *Geopolitics*, 20, 14–34

Brehm, J. and Gates, S. 1999. *Working, Shirking, and Sabotage: Bureaucratic Response to a Democratic Public*. University of Michigan Press

Brodkin, E. Z. 2012. Reflections on Street-Level Bureaucracy: Past, Present, and Future. *Public Administration Review*, 72, 940–9

Brown, W. 1992. Finding the Man in the State. *Feminist Studies*, 18, 7–34

Brown, W. 2015. *Undoing the Demos: Neoliberalism's Stealth Revolution*. Cambridge, MA: MIT Press

Brubaker, R. 2002. Ethnicity Without Groups. *Archives Européennes De Sociologie*, 43, 163–89

Brubaker, R., Loveman, M. and Stamatov, P. 2004. Ethnicity as Cognition. *Theory and Society*, 33, 31–64

Butler, J. P. and Spivak, G.C. 2007. *Who Sings the Nation-State?* New York: Seagull Books

Carr, D. 1986. Narrative and the Real World: An Argument for Continuity. *History and Theory*, 25, 117–31

Carr, H. 2010. Looking Again at Discipline and Gender: Theoretical Concerns and Possibilities in the Study of Anti-Social Behaviour Initiatives. *Social Policy and Society*, 9, 77–87

Castles, S. and Miller, M.J. 2009. *The Age of Migration: International Population Movements in the Modern World*. New York: Guilford Press

Chapman, T. and Hockley, J. L. 1999. *Ideal Homes? Social Change and Domestic Life*. London: Psychology Press

Charsley, K. and Wray, H. 2015. Introduction: The Invisible (Migrant) Man. *Men and Masculinities*, 18, 403–23

Chauvin, S. and Garcés-Mascareñas, B. 2014. Becoming Less Illegal: Deservingness Frames and Undocumented Migrant Incorporation. *Sociology Compass*, 8, 422–32

Clark, C.R. 2014. Glasgow's Ellis Island? The Integration and Stigmatisation of Govanhill's Roma Population. *People, Place and Policy*, 8, 34–50

Clark, C. and Campbell, E. 2000. 'Gypsy Invasion': A Critical Analysis of Newspaper Reaction to Czech and Slovak Romani Asylum-Seekers in Britain, 1997. *Romani Studies*, 10, 23–47

Clarke, J., Coll, K., Dagnino, E. and Neveu, C. 2014. *Disputing Citizenship*. Bristol: Policy Press

Clarke, J. and Fink, J. 2008. Unsettled Attachments: National Identity, Citizenship and Welfare. In Van Oorschot, W., Opielka, M. and Pfau-Effinger, B. (Eds) *Culture and Welfare State: Values and Social Policy in Comparative Perspective*. London: Edward Elgar Publishing

Cohen, C. J. 1999. *The Boundaries of Blackness: AIDS and the Breakdown of Black Politics*. Chicago: University of Chicago Press

Coleman, M. 2012. The 'Local' Migration State: The Site-Specific Devolution of Immigration Enforcement in the US South. *Law and Policy*, 34, 159–90

Collins, P.H. 1997. How Much Difference is Too Much? Black Feminist Thought and the Politics of Postmodern Social Theory. *Current Perspectives in Social Theory*, 17, 3–38

Connell, R.W. 1990. The State, Gender, and Sexual Politics. *Theory and Society*, 19, 507–44

Copsey, N. 2010. The English Defence League: Challenging Our Country and Our Values of Social Inclusion, Fairness and Equality. London: Faith Matters

Crawford, J. and Flint, J. 2015. Rational Fictions and Imaginary Systems: Cynical Ideology and the Problem Figuration and Practise of Public Housing. *Housing Studies*, 30, 792–807

Crenshaw, K. 1989. Demarginalizing the Intersection of Race and Sex: A Black Feminist Critique of Antidiscrimination Doctrine, Feminist Theory and Antiracist Politics. *The University of Chicago Legal Forum*, 139–67

Crossley, S. 2016. The Troubled Families Programme: In, For and Against the State? *Social Policy Review: Analysis and Debate in Social Policy*, 28, 127

D'andrade, R.G. 1995. *The Development of Cognitive Anthropology*. Cambridge: Cambridge University Press

Damer, S. 2000. 'Engineers of the Human Machine': The Social Practice of Council Housing Management in Glasgow, 1895–1939. *Urban Studies*, 37, 11, 2007–26

Das, V. and Poole, D. 2004. *Anthropology in the Margins of the State*. Oxford: James Currey Publishers

Davidoff, L. 1999. *The Family Story: Blood, Contract and Intimacy, 1830–1960*. London: Longman

De Certeau, M. 1984. *The Practice of Everyday Life*. Berkeley: University of California Press

De Genova, N. 2002. Migrant 'Illegality' and Deportability in Everyday Life. *Annual Review of Anthropology*, 31, 419–47

De Genova, N. 2013. Spectacles of Migrant 'Illegality': The Scene of Exclusion, the Obscene of Inclusion. *Ethnic and Racial Studies*, 36, 1180–98

De Swaan, A. 1988. *In Care of the State: State Formation and the Collectivization of Health Care, Education and Welfare in Europe and America During the Modern Era*. New York: Oxford University Press

Derrida, J. 2000. *Of Hospitality (Cultural Memory in the Present)*. California: Stanford University Press

Deutsch, F.M. 2007. Undoing Gender. *Gender and Society*, 21, 106–27

Douglas, M. 1966. *Purity and Danger: An Analysis of the Concepts of pollution and Taboo*. New York: Pantheon

Dubois, V. 2014a. The Economic Vulgate of Welfare Reform: Elements for a Socioanthropological Critique. *Current Anthropology*, 55, 138–46

Dubois, V. 2014b. The State, Legal Rigor, and the Poor: The Daily Practice of Welfare Control. *Social Analysis*, 58, 38–55

Duyvendak, J.W. 2011. *The Politics of Home: Belonging and Nostalgia in Europe and the United States*. London: Palgrave Macmillan

Easthope, H. 2004. A Place Called Home. *Housing, Theory and Society*, 21, 128–38

Edwards, J. and Strathern, M. 2000. Including Our Own. In Carsten, J. (Ed.) *Cultures of Relatedness: New Approaches to the Study of Kinship.* Cambridge: Cambridge University Press

Erel, U. 2011a. Complex Belongings: Racialization and Migration in a Small English City. *Ethnic and Racial Studies*, 34, 2048–68

Erel, U. 2011b. Reframing Migrant Mothers as Citizens. *Citizenship Studies*, 15, 695–709

Erel, U., Reynolds, T. and Kaptani, E. 2018. Migrant Mothers' Creative Interventions into Racialized Citizenship. *Ethnic and Racial Studies*, 41, 55–72

Essed, P. 1991. *Understanding Everyday Racism: An Interdisciplinary Approach.* Newbury Park: Sage

Eule, T. 2014. *Inside Immigration Law*, Surrey: Ashgate

European Commission 2013. Social Security Benefits: Commission Refers UK to Court for Incorrect Application of EU Social Security Safeguards. News, 30 May. Brussels European Commission

Evans, T. 2016. *Professional Discretion in Welfare Services: Beyond Street-Level Bureaucracy*. London: Routledge

Ferguson, H. 2018. Making Home Visits: Creativity and the Embodied Practices of Home Visiting in Social Work and Child Protection. *Qualitative Social Work*, 17, 65–80

Ferguson, J. and Gupta, A. 2002. Spatializing States: Toward an Ethnography of Neoliberal Governmentality. *American Ethnologist*, 29, 981–1002

Feys, C. 1997. Towards a New Paradigm of the Nation: The Case of the Roma. *Journal of Public and International Affairs*, 8, 1–19

Flint, J. 2012. The Inspection House and Neglected Dynamics of Governance: The Case of Domestic Visits in Family Intervention Projects. *Housing Studies*, 27, 822–38

Flint, J. 2018. Encounters with the Centaur State: Advanced Urban Marginality and the Practices and Ethics of Welfare Sanctions Regimes. *Urban Studies*, 31 January

Fortier, A.-M. 2000. *Migrant Belongings: Memory, Space, Identity*. Oxford: Berg

Foucault, M. 1991. *Discipline and Punish: The Birth of the Prison*. London: Penguin

Foucault, M. 1997. Ethics: Subjectivity and Truth. In Rabinow, P. (Ed.) *Essential Works of Foucault 1954–84*. New York: New Press

Foucault, M. and Miskowiec, J. 1986. Of Other Spaces. *Diacritics*, 16, 22–7

Fox, B. 2006. Motherhood as a Class Act: The Many Ways in which 'Intensive Mothering' is Entangled with Social Class. In Bezanson, K. and Luxton, M. (Eds) *Social Reproduction: Feminist Political Economy Challenges Neo-Liberalism*. Quebec: McGill-Queen's University Press

Fox, J.E., Moroşanu, L. and Szilassy, E. 2015. Denying Discrimination: Status, 'Race', and the Whitening of Britain's New Europeans. *Journal of Ethnic and Migration Studies*, 41, 729–48

Francis, N. 2012. Hatred Tearing a Town Apart. War Between Far Right and Radical Muslims Threatening Luton. 27th February. *The Sun*

Fraser, N. 1987. Women, Welfare and the Politics of Need Interpretation. *Hypatia*, 2, 103–21

Friling, T., Ioanid, R. and Ionescu, M.E. 2005. *Final Report of the International Commission on the Holocaust in Romania*. Iasi: Polirom Publishing

Ganga, D. 2007. Breaking with Tradition Through Cultural Continuity. Gender and Generation in a Migratory Setting. *Migration Letters*, 4, 41–52

Garrett, P.M. 2007. 'Sinbin' Solutions: The 'Pioneer' Projects for 'Problem Families' and the Forgetfulness of Social Policy Research. *Critical Social Policy*, 27, 203–30

Gateley, D.E. 2014. What Alternatives Post-Austerity? Importance of Targeted Employment Advice for Refugee Young People in London, UK. *Journal of Youth Studies*, 17, 1260–76

Gsy Y Blasco, P. 1997. A Different 'Body'? Desire and Virginity among Gitanos. *Journal of the Royal Anthropological Institute*, 3, 517–35

Gay Y Blasco, P. 2011. Agata's Story: Singular Lives and the Reach of the 'Gitano Law'. *Journal of the Royal Anthropological Institute*, 17, 445–61

Gedalof, I. 2007. Unhomely Homes: Women, Family and Belonging in UK Discourses of Migration and Asylum. *Journal of Ethnic and Migration Studies*, 33, 77–94

Gedalof, I. 2009. Birth, Belonging and Migrant Mothers: Narratives of Reproduction in Feminist Migration Studies. *Feminist Review*, 93, 81–100

Geddes, A. and Favell, A. 1999. *The Politics of Belonging: Migrants and Minorities in Contemporary Europe*. Farnham: Ashgate Publishing Limited

Gidley, B. 2000. *The Proletarian Other: Charles Booth and the Politics of Representation*. London: Goldsmiths University of London

Gidley, B. 2007. Sure Start: An Upstream Approach to Reducing Health Inequalities? In Scriven, A. and Garman, S. (Eds) *Public Health: Social Context and Action*. Buckingham: Open University Press

Gillies, V. 2007. *Marginalised Mothers: Exploring Working-Class Experiences of Parenting*. Oxford: Routledge

Gilson, L. 2015. Lipsky's Street-Level Bureaucracy. In Page, E., Lodge, M. and Balla, S. (Eds) *Oxford Handbook of the Classics of Public Policy.* Oxford: Oxford University Press

Goldberg, D. T. 2002. *The Racial State*, Blackwell Publishing

Goldberg, D. T. 2009. *The Threat of Race: Reflections on Racial Neoliberalism.* Hoboken, New Jersey: John Wiley & Sons

Goldring, L., Berinstein, C. and Bernhard, J.K. 2009. Institutionalizing Precarious Migratory Status in Canada. *Citizenship Studies*, 13, 239–65

Gonzales, R.G. and Sigona, N. 2017. Mapping the Soft Borders of Citizenship: An Introduction. In Gonzales, R.G. and Sigona, N. (Eds) *Within and Beyond Citizenship. Borders, Membership and Belonging.* London: Routledge

Graham, M. 2002. Emotional Bureaucracies: Emotions, Civil Servants, and Immigrants in the Swedish Welfare State. *Ethos*, 30, 199–226

Gramsci, A. 1971. *Selections from the Prison Notebooks of Antonio Gramsci.* New York City: International Publishers

Gray, M. 2014. The Swing to Early Intervention and Prevention and Its Implications for Social Work. *British Journal of Social Work*, 44, 1750–69

Green, S. 2013. Borders and the Relocation of Europe. *Annual Review of Anthropology*, 42, 345–61

Griffiths, M. 2015. 'Here, Man is Nothing!' Gender and Policy in an Asylum Context. *Men and Masculinities*, 18, 468–88

Grill, J. 2012. 'Going Up to England': Exploring Mobilities among Roma from Eastern Slovakia. *Journal of Ethnic and Migration Studies*, 38, 1269–87

Grill, J. 2018. 'In England, They Don't Call You Black!' Migrating Racialisations and the Production of Roma Difference Across Europe. *Journal of Ethnic and Migration Studies*, 44, 1136–55

Guy, W. 2001. *Between Past and Future: The Roma of Central and Eastern Europe.* Hatfield: University of Hertfordshire Press

Guy, W. 2003. 'No Soft Touch': Romani Migration to the UK at the Turn of the Twenty-First Century. *Nationalities Papers*, 31, 63–79

Hacking, I. 2004. Between Michel Foucault and Erving Goffman: Between Discourse in the Abstract and Face-to-Face Interaction. *Economy and Society*, 33, 277–302

Hall, S. 1993. Culture, Community, Nation. *Cultural Studies*, 7, 349–63

Hall, S. and Du Gay, P. 1996. *Questions of Cultural Identity.* London: Sage

Hall, S.M. 2013. Super-Diverse Street: A 'Trans-Ethnography' Across Migrant Localities. *Ethnic and Racial Studies*, 1–14

Hammer, T. 1990. *Democracy and the Nation State: Aliens, Denizens and Citizens in a World of International Migration.* Aldershot: Ashgate

Hancock, I. F. 2002. *We are the Romani People.* Hatfield: University of Hertfordshire Press

Hannerz, U. 1996. *Transnational Connections: Culture, People, Places*. Hove: Psychology Press

Hansen, T.B. and Stepputat, F. 2001. *States of Imagination: Ethnographic Explorations of the Postcolonial State*. Durham: Duke University Press

Haraway, D. 1988. Situated Knowledges: The Science Question in Feminism and the Privilege of Partial Perspective. *Feminist Studies*, 14, 575–99

Harney, N. 2006. Rumour, Migrants, and the Informal Economies of Naples, Italy. *International Journal of Sociology and Social Policy*, 26, 374–84

Hastings, A., Bailey, N., Besemer, K., Bramley, G., Gannon, M. and Watkins, D. 2013. Coping with Cuts? Local Government and Poorer Communities. York: Joseph Rowntree Foundation

Hayden, C. and Jenkins, C. 2014. 'Troubled Families' Programme in England: 'Wicked Problems' and Policy-Based Evidence. *Policy Studies*, 35, 631–49

Hats, S. 1998. *The Cultural Contradictions of Motherhood*. New Haven: Yale University Press

Herzfeld, M. 1992. *The Social Production of Indifference*. Chicago: University of Chicago Press

Heyman, J.M. 2004. The Anthropology of Power-Wielding Bureaucracies. *Human Organization*, 63, 487–500

Hochschild, A.R. 1979. Emotion Work, Feeling Rules, and Social Structure. *American Journal of Sociology*, 85, 551–75

Holt, A. 2008. Room for Resistance? Parenting Orders, Disciplinary Power and the Production of the 'Bad Parent'. In SQUIRES, P. (Ed.) *ASBO Nation: The Criminalisation of Nuisance*. Bristol: Policy Press

Humphris, R. 2013. European Union Enlargement and Roma Migrants' Welfare: The Role of Changing Migration Status in UK Education Policy and Practice. *Human Welfare*, 26–35

Humphris, R. 2017. Borders of Home: Roma Migrant Mothers Negotiating Boundaries in Home Encounters. *Journal of Ethnic and Migration Studies*, 43, 1190–204

Humphris, R. 2018a. Mutating Faces of the State? Austerity, Migration and Faith-Based Volunteers in a UK Downscaled Urban Context. *The Sociological Review*, August, https://doi.org/10.1177/0038026118793035

Humphris, R. 2018b. On the Threshold: Becoming Romanian Roma, Everyday Racism and Residency Rights in Transition. *Social Identities*, 24, 505–19

Hurtado, A. 1989. Relating to Privilege: Seduction and Rejection in the Subordination of White Women and Women of Color. *Signs*, 14, 833–55

Intke-Hernández, M. and Holm, G. 2015. Migrant Stay-at-Home Mothers Learning to Eat and Live the Finnish Way. *Nordic Journal of Migration Research*, 5, 2, 75–82

Isin, E. F. 2002. *Being Political: Genealogies of Citizenship*. Minneapolis: University of Minnesota Press

Isin, E.F. and Nielsen, G.M. 2008. *Acts of Citizenship*. London: Zed Books

Isin, E.F. and Saward, M. 2013. *Enacting European Citizenship*. Cambridge: Cambridge University Press

Jackson, S. and Scott, S. 2002. *Gender: A Sociological Reader*. London: Psychology Press

Jansen, S. 2014. Hope for/against the State: Gridding in a Besieged Sarajevo Suburb. *Ethnos*, 79, 238–60

Jefferess, D. 2011. Benevolence, Global Citizenship and Post-Racial Politics. *TOPIA: Canadian Journal of Cultural Studies*, 77–95

Jensen, O. 2013. Your Ghetto, My Comfort Zone: A Life-Story Analysis of Inter-Generational Housing Outcomes and Residential Geographies in Urban South-East England. *Identities*, 20, 438–54

Johnson, C., Jones, R., Paasi, A., Amoore, L., Mountz, A., Salter, M. and RRumford, C. 2011. Interventions on Rethinking 'the Border' in Border Studies. *Political Geography*, 30, 61–9

Johnson, P. 2013. *Spending Review Analysis*. London: Institute for Fiscal Studies

Johnson, C. and Jones, R. 2016. *Placing the Border in Everyday Life*. London: Routledge

Jones, R. 2007. *People/States/Territories: The Political Geographies of British State Transformation*. Oxford: Blackwell

Jones, H., Gunaratnam, Y., Bhattacharyya, G., Davies, W., Dhaliwal, S., Forkert, K., Jackson, E. and Saltus, R. 2017. *Go Home? The Politics of Immigration Controversies*. Manchester: Manchester University Press

Kahn, S. M. 2000. *Reproducing Jews: A Cultural Account of Assisted Conception in Israel*. Durham: Duke University Press

Katz, C. 2001. Vagabond Capitalism and the Necessity of Social Reproduction. *Antipode*, 33, 709–28

Keane, H. 2003. Critiques of Harm Reduction, Morality and the Promise of Human Rights. *International Journal of Drug Policy*, 14, 227–32

Kennedy, I. (2001) *Principles of medical law*, Oxford: Oxford University Press.

Kertzer, D.I. and Arel, D. 2002. *Census and Identity: The Politics of Race, Ethnicity, and Language in National Censuses*. Cambridge: Cambridge University Press

Keskinen, S., Norocel, O. C. and Jørgensen, M. B. 2016. The Politics and Policies of Welfare Chauvinism Under the Economic Crisis. *Critical Social Policy*, 36, 321–9

Kirkup, J. and Winnett, R. 2012. 'We're Going to Give Illegal Migrants a Really Hostile Reception'. Theresa May Interview: *The Telegraph*. 12 May. www.telegraph.co.uk/news/uknews/immigration/9291483/Theresa-May-interview-Were-going-to-give-illegal-migrants-a-really-hostile-reception.html

Klímová-Alexander, I. 2007. Transnational Romani and Indigenous Non-Territorial Self-Determination Claims. *Ethnopolitics*, 6, 395–416

Klotz, M. 2013. Genetic Knowledge and Family Identity: Managing Gamete Donation in Britain and Germany. *Sociology*, 47, 939–56

Knowles, C. 2003. *Race and Social Analysis*. London: Sage

Kofman, E. 1998. Whose City? Gender, Class, and Immigration in Globalizing European Cities. In Fincher, R. and Jacobs, J.M. (Eds) *Cities of Difference*. Guilford Press

Kofman, E. 2000. *Gender and International Migration in Europe: Employment, Welfare, and Politics*. London: Psychology Press

Kovats, M. 2002. The European Roma Question. London: The Royal Institute of International Affairs, Briefing Paper 31

Krause, K. and Schramm, K. 2011. Thinking Through Political Subjectivity. *African Diaspora*, 4, 115–34

Krummel, S. 2012. Migrant Women: Stories of Empowerment, Transformation, Exploitation and Resistance. *Journal of Ethnic and Migration Studies*, 38, 1175–84

Lamphere, L. 2005. Providers and Staff Respond to Medicaid Managed Care: The Unintended Consequences of Reform in New Mexico. *Medical Anthropology Quarterly*, 19, 3–25

Lapworth, A. 2015. Habit, Art, and the Plasticity of the Subject: The Ontogenetic Shock of the Bioart Encounter. *Cultural Geographies*, 22, 85–102

Laslett, B. and Brenner, J. 1989. Gender and Social Reproduction: Historical Perspectives. *Sociological Forum*, 14, 381–404

Laszczkowski, M. and Reeves, M. 2015. Introduction. Affective States: Entanglements, Suspensions, Suspicions. *Social Analysis*, 59, 1

Lawson, V. and ElwoodD, S. 2014. Encountering Poverty: Space, Class and Poverty Politics. *Antipode*, 46, 209–28

Lee, Y.–S. and Yeoh, B. S. 2006. *Globalisation and the Politics of Forgetting*. London: Psychology Press

Lefebvre, H. 1991. *The Production of Space (Trans. D. Nicholson-Smith)*. Oxford: Blackwell

LeGrand, J. 2003. *Motivation, Agency and Public Policy: Of Knights, Naves, Pawns and Queens*. Oxford: Open University Press

Lillrank, A. 2015. Trust, Vacillation and Neglect. *Nordic Journal of Migration Research*, 5, 83–90

Lippert, R. and Rehaag, S. 2012. *Sanctuary Practices in International Perspectives: Migration, Citizenship and Social Movements*. New York: Routledge

Lipsky, M. 2010. *Street-Level Bureaucracy. Dilemmas of the Individual in Public Service*. New York: Russell Sage Foundation

Lister, R. 1997. Citizenship: Towards a Feminist Synthesis. *Feminist Review*, 57, 28–48

Lister, R. 2003. Investing in the Citizen-Workers of the Future: Transformations in Citizenship and the State Under New Labour. *Social Policy and Administration*, 37, 427–43

Lofland, L.H. 1998. *The Public Realm: Exploring the City's Quintessential Social Territory*. New Jersey: Transaction Publishers

Lonergan, G. 2015. Migrant Women and Social Reproduction Under Austerity. *Feminist Review*, 109, 124–45

Lonergan, G. 2018. Reproducing the 'National Home': Gendering Domopolitics. *Citizenship Studies*, 22, 1–18

Luibhéid, E. 2006. Sexual Regimes and Migration Controls: Reproducing the Irish Nation-State in Transnational Contexts. *Feminist Review*, 83, 60–78

Luton Borough Council 2013. *Annual Population Survey Data on Employment and Skills in Luton*. Luton: Research and Geospatial Information

Lutz, H. 2010. Gender in the Migratory Process. *Journal of Ethnic and Migration Studies*, 36, 1647–63

Mallett, S. 2004. Understanding Home: A Critical Review of the Literature. *The Sociological Review*, 52, 62–89

Marshall, T.H. 1950. *Citizenship and Social Class*. Cambridge: Cambridge University Press

Marston, S. A. 2004. Space, Culture, State: Uneven Developments in Political Geography. *Political Geography*, 23, 1–16

Martínez Guillem, S. 2011. European Identity: Across Which Lines? Defining Europe Through Public Discourses on the Roma. *Journal of International and Intercultural Communication*, 4, 23–41

Massey, D. 2007. *World City*. Cambridge: Polity

Massey, D. B. 1994. *Space, Place, and Gender*. Minneapolis: University of Minnesota Press

Matras, Y. 2000. Romani Migrations in the Post-Communist Era: Their Historical and Political Significance. *Cambridge Review of International Affairs*, 13, 32–50

Matras, Y., Leggio, D.V. and Steel, M. 2015. 'Roma Education' as a Lucrative Niche: Ideologies and Representations. *ZEP: Zeitschrift Für Internationale Bildungsforschung Und Entwicklungspädagogik*, 38, 11–23

May, P.J. and Winter, S.C. 2007. Politicians, Managers, and Street–Level Bureaucrats: Influences on Policy Implementation. *Journal of Public Administration Research and Theory*, 19, 453–76

Mayblin, L. and James, P. 2018. Asylum and Refugee Support in the UK: Civil Society Filling the Gaps? *Journal of Ethnic and Migration Studies*, 1–20

Mayhew, L. and Waples, S. 2011. *The Growth and Changing Complexion of Luton's Population. A Structural Analysis and Decomposition.* London: Mayhew Harper Associates Ltd.

Maynard-Moody, S.W. and Musheno, M.C. 2003. *Cops, Teachers, Counselors: Stories from the Front Lines of Public Service.* Ann Arbor: University of Michigan Press

Maynard-Moody, S.W and Musheno, M.C. 2012. Social Equities and Inequities in Practice: Street-Level Workers as Agents and Pragmatists. *Public Administration Review*, 72, 16–23

Mbembe, A. 2001. *On the Postcolony.* Oakland: University of California Press

McCall, L. 2005. The Complexity of Intersectionality. *Signs*, 30, 1771–800

McClintock, A. 1995. Imperial Leather: Race, Gender, and Sexuality in the Colonial Contest. New York: Routledge

McGarry, A. 2017. *Romaphobia: The Last Acceptable Form of Racism.* London: Zed Books

McMahon, M. 1995. *Engendering Motherhood: Identity and Self-Transformation in Women's Lives.* New York: Guilford Press

McNay, L. 2009. Self as Enterprise: Dilemmas of Control and Resistance in Foucault's The Birth of Biopolitics. *Theory, Culture and Society*, 26, 55–77

McNevin, A. 2011. *Contesting Citizenship: Irregular Migrants and New Frontiers of the Political.* New York: Columbia University Press

Measor, L. 2013. Loic Wacquant, Gender and Cultures of Resistance. In Squires, P. and Lea, J. (Eds) *Criminalisation and Advanced Marginality: Critically Exploring the Work of Loic Wacquant.* Bristol: Policy Press

Menjívar, C. 2006. Liminal Legality: Salvadoran and Guatemalan Immigrants' Lives in the United States. *American Journal of Sociology*, 111, 999–1037

Mezzadra, S. and Neilson, B. 2013. *Border as Method, or, the Multiplication of Labor.* Durham: Duke University Press

Mitchell, T. 1991. The Limits of the State: Beyond Statist Approaches and Their Critics. *The American Political Science Review*, 85, 77–96

Mitchell, T. 1999. Society, Economy, and the State Effect. In Steinmetz, G. (Ed.) *State/Culture: State-Formation After the Cultural Turn*. Ithaca: Cornell University Press

Morgan, J. 2010. Family Intervention Tenancies: The De(Marginalisation) of Social Tenants? *Journal of Social Welfare and Family Law*, 32, 37–46

Mountz, A. 2003. Human Smuggling, the Transnational Imaginary, and Everyday Geographies of the Nation-State. *Antipode*, 35, 622–44

Muehlebach, A. 2012. *The Moral Neoliberal: Welfare and Citizenship in Italy*. Chicago: University of Chicago Press

Munn, N.D. 1996. Excluded Spaces: The Figure in the Australian Aboriginal Landscape. *Critical Inquiry*, 22, 446–65

Navaro-Yashin, Y. 2002. *Faces of the State: Secularism and Public Life in Turkey*. New Jersey: Princeton University Press

Neal, S., Bennett, K., Cochrane, A. and Mohan, G. 2013. Living Multiculture: Understanding the New Spatial and Social Relations of Ethnicity and Multiculture in England. *Environment and Planning C: Government and Policy*, 31, 308–23

Nordberg, C. 2015. Invisibilised Visions. *Nordic Journal of Migration Research*, 5, 67–74

Nowicka, M. 2007. Mobile Locations: Construction of Home in a Group of Mobile Transnational Professionals. *Global Networks*, 7, 69–86

Nyers, P. 2004. Introduction: What's Left of Citizenship? *Citizenship Studies*, 8, 203–15

Nyers, P. and Rygiel, K. 2012. *Citizenship, Migrant Activism and the Politics of Movement*. London: Routledge

Obeid M. 2010. Searching for the 'Ideal Face of the State' in a Lebanese Border Town. *Journal of the Royal Anthropological Institute*, 16, 330–46

OFSTED 2014. The Framework for Children's Centre Inspection. Manchester: Office for Standards in Education

Okely, J. 1983. *The Traveller-Gypsies*. Cambridge: Cambridge University Press

Okely, J. 2013. *Anthropological Practice: Fieldwork and the Ethnographic Method*. Oxford: Berg

Okely, J. 2014. Recycled (Mis) Representations: Gypsies, Travellers or Roma Treated as Objects, Rarely Subjects. *People, Place and Policy Online*, 8, 65–85

Olover, C. and Jayaweera, H. 2013. *The Impact of Restrictions and Entitlements on the Integration of Family Migrants*. Final Report of the IMPACIM Project, COMPAS, University of Oxford

Olwig, K. F. 2011. 'Integration': Migrants and Refugees Between Scandinavian Welfare Societies and Family Relations. *Journal of Ethnic and Migration Studies*, 37, 179–96

Ong, A. 2006. *Neoliberalism as Exception: Mutations in Citizenship and Sovereignty*. Durham: Duke University Press

Painter, J. 1995. The Regulatory State: The Corporate Welfare State and Beyond. In Johnston, R., Taylor, P. and Watts, M. (Eds) *Geographies of Global Change: Remapping the World in the Late Twentieth Century*. Oxford: Blackwell

Pandya, V. 1990. Movement and Space: Andamanese Cartography. *American Ethnologist*, 17, 775–97

Pantea, M-C. 2012. From 'Making a Living' to 'Getting Ahead': Roma Women's Experiences of Migration, *Journal of Ethnic and Migration Studies*, 38:8, 1251–68, DOI: 10.1080/1369183X.2012.689185

Parr, S. and Nixon, J. 2009. Family Intervention Projects: Sites of Subversion and Resilience. *Subversive Citizens: Power, Agency and Resistance in Public Services*, 101–17

Parton N. 2011. Child Protection and Safeguarding in England: Changing and Competing Conceptions of Risk and Their Implications for Social Work. *British Journal of Social Work* 41: 854–75

Pateman, C. 1989. The *Disorder of Women* Cambridge: Polity

Pateman, C. and Phillips, A. 1987. Feminist Critiques of the Public/Private Dichotomy. In Phillips, A. (Ed.) *Feminism and Equality*. Oxford: Blackwell

Pécoud, A. 2015. *Depoliticising Migration: Global Governance and International Migration Narratives*. New York: Springer

Pemberton, S. and Mason, J. 2009. Co-Production and Sure Start Children's Centres: Reflecting Upon Users', Perspectives and Implications for Service Delivery, Planning and Evaluation. *Social Policy and Society*, 8, 13–24

Perkins, M. 2004. False Whiteness: 'Passing' and the Stolen Generations. In Moreton-Robinson, A. (Ed.) *Whitening Race: Essays in Social and Cultural Criticism*. Canberra: Aboriginal Studies Press

Pfaff-Czarnecka, J. 2011. from 'Identity' to 'Belonging' in Social Research: Plurality, Social Boundaries, and the Politics of the Self. *Social Science Open Access Repository*, 368, 1–18

Phillips, A. and Taylor, B. 1980. Sex and Skill: Notes Towards a Feminist Economics. *Feminist Review*, 6, 79–88

Picker, G. 2017. *Racial Cities: Governance and the Segregation of Romani People in Urban Europe*. London: Routledge

Pine, F. 2018. Inside and Outside the Language of Kinship. Public and Private Conceptions of Sociality. In Alber, E. and Thelen, T. (Eds) *Reconnecting State and Kinship*. Philadelphia: University of Pennsylvania Press

Pink, S., Morgan, J. and Dainty, A. 2015. Other People's Homes as Sites of Uncertainty: Ways of Knowing and Being Safe. *Environment and Planning A*, 47, 450–64

Pinker, A. and Harvey, P. 2015. Negotiating Uncertainty: Neo-Liberal Statecraft in Contemporary Peru. *Social Analysis*, 59, 15–31

Powell, R. and lever, J. 2017. Europe's Perennial 'Outsiders': A Processual Approach to Roma Stigmatization and Ghettoization. *Current Sociology*, 65, 680–99

Pupavac, V. 2001. Misanthropy Without Borders: The International Children's Rights Regime. *Disasters*, 25, 95–112

Pustułka, P., Struzik, J. and Ślusarczyk, M. 2015. Caught Between Breadwinning and Emotional Provisions: The Case of Polish Migrant Fathers in Norway. *Studia Humanistyczne AGH*, 14, 117–39

Rabinow, P. 2007. *Reflections on Fieldwork in Morocco*, Oakland: University of California Press

Radstone, S. and Schwarz, B. 2010. *Memory: Histories, Theories, Debates*. New York: Fordham University Press

Ramírez C. 2014. 'It's Not How It Was': The Chilean Diaspora's Changing Landscape of Belonging. *Ethnic and Racial Studies* 37: 668–84

Rapport, N. and Dawson, A. 1998. *Migrants of Identity: Perceptions of Home in a World of Movement*. Oxford: Berg

Ravetz, A. 2003. *Council Housing and Culture: The History of a Social Experiment*. London: Routledge

Reeves, M. 2014. *Border Work: Spatial Lives of the State in Rural Central Asia*. Ithaca: Cornell University Press

Reynolds, T. 2005. *Caribbean Mothers: Identity and Experience in the UK*. London: Tufnell Press

Reynolds, T., Erel, U. and Kaptani, E. 2018. Migrant Mothers: Performing Kinwork and Belonging Across Private and Public Boundaries. *Families, Relationships and Societies*, https://doi.org/10.1332/20467431 8x15233476441573

Riccucci, N. M. 2005. Street-Level Bureaucrats and Intrastate Variation in the Implementation of Temporary Assistance for Needy Families Policies. *Journal of Public Administration Research and Theory*, 15, 89–111

Richardson, J. 2014. Roma in the News: An Examination of Media and Political Discourse and What Needs to Change. *People, Place and Policy Online*, 8, 51–64

Robson, B., Lymperopoulou, K. and Rae, A. 2008. People on the Move: Exploring the Functional Roles of Deprived Neighbourhoods. *Environment and Planning A*, 40, 2693–714

Rootham, E., Hardgove, A. and McDowell, L. 2015. Constructing Racialised Masculinities In/Through Affective Orientations to a Multicultural Town. *Urban Studies*, 52, 1523–39

Rose, N. 1999. *Powers of Freedom: Reframing Political Thought.* Cambridge: Cambridge University Press

Rumford, C. 2006. Theorizing Borders. *European Journal of Social Theory*, 9, 155–69

Rutherford, B. 2008. Conditional Belonging: Farm Workers and the Cultural Politics of Recognition in Zimbabwe. *Development and Change*, 39, 73–99

Sainsbury, D. 2013. Gender, Care, and Welfare. In Waylen, G., Celis, K., Kantola, J., Weldon, S.L. (Eds) *The Oxford Handbook of Gender and Politics.* Oxford: Oxford University Press

Schierup, C.-U., Hansen, P. and Castles, S. 2006. *Migration, Citizenship, and the European Welfare State: A European Dilemma.* Oxford: Oxford University Press

Scott, J. C. 1998. *Seeing Like a State: How Certain Schemes to Improve the Human Condition Have Failed.* New Haven: Yale University Press

Sharma, A. and Gupta, A. 2006. *The Anthropology of the State: A Reader.* New Jersey: John Wiley & Sons

Shibutani, T. 1966. *Improvised News: A Sociological Study of Rumor.* London: Ardent Media

Shore, C. and Wright, S. 1997. Policy: A New Field of Anthropology. In Shore, C. and Wright, S. (Eds) *Anthropology of Policy: Critical Perspectives on Governance and Power.* London: Routledge

Sigona, N. 2009. Ethnography of the 'Gypsy Problem' in Italy. The Case of Kosovo Roma and Ashkali in Florence and Venice. Unpublished Phd Thesis. Oxford: Oxford Brookes University

Sigona, N. and Trehan, N. 2009. *Romani Politics in Contemporary Europe,* New York: Palgrave Macmillan

Sigona, N. and Vermeersch, P. 2012. The Roma in the New EU: Policies, Frames and Everyday Experiences. *Journal of Ethnic and Migration Studies*, 38, 1189–93

Skeggs, B. 2004. *Class, Self, Culture.* London: Psychology Press

Smith, K. 2012. *Fairness, Class and Belonging in Contemporary England,* London: Springer

Sobotka, E. 2003. Romani Migration in the 1990s: Perspectives on Dynamic, Interpretation and Policy. *Romani Studies*, 13: 79–121.

Solimene, M. 2014. Discourses of Power and Life. A Group of Xoraxane Roma Confronting the State Authorities in Rome (Italy). PhD: University of Iceland

Solomos, J. and Back, L. 1996. *Racism and Society*. Basingstoke/New York: Palgrave Macmillan

Somerville, P. 1992. Homelessness and the Meaning of Home: Rooflessness or Rootlessness? *International Journal of Urban and Regional Research*, 16, 529–39

Soss, J., Fording, R.C., Schram, S.F. and Schram, S. 2011. *Disciplining the Poor: Neoliberal Paternalism and the Persistent Power of Race*. Chicago: University of Chicago Press

Stenson, K. 2013. The State, Sovereignty and Advanced Marginality of the City. In Aquires, P. and Lea, J. (Eds) *Criminalisation and Advanced Marginality: Critically Exploring the Work of Loic Wacquant*. . Bristol: Policy Press

Stevenson, N. 2014. Human (E) Rights and the Cosmopolitan Imagination: Questions of Human Dignity and Cultural Identity. *Cultural Sociology*, 8, 180–96

Stewart, K. 2007. *Ordinary Affects*. Durham: Duke University Press

Stewart, P.J. and Strathern, A. 2004. *Witchcraft, Sorcery, Rumors and Gossip*. Cambridge: Cambridge University Press

Stoler, A. L. 2002. *Carnal Knowledge and Imperial Power: Race and the Intimate in Colonial Rule*. Oakland: University of California Press

Tesar, C. 2012. Becoming Rom (Male), Becoming Romni (Female) Among Romanian Cortorari Roma: On Body and Gender. *Romani Studies*, 22, 113–40

Thelen, T. and Alber, E. 2017. *Reconnecting State and Kinship*. Philadelphia: University of Pennsylvania Press

Thelen, T. and Coe, C. 2017. Political Belonging Through Elderly Care: Temporalities, Representations and Mutuality. *Anthropological Theory*, https://doi.org/10.1177/1463499617742833

Thelen, T., Vetters, L. and Von Benda-Beckmann, K. 2014. Introduction to Stategraphy: Toward a Relational Anthropology of the State. *Social Analysis*, 58, 1–19

Ticktin, M. I. 2011. *Casualties of Care: Immigration and the Politics of Humanitarianism in France*. Oakland: University of California Press

Timmer, A. D. 2010. Constructing the 'Needy Subject': NGO Discourses of Roma Need. *Polar: Political and Legal Anthropology Review*, 33, 264–81

Timms, S. 2010. *Budget 2010. Securing the Recovery. Economic and Fiscal Strategy Report and Financial Statement and Budget Report*. London: The Stationery Office

Touraine, A. 2000. *Can We Live Together? Equality and Difference*. Redwood City: Stanford University Press

Trehan, N. 2001. In the Name of the Roma? The Role of Private Foundations and NGOs. In Guy, W. (Ed.) *Between Past and Future: The Roma of Central and Eastern Europe*. Hatfield: University of Hertfordshire Press

Tremlett, A., McGarry, A. and Agarin, T. 2014. The Work of Sisyphus: Squaring the Circle of Roma Recognition. *Ethnicities*, 14, 727–36

Tronto, J. C. 2013. *Caring Democracy: Markets, Equality, and Justice*. New York: New York University Press

Tsolidis, G. 2001. The Role of the Maternal in Diasporic Cultural Reproduction: Australia, Canada and Greece. *Social Semiotics*, 11, 193–208

Turner, B.S. 1993. *Citizenship and Social Theory*. London: Sage

Turner, V. 1969. *The Ritual Process: Structure and Anti-Structure*. New York: Routledge

Tyler, I. 2013. *Revolting Subjects: Social Abjection and Resistance in Neoliberal Britain*. London: Zed Books

Valentine, G. 2013. Living with Difference: Proximity and Encounter in Urban Life. *Geography*, 98

Van Baar, H.J.M. 2011. *The European Roma: Minority Representation, Memory, and the Limits of Transnational Governmentality*. Amsterdam: University of Amsterdam Press

Van Baar, H.J.M.. 2017. Boundary Practices of Citizenship: Europe's Roma at the Nexus of Securitization and Citizenship. In Roberto G. Gonzales, R.G. and Sigona, N. (Eds) *Within and Beyond Citizenship*. London: Routledge

Van Oorschot, W. 2006. Making the Difference in Social Europe: Deservingness Perceptions Among Citizens of European Welfare States. *Journal of European Social Policy*, 16, 23–42

Vaughan-Williams, N. 2008. Borderwork Beyond Inside/Outside? Frontex, the Citizen-Detective and the War on Terror. *Space and Polity*, 12, 63–79

Vermeersch, P. 2012. Reframing the Roma: EU Initiatives and the Politics of Reinterpretation. *Journal of Ethnic and Migration Studies*, 38, 1195–212

Vidra, Z. 2013. *Roma Migration to and from Canada: The Czech, Hungarian and Slovak Case*. Budapest: Central European University

Vincze, E. 2014. The Racialization of Roma in the 'New' Europe and the Political Potential of Romani Women. *European Journal of Women's Studies*, 21, 435–42

Vrăbiescu, I. and Kalir, B. 2018. Care-Full Failure: How Auxiliary Assistance to Poor Roma Migrant Women in Spain Compounds Marginalization. *Social Identities*, 24, 520–32

Wacquant, L. 2009. *Punishing the Poor: The Neo-Liberal Government of Social Insecurity.* Durham: Duke University Press

Wacquant, L. 2013. The Wedding of Workfare and Prisonfare in the 21st Century: Responses to Critics and Commentators. In Squires, P. and Lea, J. (Eds) *Criminalisation and Advanced Marginality: Critically Exploring the Work of Loïc Wacquant* Bristol: Policy Press

Walters, W. 2004. Secure Borders, Safe Haven, Domopolitics. *Citizenship Studies*, 8, 237–60

Wardhaugh, J. 1999. The Unaccommodated Woman: Home, Homelessness and Identity. *The Sociological Review*, 47, 91–109

Wasileski, G. and Miller, S. L. 2014. 'Bad' Victims? Understanding Social Service Providers' Responses to Roma Battered Women. *International Journal of Comparative and Applied Criminal Justice*, 38, 173–89

Weber, M. 1947. *The Theory of Economic and Social Organization.* New York: Oxford University Press

Wessendorf, S. 2013. Commonplace Diversity and the 'Ethos of Mixing': Perceptions of Difference in a London Neighbourhood. *Identities*, 20, 407–22

Wilson, H.F. 2017. On the Paradox of 'Organised' Encounter. *Journal of Intercultural Studies*, 38, 606–20

Yildiz, C. and De Genova, N. 2017. Un/Free Mobility: Roma Migrants in the European Union. *Social Identities*, 24,4

Yoo, G. J. 2008. Immigrants and Welfare: Policy Constructions of Deservingness. *Journal of Immigrant* and *Refugee Studies*, 6, 490–507

Yuval Davis, N. 1997. Women, Citizenship and Difference. *Feminist Review*, 57, 4–27

Yuval Davis, N. 2013. A Situated Intersectional Everyday Approach to the Study of Bordering. Euborder-Scapes Working Paper 2, www.euborderscapes.eu/fileadmin/user_upload/Working_Papers/EUBORDERSCAPES_Working_Paper_2_Yuval-Davis.pdf

Yuval Davis, N., Wemyss, G. and Cassidy, K. 2018. Everyday Bordering, Belonging and the Reorientation of British Immigration Legislation. *Sociology*, 52, 228–44

Yuval Davis, N. 2011. Nationalism, Belonging, Globalization and the 'Ethics of Care'. In Barrett, M.D., Flood, C. and Eade, J. (Eds) *Nationalism, Ethnicity, Citizenship: Multidisciplinary Perspectives.* Cambridge: Cambridge Scholars Publishing

Zadorozhnyi, M. 2009. Professionals, Carers of 'Strangers'? Liminality and the Typification of Postnatal Home Care Workers. *Sociology*, 43, 268–85

Index

References to notes are shown by the page number followed by the note number (eg. 205n19)

own experience as a mother 159
role boundaries 50–1, 120–1
safeguarding 41–2, 58–9, 78–9,
116–21, 129–30, 159
unannounced visits 120
Petronela (Roma) 100
Petti (Roma) 86–7
policy, anthropology of 44
Pupavac, V. 205n19
Puju (Roma) 151–2, 153–4

Q
qualifying status 46–7, 179–80

R
racism *see* Romanian Roma
identity
Radstone, S. 21
Radu (Romanian Roma) xiii, 1–2,
77–9, 105, 129
Ramírez, C. 9
Ramona (Roma) 55–6, 133–4
Reeves, M. 46
registration of families 60, 61–2,
107
religions of Roma 77
research methodology 19–21
access to the field 30–1
author's position 25–7, 32–4
choice of Luton 27–9
of the encounter 21–7
ethics 36–8
fieldwork chronology 29–30
living with the families 21,
22–3, 30–3, 39–40
negotiations with frontline
workers 34–7
right to reside 46–7, 177–8,
179–80
rights *see* legal status/rights
Rodica (Roma) 105, 185–7
Romanian-not-Roma 80, 81
Romanian Roma (general)
discrimination 6–7
framing of 2–3
identity of 4–7
lack of community organisation
5–6
lack of national home-land 6–7

racialising of 2–3, 5
terminology 73–4
see also legal status/rights;
Romanian Roma identity
Romanian Roma identity 73–98
challenging label 75–6
diversity of 76–8, 79
everyday labelling 79–82
gendered dimensions of 75
internalisation of label 75
and mothers 82–5
and nomadism 81–2
reaction to racism and
discrimination 89–97
and Romanian-not-Roma 80,
81
and state labelling 74–9
Rosemary (church volunteer) xii,
81–2, 167–71
Rosvan (Roma) xiv, 30, 31–2,
99–100
Roxana (Roma) 177
rumours 7, 92–5, 184–5
Rutherford, B. 13

S
safeguarding
and bordering effect 181–8
and cultural issues 58–9
and home encounters 41–2,
58–9, 78–9, 85–8, 116–21,
124–5, 129–30, 181–8
legal duty 45, 124
pressures of 58–9, 66
rumours about 7, 94
and state visibility 7–8, 85–8
Samantha (deputy head of children's
centre) xiii, 41, 45, 62, 83, 96,
106, 113
Sanda (Roma) xiv, 111, 148–50
schools/education 27–8, 53, 56,
83–4, 87, 88, 112
Schramm, K. 13
Schwarz, B. 21
Scott, J.C. 43, 74
Scott, S. 137
Sebastian (Roma) xiii, 109,
117–19, 120–1

Lightning Source UK Ltd.
Milton Keynes UK
UKHW011709150819
347986UK00002B/58/P